EDITOR'S FOREWORD

In our time the study of comparative government constitutes one of many fields or specialities in political science. But it is worth recalling that the most distinguished political scientists of the ancient world would have had difficulty recognizing the present-day distinction between the study of comparative government and study in other subject areas of the discipline. Think of Plato, for example, whose works abound in references to the political systems of his own and earlier days. Or consider Aristotle, whose *Politics* and related writings were based on an examination of more than one hundred constitutions. Twenty centuries after Aristotle the comparative emphasis continued strong in the work of Montesquieu and Rousseau, among others. In the nineteenth century the comparative tradition entered upon a period of decline, but there are signs that the merits of comparative political analysis are once more gaining recognition. At many colleges and universities, the introductory course in political science is no longer focused exclusively on American government. The comparative approach—in politics, in law, in administration—is becoming increasingly important in the political science curriculum.

This booklet, one of a series, is designed to reflect that approach, without, however, marking a sharp departure from the substance and method of most comparative government courses. With one exception (Arnold J. Heidenheimer, *The Government of Germany: West and East*), each booklet deals with one national government, but the booklets are distinctively comparative in at least two senses. Most of them include material descriptive of other political systems, especially that of the United States. In addition, the booklets follow a common outline, so far as possible, and are designed to promote comparative treatment. Of course, there is nothing to keep the instructor or student from treating a particular governmental system in isolation, if he chooses to do so. On the other hand, his approach to political

vii

institutions and functions can be as comparative as he wishes.

A further advantage of this series is that each booklet has been written by a distinguished scholar and authority in the field; each author is personally and professionally familiar with the political system he treats. Finally, the separate booklets make it possible for the instructor to design his course in accordance with his own interest or the interests of his students. One booklet may be substituted for another or any booklet put aside for one semester without affecting the others. The booklets, in short, unlike most one-volume textbooks, give the instructor maximum freedom in organizing his course. This freedom will be virtually unlimited as the forthcoming titles in this series complete a survey of representative governments of the world.

But to return to Aristotle once again, it remains true that the best judges of the feast are not the cooks but the guests. I have tried to indicate why, in my view, the recipe for the series is a good one. Let all those who teach comparative government, and all those who take courses in that field, proceed to judge the booklets for themselves.

ARNOLD A. ROGOW

INTRODUCTION

Once upon a time a Chicago millionaire and philanthropist named Raymond Robins—who had been head of the American Red Cross Mission to Russia in 1917–18—told a group of bitterly anti-Soviet U.S. Senators:

I believe [of the Russian Revolution] that when we understand what it is, when we know the facts behind it, when we do not libel it nor slander it or do not lose our heads and become its advocates and defenders, and really know what the thing is, and then move forward to it, then we will serve our country and our time. (*Bolshevik Propaganda, Hearings before a Subcommittee of the Committee on the Judiciary, U.S. Senate, 65th Congress,* Government Printing Office, Washington, D.C., 1919, p. 828)

More than forty years later Ambassador George F. Kennan, in commenting on these observations in his brilliant study *Russia and the West under Lenin and Stalin* (Little, Brown and Company, Boston, 1961, p. 62), observed:

I should like to say that in these words Robins was almost as close, in my opinion, as one could get to the best answer Western society can find to the problem of Russian Communism. Our success in dealing with this problem will begin on the day when we recognize it as primarily a problem of understanding, rather than one of the physical repulsion of an external force. But then we must go one step further than Robins went, and we must realize that this is at least as much a matter of understanding ourselves and our own society as it is of understanding those on the other side of the Iron Curtain.

The chapters which follow have been written in the spirit of the quotations offered above—in the hope of promoting understanding rather than libel and slander or advocacy and defense. They will not, I believe, exacerbate the anti-Communist syndrome so prevalent for so long in the USA and so likely, as has happened elsewhere, to develop into a mass neurosis or psychosis with disastrous results. Neither, I hope, will they contribute to Communist or pro-Communist myopia, infiltration, or subversion, for, like all my writings, they are written from a viewpoint which is un-Marxist and anti-Marxist. They will not be translated into Russian, any more than have any of my earlier works—since, in the official view of the Muscovite Marxists (even though I do not quite recognize the portrait), I am "an active ideologist of American Imperialism," in the words of *Pravda* (October 23, 1953) in reviewing my book on world government, *The Commonwealth of Man* (Knopf, 1952).

The objective of this effort is to set forth in brief compass the origins, nature, course, and consequences of government and politics in the USSR. Whether the objective has been well served is for others to say. This volume differs considerably in organization and scope from its companion volumes in the same series for the good and sufficient reason that government and politics in the USSR are in many respects quite different from government and politics elsewhere, particularly in the Western democracies, and require much more historical background for adequate understanding. These pages are not footnoted or documented for the good and sufficient reason that available literature on the USSR is so staggeringly voluminous that it cannot usefully be cited. My previous lengthy works, *Soviet Politics at Home and Abroad* (Knopf, 1946) and *Russia Since 1917* (Knopf, 1957), are quite fully documented. Sources of quotations are given in the text or, at least, dates are given whereby such items can be located in the Soviet or Western press. Unless otherwise indicated, statistics are from Soviet sources. All the matters here dealt with can fruitfully be pursued further with the aid of the reading list which follows the text of the Soviet Constitution.

My indebtedness to others for aid in the preparation of this study is large and variegated. My creditors include all other workers in the vineyards of Soviet studies (and of anti-Soviet studies as well); all my students and many of my colleagues during three decades on many campuses; all who proved helpful in the course of three visits of exploration to the USSR; innumerable members of many lecture audiences who asked searching questions and offered incisive criticisms; and sundry others too numerous to mention. All such help was, so to speak, indirect and impersonal. But to four collaborators I must make personal acknowledgment, along with the customary but correct absolution of all of them from responsibility for anything here set forth, whether true or false, right or wrong. The four: Professor Arnold

A. Rogow of Stanford University, editor of this series, for inspiration, guidance, and helpful comments; Mr. John T. Hawes, director of the College Department of Thomas Y. Crowell Company, for more of the same, plus gracious indulgence in the face of delays; Lily A. Schuman, my wife, for encouragement and patience during a task of writing which, by virtue of a search for brevity, clarity, and readability, took twice as long as it should have; and, last but very far from least, Jeanne Sproat—wife of my esteemed Williams colleague Professor John G. Sproat—who has cheerfully toiled, above and beyond the line of duty, in the gathering of data and in the neat and accurate typing of the entire manuscript. To these (and to others here left nameless): my thanks.

These pages are "going to press" on the eve of the "summit" reunion in Vienna of Nikita S. Khrushchev and John F. Kennedy after a disillusioning springtime of crises, befuddlements, confusions, and mounting perils in what many among us can only regard as further manifestations of an almost chronic mismanagement of human affairs in our time of troubles. Let us hope that these efforts may contribute on the world stage—as I humbly hope that these modest pages may contribute in the minds and hearts of their readers—to the avoidance of disaster through a new and creative statesmanship on both sides and thus to a brighter future for all the Family of Man.

F. L. S.

Williamstown, Mass.
June, 1961

CONTENTS

1 - Eurasian Empire

Peoples of the Steppes

During the late 1950's and early 1960's more and more thousands of Americans each year visited the Soviet Union. Most of them explored darkest Russia on standard *Intourist* itineraries: Leningrad, Moscow, Kiev, Odessa, and other cities in the Western borderlands. Others took more venturesome journeys beyond the Volga and into Central Asia and Siberia. Some Russians, albeit far fewer, visited America under inter-governmental arrangements for "cultural exchanges."

From these enterprises in mutual understanding all participants learned much. Here, as always, we learn what we learn in terms of what we have already "learned" as modified by new experience. Most Russians in America, having long learned that the United States is the world's greatest citadel of capitalistic exploitation and bourgeois decadence, have been surprised to behold a flourishing civilization exhibiting few symptoms of the inexorable workings of Marxist "laws of history." Most Americans in Russia, having long learned that contemporary Muscovy is a totalitarian despotism in which all people suffer silently in misery, suspicion, and oppression, have been astonished to discover a dynamic and creative new society whose hopeful citizens, after long years of fear and deprivation, contemplate the future with confidence.

Quite apart from these revelations, all visitors to Russia, whether flying via the planes of *Aeroflot* or traveling by train, bus, or car, have inevitably been impressed with the huge expanse of the largest of the nation-states and with the bewildering heterogeneity of its population.

1

Here, by the Soviet census of mid-January, 1959, live some 208,826,000 human beings, 55% women, 45% men, with an annual birth rate of 25 per thousand and a death rate of 7.5. Despite appalling losses in World War II, the residents of Sovietland expanded by 9.5% since 1939, with the largest increases in the Urals, Siberia, and the Far East. By early 1961 the Soviet peoples numbered 215,000,000, of whom one-half were city-dwellers. Moscow had over 5,000,000 citizens; Leningrad 3,000,000; Kiev, Baku, and Kharkov each c. 1,000,000; and Gorky, Tashkent, Novosibirsk, Chelyabinsk, and Erivan each well over 500,000.

Almost all of these peoples speak, read, and write a language difficult for Western tongues and inscribed in an alphabet strange to Western eyes. But many of them in out-of-the-way places have native languages even older and more curious and often alphabetized only recently after centuries of illiteracy: Bashkir, Buriot-Mongolian, Chechen-Ingush, Chuvash, Kabardino-Balkarian, Kalmyk, Ossetian, Yakut, Abkhazian, Koriak, Taimyr, Nargorno-Karabakh, Kara-Kalpak, etc. Within this immense empire dwell almost 200 distinct linguistic, ethnic, and cultural groups of *Homo sapiens*. But tourist and student alike may avoid total confusion by reflecting that most of these remote peoples, many of whom are remnants of ancient migrations and survivors of half-forgotten yesterdays, are few in numbers.

More than half the inhabitants of the USSR are Great Russians: 58.4% by the census of 1959. Other major language groups are the Ukrainians or "Little Russians" (16.6%); the Byelorussians (3.1%); the Uzbeks (2.9%); the Tartars (2.5%); the Kazakhs (1.8%); and the Armenians, Georgians, and Azerbaijanians (each 1.3%). In religious background, although not necessarily in current professions of faith, the Soviet peoples are 82% Eastern Orthodox, 14% Moslem, 1.5% Roman Catholic, 1.5% Jewish, 0.5% Protestant, and 0.2% Buddhist.

In the number of its inhabitants the Soviet Union is the third largest community on the planet, exceeded as of 1961 only by China (c. 670,000,000) and India (c. 420,000,000), with the United States (c. 183,000,000) in fourth place. In area the USSR is by far the largest of political entities, with 8,600,000 square miles under direct Soviet jurisdiction. Mainland China comprises some 4,000,000 square miles, continental USA and Brazil each about 3,000,000, and India less than 2,000,000. The territory of the USSR is almost equal to the areas of the USA, China, and India combined; much larger than South America; and roughly equal to the North American continent. The USA from

Atlantic to Pacific has 4 time zones. The USSR, from Kamchatka to the Gulf of Finland, has 10 time zones. When it is 7:00 P.M. in Peter's City on the Neva, it is 5:00 A.M. the next morning in Petropavlosk on the Bering Sea. During the summer months of "white nights" the sun never sets on the Eurasian empire.

But this image of immensity should at once be qualified by noting that this enormous land mass lies between the "Roof of the World" and the North Pole, with much of its expanse a perpetually frozen wasteland. Winter daylight is feeble and brief. Almost all of the USSR lies north of 45°, the half-way point between the Equator and the Pole. Most of the USSR lies north of 49°, the northern border of the USA. Leningrad is in the same latitude as the southern shore of Greenland and the southern tip of Alaska. Moscow is on the parallel of Labrador. The southernmost regions of the USSR in Turkmenistan and Tadjikistan are parallel with Reno, Kansas City, St. Louis, and Washington, D.C.

This boreal locus of Muscovy has consequences: meteorological, botanical, economic, social, and political. The great plain, bisected only by the low-lying range of the Urals, has a "continental" climate marked by sparse rainfall and extremes of heat and cold. Prior to the recording in Antarctica in 1958 of a temperature of 104° below zero, F., the coldest spot in the world was Verkhoyansk in eastern Siberia with a record of 93° below zero, F. Yet great regions which are ice-bound and snow-clad during long dark winters may enjoy temperatures in the 70's and 80's during short bright summers.

This gigantic half-saucer, extending from the Arctic coast to a rimland of the loftiest mountain ranges of Eurasia, is partitioned by Nature into three major and two minor zones of vegetation. The northernmost fringe is the *Tundra*, stretching for thousands of miles along Arctic shores. With sub-soil frozen all year long, nothing grows save lichens, mosses, and dwarf trees. Here dwell reindeer, walruses, and seals—and very few humans despite Soviet efforts to "open" the far north. In the extreme south, beyond the Caucasus, along the Black Sea coast, in the Crimea, and also in the southernmost valleys of Central Asia, is a semi-tropical borderland where frost is unknown, rainfall is abundant, and grapes, cotton, and citrus fruits flourish. Between these peripheral areas are three vast belts of plant life: the Forest Zone or *Taiga,* roughly 5,000 miles long and 1,200 miles wide, extending from the Baltic to the Bering Sea and containing an estimated quarter of all the timber reserves of the world;

the Steppe Zone, 2,600 miles long and 600 miles wide, from Bessarabia to Mongolia, barren of trees save in the river valleys, and containing, despite scanty precipitation, the richest farmland in the world: *Chernozom* or Black Earth; and the Desert Zone of salt and sand, 1,800 miles long and 600 miles wide, encompassing the flatlands north of the Caspian Sea and eastward across Central Asia.

For ten centuries and more, most Russians, as well as most non-Russian migrants into these endless woodlands and grasslands, have dwelt and loved and earned their livelihoods on the steppes, with scattered settlements in the forest and in the desert. Their "national character" may have been subtly shaped by the impact upon them of an infinity of prairie under an eternity of sky; by the age-old Slavic custom of swaddling infants; by alternating political experiences of anarchy and despotism; or by some mystical aspect of the "Russian soul." Among these various explanations of how Russians of the past came to be Russians of the present we need not choose. More light is to be had by noting the origins, growth, and tragic destiny of the Russian community during a life span which began over a thousand years ago.

Birth, Death, Resurrection

It is probable, though unproven, that all the ancestors of all Western peoples (perhaps including the vanished race of the Cromagnons and long lost Neanderthal Man) wandered into Europe from the high plateaus of northeastern Asia by way of the "Steppe Road" from Lake Baikal to the delta of the Danube. If so, then among peoples still extant those speaking Celtic tongues must have come first and farthest, followed by Greeks and Romans and by the forebears of the Germanic-speaking tribes. The migrants whose language was Slavic are first mentioned in historical records in the 1st Century, B.C. Called by Pliny *Venedi,* by Ptolemy *Venedae,* and by the Germans *Wends,* they then lived not on the steppes but in the forests and meadowlands between the Baltic, the Carpathians, the Vistula, and the Dnieper. From this center they slowly spread out. In new lands they mixed with other peoples and begot the precursors of the West Slavs (Poles, Czechs, Slovaks, and the original Prussians), the South Slavs (Serbs, Croats, Slovenes, Bulgarians), and the East Slavs (Great Russians, Byelorussians, and Ukrainians).

But these Slavic tongues, each distinct but all akin, emerged belatedly. The origins of "Russia" must be sought elsewhere.

Between 800 and 700 B.C. the Greeks were aware of barbarian tribes they called "Scythians," dwelling north of the Black Sea as successors to earlier peoples called by the Greeks "Cimmerians" and, before them, "Maeotians." In the days of Alexander the Great (356–323 B.C.), the Scythians were assailed and ultimately ousted or subjugated by new nomads of Asia variously called "Sarmatians," "Alans," or "Antes," who centuries later mingled and intermarried with Slavic peoples from the north. These intruders came into the western reaches of the Steppe Road by way of what was later to be known as the "Water Road," or "River Road" of western Russia: a much traversed route from Scandinavia to Byzantium via the Gulf of Finland, the Neva, Lake Ladoga, the Volkhov River, Lake Ilmen, the Lovat River, portage to the headwaters of the Dnieper, and thence southward to the Black Sea.

The first "Russian" community originated at the junction of the Steppe Road and the River Road. Between 200 and 300 A.D. the Sarmatians were conquered by the Goths, a Germanic people coming down the River Road from the Baltic island of Gotland. The Goths were soon assailed by new Asiatic invaders, the Huns, who pushed sundry German tribes—Ostrogoths, Visigoths, Franks, Lombards, Vandals, Angles, Saxons, Jutes, etc.—across the frontiers of the now decadent Roman Empire. Under Attila, the "Scourge of God," the Hunnish hordes overran Europe until they were beaten back at Chalôns-sur-Marne in 451 A.D. These barbarian migrations, confused, aimless, and fatal to an already dying civilization, had their sources in the lands of Russia long before "Russia" existed as a community or a State. They brought the Western Roman Empire to an end in 476 A.D. The Eastern Empire, with its glittering capital at Constantinople or Byzantium, was to endure for another thousand years. It was destined, as we shall see, to influence profoundly the belatedly emerging "Russia" of the 9th and 10th Centuries of the Christian era.

Meanwhile, successive groups of nomads continued to flow westward across the prairies, partly because of the slow erosion of their original Asian grazing lands and partly because the Great Wall of China forbade any migration to its south. After the Huns came the Bulgars (400–500 A.D.); after the Bulgars, the Avars (500–650); after the Avars, the Khazars (650–750); and after the Khazars, the Magyars (750–850) who were later to establish in the mid-Danubian plain the kingdom of Hungary. The Khazars, as overlords of Sarmatian and Slavic subjects, established an "empire" north of the Black Sea in the 700's and

800's and were the first among these nomads to abandon animism and polytheism in favor, by decree of their Kaghan or Kakhan, of a monotheistic "higher religion." Their choice was Judaism. The date is uncertain. This "Jewish kingdom" was progressively weakened by Arab invaders who crossed the Caucasus and sought to emulate their fellow-Moslems engaged in carrying the sword of Allah all across North Africa, through Spain, and into the Kingdom of the Franks—where they were halted and driven back to the Pyrenees by Charles Martel at Tours in the year 732. The subject peoples of the Khazars, so say the earliest chroniclers of later times, sought "protection" elsewhere in view of the waning of Khazar power.

What followed is clouded in myth and legend. There is no conclusive evidence that people in Kiev, oldest of "Russian" cities, or in Novgorod, far to the north on the River Road, ever "invited" strangers to protect them. What is not in doubt is that the barbarian strangers in question were the daring pioneers and pirates who poured out of Scandinavia during the 9th, 10th, and 11th Centuries—and, among other exploits, ravaged the coasts of Western Europe, settled themselves in Sicily, founded a kingdom in Normandy, conquered Anglo-Saxon England (1066), and explored Iceland, Greenland, Labrador, and perhaps New England and even Minnesota some 500 years before Columbus reached America. By their victims they were variously named "Norsemen," "Vikings," or, as by the Byzantines, "Varangians." Some of these voyagers, whether invited or no, traveled southward along the River Road and vainly raided Byzantium as early as the year 860.

These Norse assailants of what was then the largest and wealthiest metropolis of Christendom were dubbed "Russians" by some of the chroniclers. The source of the name is uncertain. The *Rukh-As* or "light clan" of Alans, living near the Sea of Azov, were long called *Rus, Ros,* or *Hros* by their neighbors. Vikings from Sweden, arriving at Azov, took the name *Rus* and founded a realm later called the "Russian Kaganate." *Russus,* however, is Latin for red. The Varangians, some of them redheaded and red-bearded, often sailed the rivers and seas in redpainted ships with red sails. *Ruotsi,* moreover, is a Finnish term for oarsmen or rowers, early applied to Norsemen from Sweden. While the semantic problem remains unsolved, it is evident that some or all of the mixed tribes of migrants north of the Black Sea were already known as "Russians" by 800 A.D. when Charlemagne, King of the Franks, was crowned "Emperor of the Romans" by Pope Leo III in a futile attempt to restore a vanished imperium.

It is equally clear that a certain Rurik of Jutland (Denmark) became ruler of Novgorod, probably in the year 862, and subsequently sent barons or *Boyars* named Askold and Dir to wrest control of Kiev from the Khazars. About the same time patriarch Photius, head of the Byzantine Church, sent two missionaries, St. Cyril and St. Methodius, to "Khazaria," where they failed to make converts. The year 862 found them in Moravia. Here they converted the Western Slavs (temporarily) to Greek Orthodox Christianity and allegedly adapted the Greek alphabet to the needs of the speakers of Slavic tongues—none of whom as yet had a written language—by devising the "Cyrillic" alphabet which later became the medium of "Church Slavonic" throughout Slavdom and is the matrix of the modern Russian language. Meanwhile, Rurik having died, his Norwegian kinsman, Helgi or Oleg, ruled Novgorod in the name of Rurik's infant son, Ingvar or Igor. Norse names henceforth become Slavic. Oleg seized Kiev from Askold and Dir, who were slain, and, c. 882, made himself "Prince of Kiev." He was succeeded by Igor and then by Igor's widow, Olga, who was baptized in Byzantium in 957, and then by Olga's son, Svyatoslav I (the name means "Glory of Sanctity"), who conquered the Khazars, defeated the Bulgars, and ruled a far-flung kingdom.

The tangled and troubled tale of Kievan Russia (882–1240) is best left to the historians. Suffice it to say that here was a widespread feudal realm, dominated by a land-holding nobility of *Boyars,* protecting and exploiting masses of serfs or slaves, and ruled by Princes who traced their ancestry to Rurik of Jutland as did all their successors down to 1917. In Novgorod and other northern trading towns a popular assembly or *Veche* shared power with a *Soviet Gospod* or Council of Masters. Government, always at best an uncertain and disorderly process in these anarchic times, was thus a fusion of democracy, aristocracy, and monarchy.

Among the rulers deemed most memorable by later generations was the grandson of Olga, Prince and Saint Vladimir ("Lord of the World") who renounced paganism and—after considering the merits of Judaism, Islam, and Roman Catholicism among the higher religions—converted his subjects to Greek Orthodox Christianity. His 19th-Century statue, wearing Cross and Crown, still stands in Kiev's riverside park, gazing across the Dnieper and the lands beyond. The year of conversion was

989. The source was Byzantium, the common inspiration of much else in the culture of early Russia. Vladimir later married Anne, sister of the Byzantine Emperor. Among other Slavs, the Serbs and Bulgars also embraced Greek Orthodoxy, but the Poles (968 A.D.) and also the Czechs, Slovaks, Croats, and Slovenes became Roman Catholic, thus leaving Slavdom religiously divided ever since.

Of later Princes, the best remembered were Yaroslav the Wise who died in 1054, the year of the final breach between the Roman and Greek churches; Vladimir Monomach (d. 1125), direct ancestor of subsequent rulers; and Yuri Dolgoruki (George the Long-armed), originally Prince of Suzdal and Vladimir in the north and alleged founder of Moscow c. 1147. The site of the little wooden town on the Moskva River was ultimately to prove fateful for it lay near the mid-point among the headwaters of the Volga and the Western Dvina, both arising in the Valdai Hills to the northwest, and of the Dnieper and Don to the southwest and south. For centuries these waterways were channels of trade, travel, and power through the wilderness of forest and steppe. But Moscow meant little in Kievan Russia.

Holy Kiev was recurrently menaced by new nomads from Asia. As early as 895 the Pechenegs or Patzinaks reached the Dnieper, drove the Magyars into Hungary, and raided the frontiers of the Byzantine Empire. In 972 they vanquished and slew Svyatoslav I, whose skull was fashioned into a drinking cup for a Pecheneg chieftain. In 1036 the invaders were beaten by Prince Yaroslav and fled into the Balkans. In 1095 other barbarians along the Steppe Road arrived at the Dnieper. They were called by the Russians the Polovtsi, and by others Falven, Cumans, or Kipchaks. After many decades of intermittent warfare the Polovtsi in the year 1185 vanquished and slew a certain Prince Igor, whose tragedy was mournfully celebrated in the first Russian epic poem, "The Tale of the Host of Igor." Despite this disaster, Kievan Russia survived for another half-century.

The decline and fall of this first Russian State may be attributed in part to the incapacity of its rulers and subjects to organize an effective polity, despite the repeated challenges of anarchy within and assault from without. The kings, barons, and burghers of the Western European communities during the same era did only slightly better in the face of comparable challenges. They were in no instance menaced by such formidable foes. Had they faced the same test, they would doubtless have suffered the same fate. It is, nonetheless, plain from the record that

the early Russia which was now about to die was more grievously
afflicted than other segments of Christendom with anarchy,
violence, and man's chronic inhumanity to man. The first function of all government is to restrain these destructive manifestations of Original Sin within the State and to protect the State
against attack from without. In their groping attempts to ac-
complish these tasks the Kievan Russians of days of old were
finally to fail.

In June of the year 1223, at a season when the steppe-
dwellers rejoice that soggy springs give way to sunny summers,
a fearful apparition materialized. Another army of Asian invaders approached the lower reaches of the Don, coming from
nowhere as far as the Russians knew. They had come, in fact,
across the Caucasus, after vanquishing the knights of Georgia and
traversing passes through mountains higher than the Alps. They
were not barbarians but organized, disciplined, and superbly
led warriors, riding swift horses, bearing lacquered black shields
and armor, and wielding compound bows, then unknown in the
west, with deadly range and accuracy. Their cavalry fought in
troops of 10, squadrons of 100, regiments of 1,000, and divisions
of 10,000, with each army comprising 3 divisions. Their battle-
standard was a weird device of 9 yak-tails.

Such was the army which arrived mysteriously on the Don.
Its commanders sent envoys to parley. Prince Mstislav the Daring ordered them put to death. A reply came from the men who
commanded the strange horsemen: "As you wish for war, you
shall have it. We have done you no harm. God is impartial. He
will decide our quarrel."

Mstislav—responding to appeals from a Polovtsi chieftain
who said "Today they have taken our land, tomorrow they will
take yours"—led 80,000 warriors to face the foe. Battle was
joined near the River Kalka, north of the Sea of Azov. By day's
end all the Russian fighters were slain or in flight. Mstislav and
his aides were crushed to death under heavy planks by a merciless enemy. The invaders raided the Crimea and then vanished
eastward along the Steppe Road. Wrote a Russian chronicler:
"Only God knows whence they came and whither they went."

The victors in this encounter were the Mongols, last of the
Asian nomads to invade Europe and quite incredibly the build-
ers, by virtue of military invincibility, of the greatest land empire
of all time. The dark riders who crushed Mstislav's soldiery in
1223 were a segment of the armies of Jenghis Khan (1162–1227).
This tribal chieftain in far-off Asia, having united his tribesman

into the most powerful of the "Great Powers" of his day, had received in 1206 the title by which he has ever since been known and, in 1215, had breached the Great Wall, taken Peking, and conquered Cathay. His hopes for peace and quiet were frustrated when the envoys he sent to the Shah of Khorezm, a huge Moslem empire of Central Asia, were put to death, thus leaving Jenghis no decent choice save war. In 1219 a quarter of a million Mongol horsemen, led by two superlative strategists named Chepé and Subotai, overran Khorezm, pillaged Bokhara and Samarkand, and in vain pursuit of the Shah invaded northern India and Iran. It was one of these armies that had crossed the Caucasus, annihilated the Russians at the Kalka, and then returned across the prairies to the remote Mongol capital of Karakorum: City of the Black Sands.

Having already founded the most extensive of realms, now only at the beginning of its expansion, Jenghis was gathered unto his fathers in the Christian year 1227. His son, Ogdai Khan, pondering reports of the wealth and weakness of the Russians, presently ordered a nephew, Batu the Splendid, to embark upon a new enterprise in conquest. Expeditions over thousands of miles were routine for these mounted warriors. In 1236 Batu appeared on the Volga in command of 300,000 horsemen. They proceeded up the river, burned the petty town called Moscow, razed the local metropolis of Vladimir (1237), and overtook and destroyed the army of Grand Prince Yuri. From northwestern Russia they rode southward along the River Road and besieged Kiev. In December, 1240, they overwhelmed the defenders and demolished the city, putting most of its inhabitants to the sword. So passed into gloom the hopes of medieval Russia.

The black cavalry of the grasslands, curious as to what lay beyond, pressed on. Batu and Subotai reached Galicia in the spring of 1241. Kings and barons, knights and townsmen, rallied to the defense of Christendom. All their efforts were vain. In April, 1241, at Leignitz in Silesia, a Mongol host led by Kaidu and Baibars, both grandsons of Jenghis, cut to pieces a joint Polish-German-Bohemian-French army. At the same time other horsemen under Subotai and Batu entered Hungary and on the fatal field of Mohi, near the dark hills of Tokay, slaughtered the soldiery of King Bela IV. The indomitable horsemen stormed Budapest, invaded Austria, and sacked all the towns of the Dalmatian coast, save only Dubrovnik behind its mountain-girt walls. All Europe was helpless before the armies of the Khan.

Christendom was saved by happenstance. Ogdai died. When

they received the news in 1242, his commanders decided to go home. They abandoned Dalmatia, Hungary, Bohemia, East Germany, and Poland, but left agents and garrisons to rule over subjugated Russia.

Before considering the fate of the surviving Russians under Mongol rule, it will be well to note the later enlargement and slow decline of the most extensive and most populous of all empires, at times encompassing half of the territory of Eurasia and perhaps two-thirds of the human race. When a monarch in an ancient legend asked his wise men to devise an aphorism suitable for all occasions, they framed their response: "And these things too shall pass away." So it came to pass with the Mongol Empire, as with all things human, but only after many generations of mankind had suffered evil or enjoyed good or trembled in fear before the riders from Mongolia. Jenghis's grandson, Hulagu Khan, took Baghdad and founded the Ilkahn dynasty in Persia. Pushing on toward Africa, his armies, never thus far halted by Christian arms, were defeated by Moslem arms from Egypt at Ain Jalut in Syria in September, 1260. Mongol warlords abandoned the Levant, but forced the Seljuk Turks of Anatolia to pay them tribute.

Another grandson of Jenghis, Mangu, was named Great Khan in 1251 and made his brother, Kubla, ruler of China. In 1260, as the Mongol tide ebbed in the Near East, Mangu died. His brother became Great Khan and moved his capital to Peking. The imperium of Kubla Khan (1260-94) was visited and described to an incredulous West by Marco Polo and his father and uncle, all merchant-gentlemen of Venice, who lingered at Kubla's court for sixteen years and served him on sundry missions. Kubla's kingdom exacted obedience from all peoples dwelling between Korea and Poland and between Indo-China, the Punjab, Arabia, and the northern valleys of Siberia and Russia. His expeditions against Java, Cochin-China, and Japan came to nothing. But the domain of this tolerant and widely respected monarch covered half of the then known world.

Its disintegration was slow and chaotic. Vast provinces or Khanates went their own way and ignored Peking. In the year 1369 the disputed title of Great Khan was assumed by a scion of Jenghis: Timur the Lame or Tamerlane. His efforts to restore Mongol unity of the days of old led to victories, conquests, and monstrous atrocities throughout the Middle East. His failure left only a fearful memory of burning cities and mounds of skulls. He died in 1405 and was placed in an ebony coffin within an ornate tomb in Samarkand, still standing but now empty. Tamerlane left nothing to posterity but ruin and a sense of horror—never to be exceeded save by the deeds of German Christians of the 20th Century.

One of his descendants, Baber (d. 1530), fled from Samarkand to Kabul and thence subjugated most of India, making himself "Emperor of Hindustan" and founder of the Mogul (Mongol) dynasty which endured until the advent of the British Raj in the 17th Century. Baber's grandson, Akbar (1556–1605), a contemporary of Elizabeth I of England, Catherine de Medici of France, and Ivan IV of the new Russia, was widely regarded as the wisest and most beneficient monarch of his generation.

By this time the original Mongol Empire was long gone. Under Uzbek Khan (1314–41), the Western Mongols embraced Islam. In the Middle Kingdom the Mongol dynasty gave way to the Mings in 1368, with the Eastern Mongols unwittingly absorbed into the human sea of China. The Eurasian *Pax Mongolica* was the most nearly successful effort at the "conquest of the world" in all recorded time. Had the black-armored archers on horseback persisted in winning Western Europe, succeeded in penetrating Africa, and built an imperium as enduring as that of the Romans, the world of today, for better or worse, might enjoy World Government rather than the anarchy of rival sovereignties. This was not to be.

The final failure of the Mongols to unify the world was doubtless due to the very methods which enabled them to do what they did. Militarism in human society always produces spectacular results when it creates "invincible armies." But since militarism is destructive, coercive, and divisive, its devotees sooner or later, among themselves, become divisive, coercive, and destructive in their persisting devotion to a false god. The early pagan Mongols, moreover, had no "ideology" and no Messianic mission, for they were tolerant of all faiths and had no thought of "saving the world." This attribute long served them well in the governance of alien peoples but finally weakened their unity as their far-flung local rulers yielded to the persuasions of missionaries of the "higher religions": Mohammedanism, Buddhism, and Confucianism.

Let us return to Russia under the Mongol or "Tartar" yoke. The Asian conquerors of 1236–40 were not merciless destroyers. Almost always they offered their victims a choice: acknowledge the authority of the Great Khan and pay tribute to his agents or face destruction. Most of the local potentates of Russia made the wrong choice seven hundred years ago. One was an exception: Alexander, Prince of Novgorod. This Russian "national hero" defeated Swedish invaders near the Neva in 1236 and was henceforth known as Alexander Nevsky. In April, 1242, again in an encounter at arms long cherished by posterity, he vanquished the Teutonic knights of the Baltic at Lake Peipus. In the interim he had acknowledged Mongol invincibility, gone to Batu as a subject, agreed to pay tribute, and thereby achieved political survival and a semblance of local independence. When he died in 1253, he had won a measure of authority, with Mongol consent, over all the thinly scattered settlements in the northlands toward the White Sea and the Urals. All other Russian communities were servile and asleep.

The Russians of long ago under Mongol rule lived simply and doubtless welcomed the surcease from internal anarchy and alien invasion afforded by the *Pax Mongolica*. Their conquerors imposed no "alien way of life." Mongol governors and commanders asked no more than obedience, tribute, and maintenance of law and order—with all resistance, to be sure, ruthlessly suppressed by Mongol armies. Local Russian rulers who yielded were tolerantly treated. Their duties consisted in traveling periodically to Sarai, capital of the "Empire of the Golden Horde" east of the lower Volga near modern Tsaritsyn or Stalingrad, and there rendering obeisance and payment and accepting *yarliki,* or investitures, authorizing them to assume functions of local administration and tax-collection in the name of the Great Khan. So lived Russia for 240 years (1240–1480).

During these centuries of shadow—longer than the whole span to date of the independence of the USA—Russians were isolated from Western Europe and thus knew nothing of the Renaissance and the adumbrations of the Reformation. Silence enveloped the peoples of the steppes. Yet their Mongol masters taught them skills they had not hitherto known: census-taking, tax-gathering, coinage, customs dues, postal communication, military conscription, and ultimately the uses of militarism and absolutism, as counter-weapons of emancipation. As in Spain under the Moors, rulers and subjects united Church and State in a holy war for liberation from Moslem overlords.

This crusade, in Russia as in Spain, was long delayed in reaching its goal. Rulership of the Mongol subject state of Moscow or Muscovy passed in the late 1200's to Daniel, son of Alexander Nevsky. His successors in Central Russia were Ivan Kalita (John Moneybags), Ivan II, Dmitri, Basil the Blind, and Ivan III.

During these years the Duchy of Muscovy became the sole focal point of Russian resistance to Mongol rule. In the year 1380 Prince Dmitri of Moscow (henceforth known as Dmitri Donskoi or Dmitri of the Don), supported by St. Sergius of Radonezh, rebelled and for the first time defeated a Mongol army at Kulikovo near the Don. His triumph was "Pyhrric." Two years later Mongol horsemen plundered Moscow and put it to the torch. This Muscovite enterprise in emancipation failed, but it identified the prospective liberators.

A hundred years later Ivan III (1462–1505), Grand Duke of Muscovy—later called "Ivan the Great"—succeeded, in alliance with the Khan of the Crimea and without open warfare, in discontinuing tribute to the Golden Horde. He thus restored at long last the political independence of a new Russia whose center was Moscow. He hired Italian architects to build the Moscow Kremlin, annexed Tver and Novgorod, and recreated a Russian realm which, like its precursor of earlier times, owed much to Byzantium.

The Byzantine or Eastern Roman Empire perished in the year 1453 when the Ottoman Turks besieged its fabulous capital, breached the Roman walls whose defenders had thrown back all assailants for a thousand years, and built on the ruins a new Ottoman Empire with Constantinople as its metropolis. The last of the Byzantine Caesars, Constantine Paleologus, died in battle. Ivan of Muscovy married his niece, Sophia, and took unto himself the Byzantine title of "Autocrat" and, as a symbol of power, the Byzantine double-headed eagle.

The Anatomy of Autocracy

Basil III, son of Sophia and Ivan the Great, inherited the Muscovite throne in 1505. In the year of his succession, Abbot Philotheus of Pskov Monastery addressed a memorable message to the new sovereign:

> The church of ancient Rome fell because of the Apollinarian heresy; as to the Second Rome—the church of Constantinople—it has been hewn by the axes of Ishmaelites, but this Third new Rome—the Holy Apostolic Church, under thy mighty rule—shines throughout the entire world more brightly than the sun. All the Orthodox Christian realms have converged in thine own. Thou art the sole Autocrat of the Universe, the only Caesar of the Christians. . . . Two Romes have fallen, but the Third stands, and no fourth can never be . . .

This early vision of Russia's Messianic mission to "save the world" was to persist in sundry guises for many centuries, including the 20th. The benighted and half-barbaric Muscovy of the 16th Century emerged as a "Great Power," but soon proved incapable of saving even itself from the evils of anarchy at home and assault from abroad. The stage on which was to be enacted a fantastic and mournful drama was set during the long reign of Ivan IV (1533–84) who, at the age of three, succeeded his father, Basil III. As he matured, this contemporary of Emperor Akbar and Elizabeth I took the title of "Tsar" (probably a Slavic contraction of "Caesar") and is known to posterity as *Ivan Grozny:* "Ivan the Terrible" or "John the Dread."

This appellation was merited by his many crimes, some of which were followed by repentance, abdication, withdrawal to a monastery, and return to power. His sins, in addition to indecent debaucheries, included the murder of his son, the execution of the Metropolitan of the Church, the killing by torture of all who evoked his displeasure, and the butchery of the burghers of Novgorod for allegedly treasonable negotiations with the kingdom of Poland. This sovereign was at once a statesman and a madman—a combination of qualities destined to recur at intervals in Tsarist Russia and in the USSR of our own time. Such incongruous attributes of power-holders reflect the ignorance, disorder, and passion for anarchy of a "backward" people, constantly assailed by foreign foes and chronically incapable during most of the unhappy past of achieving any semblance of internal peace or external efficacy save through utter subjection to cruel and ruthless despotism.

The major aims which Ivan Grozny set for himself were fourfold: to break the bonds against Muscovite expansion imposed by the still formidable might of the Mongols or Tartars, often allied with the Ottoman Turks; to recover the "lost provinces" of western Russia, seized by Swedes, Germans, Lithuanians, and Poles during the era of the Mongols, who took little interest in the far frontiers of their Russian subjects; to make Muscovy once more a part of Europe; and to vanquish invaders from the West. In pursuit of these goals Ivan experienced some successes and many failures.

As means to his ends, he crystallized the Muscovite polity into an unlimited, divine-right Autocracy and brought into being the first of the forces of political police, destined to persist for centuries in Tsarist Russia and to be revived in even more terrifying form in the post-1917 USSR. Ivan's *Oprichniki,* garbed in black, wielding whips, and wearing dog's heads, tormented and killed all suspected of dissent.

He also hired mercenary soldiers, including *Streltsi* or musketeers; authorized adventurers or "Cossacks" to seek fame and fortune at the expense of the Turks and Tartars in the wild southern borderland of the "Ukraine," which originally meant "beyond the frontier"; beat down the *Boyars* or old nobility and created a new nobility of *Dvoryane* or courtiers and *Pomeshchiks* or estate-owners who, in return for fighting for the Tsar, were rewarded with lands whose cultivators were reduced to serfdom so that their masters might profit by their labor. Absolutism, terrorism, feudalism, and militarism thus became the bases of royal power in what was long to remain a nightmare realm of dread.

With the record of Ivan's triumphs and tragedies and those of his successors we cannot here concern ourselves. Yet a few features of lasting import in this bizarre chapter of the human adventure must be noted lest we lose perspective on the Russian present by forgetting that it is a product of the Russian past. In 1552 Ivan Grozny, carrying the cross of Dmitri Donskoi at the head of a hundred thousand troops, smashed the Mongols at Kazan and in 1556 took Astrakhan at the delta of the Volga. The grotesque Cathedral of St. Basil was erected in Red Square in Moscow in honor of victory. The door to the East was now broken open. In 1581–82 the Cossack Yermak and his freebooters reached the Ob-Irtish and made central Siberia a gift to the Tsar. The Steppe Road, long a highway of Asians moving westward, now became a highway of Russians moving eastward.

By way of anticipating things to come, the first Russian treaty with China, 1689, left the Amur Basin in the hands of the Manchus and confined Russian migrants (who were fur-trappers, gold-seekers, explorers, and adventurers rather than settlers) to the northern wilderness. By 1750, following the explorations of Captain Bering, a Danish navigator in the Russian Navy (d. 1741), Russians had reached North America. By the 1820's they had penetrated as far south as California—a circumstance which contributed to the promulgation of the "Monroe Doctrine" of 1823, forbidding further European colonization of the Americas, and led to the relinquishment of Russian claims south of 54°40′ and to the first Russian-American treaty in 1824. The sale of Alaska to the USA in 1867 made Bering Strait the easternmost limit of Muscovite aggrandizement. Given this

tradition of discovery and expansion across unbelievable dis-
tances of wasteland, vaster and far less hospitable than the great
plains crossed by America's westward-moving pioneers in the
19th Century, it is not incongruous that Russians in the middle
decades of the 20th Century should have participated actively in
the exploration of Antarctica and should have "beaten America"
in probing extraterrestrial space and first sending rockets to, and
around, the moon.

No such unlikely future could have been foreseen by anyone in his senses as he viewed the dismal Russia of Ivan IV,
during whose reign the quest for space began. Successful in the
East, he failed altogether to "break open the window" to the
West. He negotiated trade relations with England, but was
spurned in his attempts to marry Lady Mary Hastings and to
conclude an alliance against Poland with Queen Elizabeth I. His
wars against Poles, Germans, and Swedes in a futile effort to
recover the River Road and reach the Baltic led only to another
sacking and burning of Moscow by Tartars and Turks from the
Crimea in 1571.

The curse of impotence and anarchy, sometimes exorcised
but ever resumed, lay heavily upon the Tsardom from beginning
to end. When Ivan died in 1584 the throne passed to his feeble-
minded son, Fedor, previously judged by his father to be better
qualified to be a convent bell-ringer than a Tsar. One of the
eternal problems of all politics and all government is how to
assure an orderly transition of authority from a passing group of
power-holders to a coming group of power-holders. The method
of monarchism, to which the Russians of old aspired, sometimes
works via dynastic succession and sometimes fails. The method
of democracy—once described by Winston Churchill as "the
worst form of government ever devised, except for all the other
forms which have been tried"—postulates free elections among
competing candidates for office with political majorities tolerat-
ing political minorities and all cheerfully acquiescing in the results of polling in parliaments or publics or both. The Russians
of 400 years ago knew nothing of the latter device and often
fumbled in their efforts to apply the former formula. Even today, as we shall see, this problem, albeit ameliorated since the
death of Stalin, has still not been wholly solved by Russia's
rulers.

Under the nominal rule of dim-witted Fedor, power passed
to his father-in-law, Boris Godunov. When Fedor died in 1598,
Boris was "elected" Tsar by the *Zemsky Sobor* or Assembly of

the Land, a transitory "parliament" of feudal nobles—whose existence was unknown to the mass of the population and whose authority was denied by the *Boyars,* including many of its own members. Some among them championed a "false Dmitri," pretending to be Fedor's brother who had been killed in 1591. Boris died, amid waxing chaos, in 1605. Cossacks and Poles brought the false "Dmitri" to Moscow where he was swiftly slain. A faction of *Boyars* elevated Boris Shuisky to the Tsardom, as others supported a second "false Dmitri." Meanwhile a great peasant rebellion (1608–10) boiled up under the leadership of Bolotnikov as the first of a series of such outbursts—of which the more notable later examples were the serf revolts led by Stenka Razin in 1667–71 and by Pugachev in 1773–74. All were drowned in blood. Until 1917 Russia's landlords, aided by the full military might of the Autocracy, always managed in the end to suppress by violence these outbursts of rage among the *Muzhiks,* in which furious farmers, driven to desperation by poverty and oppression, burned the manor houses and murdered their masters.

But in the "Time of Troubles" (1598–1613), class conflict, coupled with brutal contests over succession to rulership, led to anarchy and, almost, to another demise of the Russian polity. Western neighbors, always eager to cast down the potentially threatening "Colossus of the North," moved in. Narva and Novgorod were seized by the Swedes, and Smolensk by the Poles. In 1610 a Polish army occupied Moscow. Russia once more appeared doomed as an independent community. But the second "false Dmitri" was killed, and a popular uprising ensued. The rebels were led by Cosmo Minin, a butcher of Nijni Novgorod, and by Prince Pozharsky. Their statues still stand today before the Cathedral of St. Basil in Red Square. The Polish invaders were ousted from Moscow in the year 1612. A year later the *Zemky Sobor* elected to the Tsardom 17-year-old Michael Romanov, distantly related to earlier rulers and destined to found the dynasty which endured until 1917.

In the reign of Alexis (1645–76) the Cossacks of the southland, under Hetman Bogdan Hmelnitsky (whose equestrian monument still graces Kiev's central square), waged war against Poland and against the Polish landlords of the Ukraine—with both contestants perpetrating hideous atrocities. In 1667—ever since celebrated as the year of the "reunion" of Russia and the Ukraine—Muscovy regained Kiev, Smolensk, and most of the eastern shore of the Dnieper, though not yet all the lost western lands. Peter the Great (1682–1725) broke open the "window to the West" by abandoning Moscow, building a new capital on the Neva, and traveling *incognito* (1697–98) in Europe to learn Western skills in ship-building, architecture, and armaments. On his return he savagely suppressed a revolt of the *Streltsi;* cut off beards and heads to force the nobles to "Westernize"; assumed the title of "Emperor"; and founded, among other enduring institutions, the Russian navy, the Academy of Sciences, the Senate or highest administrative court, and the Holy Synod as an agency for State control of the Church.

In the "Great Northern War" against Sweden (1699–1721) Peter's forces suffered defeat at Narva in 1700 at the hands of King Charles XII. Peter later tasted victory. Charles vanquished Russia's feeble allies in Denmark and Poland and invaded the Ukraine in alliance with Hetman Mazepa, a Cossack chieftain who welcomed Swedish aid as a means of freeing his country from Great Russian rule. (This design for violence, born of a persistent and forever frustrated Ukrainian nationalism, was often to recur in later centuries.) In 1709 at Poltava, Peter's army crushed his foes and sent Sweden's king in flight to Turkey. (The saddles and accoutrements of both monarchs, along with painted depictions of their encounters, are still to be seen in the Winter Palace in Leningrad.) By the "Peace of Nystad" (1721), concluded after a Russian invasion of Sweden, Peter annexed most of Karelia along with Estonia and Livonia on the south shore of the Gulf of Finland.

The later fortunes of the Romanovs and their subjects cannot here be recounted. It is enough to note that Russia's rulers, in their ceaseless striving to overcome Russian backwardness and weakness in the face of more efficient and aggressive Western Powers, sought security through despotism, militarism, and feudalism at home and through territorial aggrandizement and Messianism abroad. These devices of adaptation worked well enough for a century and more but finally brought the realm to ruin by prolonging old ways into new times when new ways were needed and by confronting a ramshackle and obsolescent polity with foreign foes who had long since become "modernized."

Under Peter's daughter Elizabeth (1741–61) Russian troops fought against Prussia in the "Seven Years War" and took Berlin in 1760—but to no avail since the mad Tsar, Paul III, made peace with Frederick the Great on Prussian terms. Catherine the Great (1762–96), originally a German princess and long addicted to "liberalism" and a multiplicity of lovers, warred with Turkey; made possession of Constantinople a goal of Russian foreign policy; and joined Austria and Prussia in partitioning the impotent kingdom of Poland in three stages: 1772, 1795, and 1796. Her able commander, Alexander Suvorov (1729–1800), defeated the Turks, crushed Polish rebels, and, had he lived longer, might have thwarted Napoleon's conquest of Europe. Catherine's "liberalism" turned "reactionary" in her horror at the French Revolution and allowed of no "reforms" which might imperil the privileges of the nobles.

Like Catherine, Alexander I (1801–25) began his reign as a liberal and ended it as a reactionary. He toyed with Western notions of constitutionalism and of emancipation of the serfs and even gave thought to the proposals of his adviser, Mikhail Speransky, for a representative system of local and national government. Nothing came of these projects. Alexander's interests were elsewhere. He joined Austria, Prussia, and Britain in fighting Napoleon, acknowledged defeat, divided Europe with Bonaparte at Tilsit (1807), and thereafter wrested Finland from Sweden (1809) and Bessarabia from the Ottomans (1812). In June of 1812 his realm was again menaced with political extinction at the hands of Napoleon's "Grand Army" of invasion.

In the "Great Patriotic War" Napoleon's soldiers took Moscow and then died of cold and hunger amid the ashes of the burned city and on the long retreat to the West. In renewed alliance with Britain, Austria and Prussia, Alexander brought the French empire to ruin and entered Paris in triumph in March of 1815—heroized by all of reactionary Europe, idolized at the Congress of Vienna by the would-be restorers of the *status quo,* and widely praised in conservative circles for his sponsorship of the mystical "Holy Alliance," designed to suppress all revolutions everywhere in the name of Christianity.

These successes abroad had no relevance to the problems of a sick society at home. Nicholas I (1825–55) evolved a simple formula for dealing with discontent: suppress critics at home and win victories abroad. He reactivated the "third section" of the Imperial Chancery as a political police, later called the *Okhrana,* to root out and crush all opponents of the regime. He waged war on Turkey and contributed to the independence of Greece. As "keeper of order" in Europe, he sent his troops to put down the Polish rebellion of 1830–31 and to smash the liberal Hungarian revolutionists of 1848–49. Another war against Turkey led Britain, France, and Sardinia to come to the aid of the Ottomans as a means of "containing" Tsarist ambitions to dominate the Near East. In the ensuing Crimean War of 1854–56, limited and local but no less lethal to its participants, Nicholas suffered humiliating defeat and promptly died.

His son and successor, Alexander II (1855–81), made peace in Paris with the Western Powers and soon became the memorable "reforming Tsar." His innovations were many but, as time would tell, inadequate to the exigencies of the occasion. His major reform, achieved without civil war, was the abolition of serfdom in March, 1861, decreed almost two years before the outlawing of slavery in the USA in the midst of civil war. The freed serfs, however, received only part of the land they deemed to be theirs—with all such lands held collectively by the village *mir* rather than partitioned into individual farms. The peasants, moreover, were obliged to pay "redemption dues" to the State as a means of compensating the landlords. The chronic hunger of the peasants for land, along with their hatred of the estate-owners, thus persisted despite the end of serfdom. Alexander likewise brought into being county councils or *Zemstvos* as agents of local self-government, albeit controlled by the landlords (1864); introduced trial by jury in a reorganized court system (1864); initiated a measure of municipal self-government (1870); recast the military service (1874); and was contemplating plans for a national constitution when a terrorist bomb ended his life (March 13, 1881).

Alexander III (1881–94) symbolized black reaction. Nicolas II (1894–1917) was dominated by his wife, Princess Alex of Hesse, who in turn relied for advice on mystics and quacks, including at the end the debauched monk Rasputin. The last of the Romanovs epitomized weakness and folly both at home and abroad. National defeat at the hands of Japan (1904–05) provoked an abortive revolution. National defeat at the hands of the Central Powers (1915–16) unleashed the great revolution which ended the dynasty and plunged Russia into an era of anarchy from which once more escape was to be had only through a new form of despotism.

The Tsarist regime from beginning to end was a divine-right Autocracy with no semblance of public participation beyond the provincial *Zemstvos* and the village *mir*. Earlier quasi-parliaments, such as the Duma of the Boyars and the *Zemsky Sobor*, had long since vanished. The Tsar alone appointed and removed Governors of provinces; members of the Council of

Ministers or Cabinet, and of the Imperial Council which drafted legislation; the Privy Counselors, comprising the Senate or highest administrative and judicial body; and the Procurator of the Holy Synod. The Manifesto of October 17, 1905, promised civil rights and popular elections for an effective parliament, but the pledge was soon ignored. The Imperial Duma (1906–17) was checkmated by an upper house in the form of an enlarged Imperial Council, restricted to reactionary men of wealth by limiting the franchise and devising an indirect system of class elections, and given no authority whatever over the Ministry, the budget, or even legislation—all of which could be vetoed by the Autocrat. Such a structure of power could function effectively in Tudor England or Bourbon France. In the 20th Century it was hopelessly obsolete as a device for serving human needs, even in backward Russia.

The Pathology of Revolution

Political scientists, who are usually neither scientists nor politicians but scholars and teachers, have grappled inconclusively with the phenomenon of revolution for thousands of years—ever since Plato and Aristotle, and long before among the thinkers and writers of ancient India and China. The results—alas!—are unclear, unlike those of the physical and biological scientists. Whether this discouraging consequence is due to the incompetence of political and social "scientists," or to the extraordinary complexity of the patterns of human behavior they try to study, is debatable. The fact remains that no generally acceptable "theory" of revolution has emerged save among the Marxists, whose misconceptions we must consider in the next chapter.

With the wisdom of hindsight, we can see that the Tsarist Russia of the late 19th and early 20th Centuries was "ripe for revolution." The question of "Why?" is perhaps best answered by noting that the Russian community had become bitterly divided against itself during a troubled time of economic and social change. Autocracy often proves to be a workable form of power in agrarian feudal communities dominated by a landed aristocracy. But let such a community experience the beginnings of "modern" commerce, finance, and industry, bringing into being an urban middle class sharply different in life-ways and outlook from nobles or peasants, and the old order is jeopardized —the more so as such a middle class is soon bifurcated into antagonistic groupings of businessmen and factory-workers, each at odds with the other but both opposed to the *ancien régime* of absolutism and feudalism.

This familiar source of revolutions in contemporary Western Civilization was the matrix of the violent upheavals which from time to time convulsed England, France, and America in the 17th, 18th, and 19th Centuries, with later counterparts in Asia, Africa, and South America. In Tsarist Russia of a hundred years ago, despite its backwardness, the process had already begun. Here too, albeit belatedly, modern science and technology, as applied by entrepreneurs to the tasks of producing goods and services for sale to consumers, created a growing and prosperous middle class of owners, managers, and professional people and a growing and impoverished working class of urban wage-earners. Both groups, in search of gain or redress of grievances, aspired to participation in public policy-making.

Both were resisted in their aspirations by most of the members of the old aristocracy and the Tsarist bureaucracy, alike determined to safeguard their privileges against all challengers. To the chronic land-hunger of a primitive peasantry, imbued with perennial hatred for the landlords, was added the discontent of a rising *bourgeoisie* and a waxing *proletariat*—to use Marxist jargon which, in this case at least, bears some resemblance to reality. Both questioned and threatened the old order and confusedly pursued dreams of a new order in which somehow (nobody knew how) Russia could achieve some semblance of the liberty, equality, and fraternity reported to prevail in the democracies of Western Europe.

These formless hopes were given shape and substance by the emergent Russian "intelligentsia." These thinkers, writers, and artists were socially sensitive and conscience-stricken sons and daughters of aristocrats, searching for salvation, or, in some instances, children of the new businessmen or, occasionally, of illiterate farmers or factory hands. Their talents and ambitions, reflecting the genius of a greatly gifted people, found expression in the most impressive music, drama, poetry, and fiction of the 19th Century. Their political beliefs lacked any common denominator save for a widely shared conviction that better days in a freer society could be achieved through reform or revolution.

Some of the intellectuals, to be sure, rallied to the defense of the *status quo*. Among them were the anti-Western "Slavophiles" of the mid-century whose conservatism was shared by

Nikolai Y. Danilevsky (1822–85), Pan-Slavist philosopher of history, and also, in his later years, by the literary immortal, Fyodor N. Dostoevsky (1821–81). Perhaps the most eloquent voice of reaction was that of Konstantine P. Pobedonostsev (1827–1907), Procurator of the Holy Synod for 25 years, who held that democracy was a "lie" and that Russians were so slothful and violent as to require authoritarian rulers willing and able to suppress all dissent.

Yet republicans, radicals, and rebels were more numerous than reactionaries in the ranks of the intelligentsia. One of their early heroes was Paul Pestel, leader of the "Decembrists" of 1825: a group of liberal army officers who attempted revolution and suffered exile or death. In later decades Alexander Herzen, Vissarion Belinsky, and others of like mind at the University of Moscow espoused a vague "socialism" inspired by the village *mir* of the peasantry. Philosophical anarchism found a spokesman in Peter Kropotkin (1842–1921) and revolutionary anarchism in fiery Mikhail Bakunin (1814–71), who participated in most of the European revolutions of his day. Among the terrorists were Sergei G. Nechaev (1847–82) and Peter N. Tkachev (1844–86), both of whom foreshadowed things to come in preaching revolt by way of a small, disciplined, conspiratorial brotherhood of professional revolutionaries.

Other violent spirits, in the name of *Zemlya i Volya* (Land and Freedom), sought in vain in the 1860's to stir up a peasant rebellion and to kill the Tsar. By 1879 Peter Lavrov had organized the *Narodniki* or Populists who looked to the peasantry for liberation, championed a Constituent Assembly, and assassinated Tsarist officials. Their political heirs, first organized as a party in 1902 and successful by 1917 in converting most of the peasants to their cause, were the Social Revolutionaries, led by Victor M. Chernov (1876–1952). The SR's, as they came to be called, also practiced assassination and preached a misty gospel of agrarian socialism.

These and other embittered souls were first called "nihilists" by Turgenev and were caricatured by Dostoevsky in *The Possessed*. Most of them were "socialists" in the sense of seeking salvation through common ownership of property after the overthrow of the Autocracy. Through genius or destiny or accident, one such group of socialists, after the turn of the century, was to become more significant, or at least more successful, than all the rest. But in this there was nothing "inevitable" nor could anyone in the 1890's or early 1900's have foreseen the final outcome. All that was clear was that agitators of sundry persuasions were appealing to disgruntled workers, peasants, and businessmen against the nobility and the Tsardom and that the old order might some day be doomed unless its defenders were prepared in time to redress grievances and to make new departures. This they were unable or unwilling to do.

2 - Messiah and Millennium

The Gospel of Salvation

In the world of the 1960's well over a billion people, comprising more than a third of the human race, are ruled by disciples of Marxism. How this came about is not our present concern. But at the same time government and politics in the USSR must forever remain impenetrable mysteries to all who lack any knowledge of the secular belief-system and value-system which its rulers profess. This subversive ideology—called by Bertrand Russell the "fourth of the Judaic higher religions" and by Arnold J. Toynbee the great "Jewish-Christian heresy" of our time—is odious to all believers in free enterprise in business and in civil liberty and democracy in the governance of men. Yet it must be understood, if possible. And since it has spawned vast libraries of literature, both *pro* and *contra,* understanding is to be had by those who seek it.

The father and founder, son of a Jewish lawyer of Treves who soon became a Protestant Christian, was born in the Rhineland in 1818 and died in London in 1883. During his sixty-five years Karl Marx earned his Ph.D. at the age of twenty-three, embraced atheism and radicalism, married Jenny von Westphalen, raised three daughters, got himself expelled from Prussia and France, lived in poverty in Soho, worked for a time as foreign correspondent of Horace Greeley's *New York Tribune,* toiled in the library of the British Museum, and published prodigious numbers of books and articles, among them *The Communist Manifesto* of 1848 and *Capital.* His life-long collaborator and wealthy patron was genial, generous, German-born Friedrich Engels (1820–95), lover of Irish-born Lizzy Burns. Said Engels soberly at Marx's simple funeral in Highgate Cemetery: "The greatest living thinker has ceased to think. . . . His name will endure through the ages and so also will his work!"

The well-articulated cult concocted by Marx and Engels is many things in one. Marxism is first of all a theory of the Universe. Marx rejected George Hegel's philosophical idealism in favor of philosophical materialism, which holds that Matter is primary and Mind is derivative. But Marx borrowed from Hegel his formula of the "dialectic"—thesis, antithesis, synthesis— which purports to explain all processes of change. The cosmology of Marxism is thus "dialectical materialism," whose intricacies and implications we need not here explore.

Marxism is also a hypothesis of history and a system of sociology, commonly called "historical materialism." All human societies are alleged to be shaped or "determined" as to their structure and institutions by their levels of technology and their methods of production. These are the "base." All else is "superstructure." From the base emerge social classes which are assumed to be typically bi-polarized into propertied exploiters and propertyless victims of exploitation: masters and slaves, landlords and serfs, *bourgeoisie* and *proletariat*. Class conflict is thus the clue to history, the key to social change, and the secret of all politics and all government.

Marxism, moreover, is a doctrine of economics, called "political economy" in Marx's time. The owners of "means of production" constitute the "ruling class" in all societies. With the advent of the machine and of modern "capitalism," the owners are the entrepreneurs of business. According to the Marxist "labor theory of value," borrowed from earlier British political economists, the price of every commodity is in the last analysis determined by the amount of labor devoted, directly or indirectly, to its production. The sinister secret of capitalism is that capitalists make profits by paying workers less than the workers produce. The difference is "surplus value," expropriated by the owners of the means of production. Capitalism is thus revealed to be an unethical scheme of exploitation whereby the rich rob the poor of what the poor create.

The system, however, is self-destructive according to the Marxist analysis. The passion of the capitalists is accumulation by maximizing profits. This can only be done by exploiting workers. Hence the operation of the "iron law of wages," borrowed from David Ricardo, according to which wages will always tend to be pushed down to a bare subsistence level and be kept there by competition for jobs among the members of the "reserve army of the unemployed." In this process the middle class will be ultimately ground to pieces between the "upper and nether millstones" and become "proletarianized." Finally, after successive crises of the business cycle of ever-increasing severity and duration, a small minority of bloated capitalists will confront a vast majority of starving proletarians. Then comes the Revolution. "Workers of the world, unite! You have nothing to lose but your chains."

To continue our effort to separate out the threads in a tangled fabric, Marxism is likewise a theory of the State and a proposition about politics. The premise is "economic determinism." All Marxists are economic determinists. But be it noted, lest confusion be worse confounded, that not all economic determinists are Marxists—e.g., James Harrington, Alexander Hamilton, James Madison, Charles Beard. By the Marxist dispensation, the State is always no more and no less than an "executive committee" of the ruling class, perpetuating the prevailing system of exploitation through force, fraud, and favors. Politics is thus seen to be a competition among rivals for material gain and, when clearly comprehended, a surface mirror of an underlying "class struggle" between irreconcilably antagonistic social groups.

Finally—albeit finality is lacking in such matters—Marxism is a Messianic and Millennial vision of a Golden Age. The "inevitable" collapse of capitalism means the "proletarian revolution." But this transition, unlike all its precursors in earlier rebellions of slaves or serfs or burghers against aristocrats and kings, will inaugurate a wholly new era in the human adventure. The outraged workers will smash the "bourgeois State" and establish a "dictatorship of the proletariat." Marx was foggy as to the nature of this predicted form of political power but saw, or thought he saw, some of its lineaments in the revolutionary Paris Commune of 1871, finally drowned in blood by the troops of the bourgeois National Assembly. The proletarian dictatorship will "expropriate the expropriators"—i.e., confiscate and socialize all means of production—and thus initiate the "cooperative commonwealth."

How this new Heavenly City would function was left vague in the pristine Marxist prognosis. But it was postulated that somehow the willing labor of each would contribute to the wealth and welfare of all in a social order freer and more perfect than any hitherto known. Under a transitional regime of "socialism" the distributive principle would be: from each according to his ability, to each according to his work; and in the ultimate regime of "communism": from each according to his ability, to each according to his needs. The result would be an egalitarian "classless society" in which, at long last, the exploitation of man by man would be at an end. And since the State is merely a vehicle of coercion whereby exploiting classes dominate exploited classes, there will be no need of the State in the classless society of times to come. The State will "wither away." True freedom will for the first time dawn in man's endless striving toward the Open Society. Each and all will know liberty as men have never known it before. The perfectability of mankind will become possible beyond the fondest dreams of the prophets of ancient days.

Here is a noble vision of the emancipation of humanity from age-old injustice and evil. Here is also a formula in whose name its converts were to establish tyrannies among the most monstrous in all human experience. The paradox admits of various levels of explanation. Man, say some, is always a bearer of Original Sin. Therefore, dreams of freedom, alienated from God and divorced from the problem of the salvation of each human soul, eventuate in despotism and new injustices. Marx and the Marxists, say others, stultified their purpose by embracing the pernicious idea that the end justifies the means. When means to ends include violent revolution and mass robbery and murder in the name of "class conflict," the final end will not be liberty but more oppression and persecution. Still others see the sources of the fading of the Marxist vision in the historical legacy of Russia—and of China. Some would solve the problem by noting that Marxism is simply wrong in all or most of its postulates. A few non-Marxists assume that the Marxist adventure of our time, despite hideous tragedies and recurrent frustrations, may yet attain some facsimile of the Good Life in the Good Society. Among convinced Marxists there can be no doubts for here, as with all true believers, the test of faith is to believe what is absurd. But these are anticipations of the balance of our inquiry.

Refutations of Marxism are a dime a dozen. Marx and Engels and some of their later converts, most notably Lenin, arrived at new and fruitful insights into human affairs. Marx's description of capitalism in mid-19th-Century England was not wholly inaccurate. It paradoxically resembles Soviet "socialism" in the

1930's. All industrialization in its early stages is painful, exploitive, and productive of grave abuses, whatever its ideological or institutional framework. But the major premises of Marxism, viewed in retrospect, are demonstrably false.

The ancient quarrel between philosophical "idealists" and "materialists" is meaningless in the light of modern physics which has shown, with terrifying conclusiveness, that all matter can be converted into energy and *vice versa*. The validity of the "dialectic" is questionable. Class conflict is not normal but abnormal in human communities. The "labor theory of value" is erroneous. Capitalism is no more and no less a system of exploitation than any other system which inspires or compels people to produce more than they consume with the balance available for investment and economic growth. In mature capitalistic economies the "proletariat" does not become larger and poorer but smaller and richer, while the "doomed" middle class waxes ever mightier and more affluent. No civilized society has ever been, or can ever be, "classless" or "stateless." Total socialism, where achieved, thus far resembles Aldous Huxley's *Brave New World* or George Orwell's *1984* far more than Plato's perfect polity or Sir Thomas More's *Utopia*.

While the refutation could readily be continued over many pages, it is operationally important to note that all refutations of cults and creeds are irrelevant to believers and even to many potential believers. Endless efforts at demolishing Marxism are comparable to Mark Twain's comment on nicotine: "Giving up smoking is the easiest thing in the world. I've done it hundreds of times." Any ideology which makes a powerful appeal to the discontents and the hopes of large numbers of human beings will, quite inevitably, make converts, regardless of repeated demonstrations of the errors of its major premises. Such has been the fate during the centuries of Buddhism, Hinduism, Christianity, Islam, Democracy, Fascism. Such is also the destiny of Marxism and the Marxists.

The scope of the "market" for Marxism, as for earlier revolutionary cults and subversive creeds, is in large part a product of the skills or unskills of power-holders in remedying abuses and in giving masses of men and women the experience, or at least the hope, of a tolerable life in a just and orderly society. Power-holders in the global State System of the 20th Century have thus far failed to fulfill this responsibility. To successive generations experiencing disastrous World War, calamitous Depression, and catastrophic World War once more, followed by prospects of the desperate impoverishment and possible thermonuclear suicide of mankind, the Marxist formula of salvation, however fatuous in logic or discredited by the horrors perpetrated in its name, will continue to seem plausible and appealing to all who feel alienated from a world they never made. If people are to be immunized against the seductions of false philosophies, they must be able to convince themselves that things as they are offer opportunities for personal self-fulfillment rather than a prospect of poverty, violence, and disorder in human relations. By this test the rulers of all the nation states in the world of the 20th Century have, to date, failed more often than they have suc-ceeded. The rulers of Tsarist Russia failed most abysmally and, in failing, finally abdicated their rulership to the Marxists.

The Spark

During the final decades of the 19th Century the cult of Marxism won converts among alienated Russian intellectuals. Workers and peasants, being largely illiterate, knew nothing as yet of such matters. Some of these converts were to fashion the "Party" which was to seize power in the revolutionary Russia of 1917. The name is misleading, for this conspiratorial fraternity of disciples and of prospective oligarchs bore no resemblance, and still bears no resemblance, to political parties in the Western democracies where politicians of various persuasions compete with one another for public support in a relatively free market for civic discussion and partisan activity.

The Russian Marxists became more Russian than Marxist by virtue of the circumstance that they were compelled, willy-nilly, to pursue their purposes in a context not of democracy but of the repressive and intolerant Tsarist Autocracy. Like other humans in other times and climes, many among them subtly absorbed the attitudes and attributes of the enemy they fought against. Ancient folk-wisdom tells us that those who sup with the Devil must use a long spoon. It tells us also that fire must be fought with fire. But those who confront the Devil often become devilish. And those who fight fire with fire often become fiery and frequently end by burning or being burned. This destiny, perhaps implicit in the human condition, was not to be escaped by the Marxists of Russia.

The revolutionary creed, borrowed from the West, slowly permeated the ranks of the intelligentsia. It competed with other creeds—some of them natively Russian (e.g., Pan-Slavism, "Nihilism," Popularism, and the nascent agrarian-socialist doctrines of the SR's) and others imported from abroad (e.g., "Utopian Socialism," anarchism, syndicalism, individualism, liberal democracy, and the "revisionist," non-revolutionary, and "reformist" Marxism of the German Social Democrat, Eduard Bernstein, whose moderation of the original gospel found more and more followers among Western Marxists after 1900). How and why pristine Marxism finally vanquished all its Russian rivals is a problem which, by the 1960's, has been explored in minute detail in hundreds of books in dozens of languages by scores of scholars, Marxist, un-Marxist, and anti-Marxist. The results, albeit often dull, are priceless for serious researchers into the timeless question of how the now came out of the then. But these results cannot here be reviewed nor are they germane, save deviously, to the issue of how and why and to what ends Marxists rule Russia today. Let us content ourselves with the bare bones of the matter here in hand.

In 1870 Marx and Engels in London were surprised to learn that the first foreign translation of Vol. I of *Capital* from the original German had been authorized in St. Petersburg. The Tsarist censors regarded it as harmless because unreadable, even though "completely socialist." This fortuitous literary transaction had no immediate visible effect, but contributed to startling consequences later. The members of *Zemlya i Volya* reached a parting of the ways in the year 1879. Some among them, resisted by others, opposed assassination as a political weapon, less out of moral scruples than out of Machiavellian calculation of expediency. The dissidents included George V. Plekhanov (1856–1918), who was converted to Marxism while abroad in 1881 and was to be known, because of his later propaganda activities, as "the Father of Russian Marxism." In September, 1883, six months after Marx died, Paul Axelrod, Leo Deutsch, Vera Zasulich, and other Russian Marxists in exile joined Plekhanov in Geneva in founding what they called the "Emancipation of Labor Group," aimed at converting the Populists to Marxism. These revolutionists, to be followed by many more, toyed during the 1880's with "programs" for a Russian Social Democratic Party. Their smuggling of Marxist literature into Imperial Russia contributed to further conversions among intellectuals, even though without impact as yet among the gray masses to whom such appeals were ostensibly addressed.

Among the few thousands of Russian "egg-heads" thus influenced, three—later destined for fame or infamy—are worthy of special mention. One was the child, born April 22, 1870, in Simbirsk, of the daughter of a Volga-German army doctor. Her husband was a high school teacher of mathematics and physics: Ilya N. Ulianov. His educational efforts in the valley of the Volga won him rank in the honorary nobility. Little Vladimir Ilyich had an older sister Anna (1864–1935) and an older brother Alexander (1866–87), and was to have three younger siblings, christened Olga, Dmitri, and Maria. The family was conservative and Orthodox. Young Vladimir grew up in Simbirsk and attended the local Classical High School—whose principal was Fyodor Kerensky, father of Alexander Kerensky (1881–   ). Vladimir's own father died of a stroke when the boy was 16. During his 17th year sister Anna and brother Alexander, both students in St. Petersburg, were arrested on charges of belonging to *Narodnaya Volya* and conspiring to kill the Tsar. Anna was acquitted. Alexander proudly confessed his guilt and, with four fellow-conspirators, was hanged in 1887, despite his mother's efforts in the capital to secure mercy.

The bereaved Ulianovs moved to Kazan, where Vladimir entered the local law school, only to be expelled for "subversive" activities. In 1888 he began reading Marx. In 1891 he passed the law examinations in St. Petersburg and briefly practiced law in Samara. The year 1893 found him back in the capital; then abroad in Germany, Switzerland, and France, writing revolutionary pamphlets; and in 1895 again on the Neva, where he was soon arrested and exiled to Siberia (upper Yenesei), 1897–1900. Here he married Nadezhda K. Krupskaya, a Marxist comrade, and continued his writing under the pen name of "Ilin," and then of "Lenin."

Another early convert was Lev Davidovich Bronstein, son of Jewish *kulaks* ("fists") or rich farmers in the southern Ukraine. Born November 7, 1879, he did brilliantly in school in Odessa, and in his youth became a "radical" of indefinite persuasion. When arrested in 1898, he pursued his literary and philosophical studies in jail—by which time he was already a convinced Marxist—and then departed for Siberian exile (1900–02) with the woman he had married in the transfer prison in Moscow: Alexandra Sokolovskaya. Despite the birth of two daughters, she approved his decision to flee abroad to further the cause. This he achieved by a fake passport signed with the name of one of his Odessa jailers: Leon Trotsky.

In October, 1902, he arrived in London and called, impoverished, on "Mr. and Mrs. Richter," living precariously in a one-room flat near King's Cross. The "hosts" were Lenin and wife. In the same year the guest married Natalia I. Sedova, whom he had met in Paris and with whom he lived happily ever afterwards, despite further Siberian exiles, weird escapes, wild wanderings abroad, and final return to his homeland to become, incongruously, Lenin's chief aide in the founding of the Soviet State.

The third major character in the drama to come was born December 21, 1879, in the little Georgian town of Gori. Apart from Khrushchev and a few other later notables who survived the "Great Purge," he was among the few of the early Russian Marxists who could claim a "proletarian" background. His father, Vissarion I. Djugashvili, was once a serf who became a cobbler and married the daughter of a serf, Ekatarina Gheladze. These parents lived in a shack and spawned three babies, all of whom died in infancy. The fourth, christened Josef Vissariono-vich, survived. His irresponsible and alcoholic father, who opined that his son might make a good cobbler, died when Joseph was 11 years old. His mother, who earned her living as a washer-woman, wanted him to become a priest. This slum-child of a shoemaker finally arrived at the Theological Seminary of Tiflis —from which he was expelled in 1899 as a "subversive."

After this event he embarked as a converted Marxist upon a fantastic career of revolutionary agitation; repeated arrests, exiles, and escapes; and intermittent connivance in terrorism and brigandage. His first wife, Ekaterina Svanidze, bore him one son, Jacob. She died in 1907. In 1919 he was to marry Nadezhda Alliluyeva, mother of Vassily and Svetlana. Nadezhda killed herself in 1932, embittered by her husband's brutality. This revolutionary fanatic from Georgia, who, like all others of his ilk, adopted aliases to deceive the police, was first known as "Sosa," then as "Koba," and finally as "Stalin."

To return to the seed-time: The Bund or Union of Jewish Marxists clandestinely collaborated with other scattered Marxist groups calling themselves "Leagues of Struggle" in sending delegates to a secret "Congress." The place was Minsk. The time was March, 1898. The delegates numbered only nine—none of them later well known and all soon arrested. They issued a "Manifesto," written by Peter Struve, appointed a "Central Committee," and announced the founding of the "Russian Social Democratic Labor Party" (RSDLP). This apparently futile meeting of obscure conspirators was "Congress I" of the Party which was to seize power nineteen years later.

Spring of 1900 found Lenin back in St. Petersburg. He conferred with Struve, Vera Zasulich, Julius O. Martov (Tsederbaum, 1873–1923), and other Marxists and then went to Germany and Switzerland to visit Plekhanov, Axelrod, and other exiles. His purpose was to establish a Party journal to be edited and printed abroad and to be smuggled into Russia. He and Vera Zasulich, along with A. N. Potresov, became editors with HQ in Munich. They borrowed a name from the reply of the exiled "Decembrists" of 1825 to greetings from Alexander Pushkin: "From the spark will spring the flame!" The first issue of *Iskra* (The Spark) was dated December 11, 1900, by the old Russian calendar in use until 1918. By the Western calendar the date was Christmas Eve. During the next four years the new periodical was successively printed in Leipzig, Stuttgart, London, and Geneva.

In the fourth issue of *Iskra*, May, 1901, in later issues, and in a pamphlet, *Shto Dyelat?* (What Is to Be Done?), published in Stuttgart in March, 1902, Lenin argued against efforts to build a large mass movement and in favor of a small, select, disciplined, conspiratorial organization of full-time professional revolutionists to be financed by Party funds. In accordance with what was soon to be called "Democratic Centralism," members should elect delegates to periodic "Congresses" which should choose a "Central Committee" to direct the revolutionary struggle. At the Congresses decisions regarding program, strategy, and tactics should be arrived at by free debate and majority vote, but once a decision was reached all members must be solemnly pledged to carry it out regardless of personal opinion. Lenin's "hard" view was finally to prevail over the "softs." Such has been the structure of the Party from that date to this—with, as we shall see, "centralism" prevailing over "democracy" during most of the intervening years.

The Plotters

The Russian Marxists early in the century dedicated themselves to the overthrow of the Autocracy and, more vaguely, to the building of a Socialist Russia. Later in the century the Autocracy was overthrown and a Socialist Russia came into being. But to assume that the later events were results of the former purposes would be to commit the logical and historical fallacy of *post hoc, ergo propter hoc*. The demise of the Autocracy was effected by the corruption and ineptitude of its own defenders and by the indignation of an outraged people, only a few of whom initially followed Marxist leadership. The "building of socialism" was a vision long cherished by most Russians and embarked upon belatedly, and almost as an afterthought, by the Marxist faction which the revolution brought to power. No "Grand Design" connects the conspirators who founded the RSDLP and *Iskra* with the world-shaking events of 1917 and thereafter, despite certain continuities of programs and personalities.

During the years between, the history of Russian Marxism is a record, not of unflinching devotion to a goal clearly seen, but rather of frictions and feuds, bitter scholastic disputations, insults and quarrels, and endless failures and frustrations. This tangled record has been minutely dissected by historians of the Party, in the USSR and the West alike. We need here concern ourselves only with those themes of detail which were subsequently to be woven into the fabric of Soviet politics and government.

During August, 1903, half a hundred Russian Marxists met in a warehouse in Brussels and then, in flight from police and fleas, in a church in London. These delegates to "Congress II" of the RSDLP voted a platform (to remain unchanged until 1919) containing minimum demands for social reforms and a democratic republic and maximum demands for social revolution and a "dictatorship of the proletariat." Angry argument followed Lenin's plea, initially supported by Plekhanov, for a small monolithic comradeship of professional rebels and Martov's plea for a broad democratic movement of all sympathizers. By a vote of 28 to 22, the "softs" prevailed over the "hards"—until 5 Bundists and 2 so-called "Economists" (Marxist revisionists) quit the Congress in pique at demands for complete centralism. Lenin's "hard" faction now had a majority over Martov's "softs" and wrote the Party statutes to conform with its own organizational conception.

This cleavage, which both sides deemed temporary, was to become permanent. *Bolsheviki* means members of a majority; *Mensheviki,* members of a minority. These originally colorless words became names of two causes, "Bolshevism" and "Menshevism," whose adherents, both equally Marxist, came finally to hate one another with the hot rage of all orthodoxies for all heresies. At Congress II an allegedly "neutral" but actually Leninist Central Committee was chosen. Of its three members (the other two were V. A. Noskov and F. B. Lengnik), only one, G. M. Krzhizhanovsky (1872–1959), survived to hold office in the Soviet regime. But Lenin's triumph was ephemeral. After the delegates adjourned, Plekhanov joined Martov, Axelrod, and Trotsky in assuming control of *Iskra,* which henceforth opposed Lenin's views. By the turn of the year even the Central Committee, enlarged to nine (including Lenin) by "co-optation" or selection of new members by present members, voted against Lenin's demand for a new Congress. By mid-year, 1904, Mensheviks controlled the Central Committee. When Congress III met in London in April, 1905, the Mensheviks refused to attend and convened their own Congress in Geneva.

Lenin was uncompromising, for he was convinced that only a select, silent, and secret organization of trained conspirators, carrying out orders from above, could effect successful revolution in Tsarist Russia. He called the Mensheviks "revisionists," "opportunists," and betrayers of Marxism. Plekhanov accused Lenin of "Bonapartism" and of "confusing the dictatorship of the proletariat with the dictatorship *over* the proletariat"—a concept which could only lead to one-man rule. Martov equated Bolshevism with "martial law." Trotsky wrote that the Bolshevik view would mean that "the Party is replaced by the organization of the Party, the organization by the Central Committee, and finally the Central Committee by the Dictator." He and Parvus (Alexander I. Helfand) repudiated Lenin's idea of the Party, but espoused a revolutionary regime to be ruled only by Marxists— an idea which Lenin long resisted. When Trotsky and Lenin joined forces in 1917, the former, in effect, accepted the latter's notion of the Party, while the latter, in effect, accepted the former's notion of the State—thus contributing unwittingly, out of their polemics of 1905 f., to that dichotomy and synthesis of State and Party in the USSR which was, indeed, to lead after Lenin's death to Trotsky's own downfall and to the establishment of the Stalinist Autocracy.

Yet no one could have foreseen such results in the quibbling and sparring among the Russian Marxists during the early 1900's. It is an article of faith among Marxists that Matter determines Mind—i.e., that material conditions, technological, economic, social, and political, shape ideas and motivations which in turn are but pale reflections of the "historical forces" which decide human destinies. Such in truth is sometimes the case. But the future fortunes of the Russian Marxists were to constitute a persuasive demonstration of the opposite thesis—i.e., that ideas and purposes often "determine" the ways of men: political, social, economic, and technological. This pragmatic refutation of the premises of "historical materialism," evidenced by the dreams and deeds of the Russian Marxists themselves, never caused them (save for dissenters and deserters) to question the canons of their faith, nor do the faithful ever question them today.

During the dawn-years of the 20th Century Bolsheviks and Mensheviks alike were puzzled by the obvious inapplicability of their dogmas to the facts of life. If "feudalism" is to be followed by "capitalism," with the waxing of industry and commerce, and if "capitalism" is to be followed by "socialism" after its fulfillment and breakdown in "proletarian revolution," then the ultimate event was plainly far-off in backward Russia. A still feudal society was in the grip of a medieval Autocracy. According to the Marxist formula, change could come only with the emergence of a *bourgeoisie* committed, as in the West, to laissez-faire individualism, nationalism, and republicanism. Only when "bourgeois capitalism" had fully matured and decayed could the "proletariat" come to power and build a new heaven and a new earth. This process would manifestly require decades and generations, if not centuries. How then could the Russian Marxists, operating as revolutionary conspirators against the Tsardom, achieve their cloudy goals during the lifetime of their disciples?

The answer was to be found in war, which is often the midwife of revolution. In February, 1904, the emergent warlords of Japan attacked the Tsarist Empire in Manchuria. In the ensuing conflict the Romanov regime suffered humiliating defeats on land and sea which sparked revolt at home. Peasants killed landlords. Workers struck. Sailors and soldiers mutinied. Terrorists murdered officials. Millions of Russians not only refused to rally patriotically to the cause of the Autocracy but seized upon the occasion to demand reform or revolution. In November, 1904, a conference of *Zemstvos* representatives drew up an "eleven-point-petition" for civil liberties and constitutional government. For a time the defenders of the *status quo* remained deaf.

In January, 1905, a Father Gapon (possibly a police agent, probably an honest reformer, and in any case soon to be slain by SR terrorists) led a peaceful demonstration of thousands of St. Petersburgers to the Winter Palace to plead for redress of grievances. As they entered the great square, police and soldiers, whether by order or through panic, opened fire, killing hundreds and wounding thousands of the paraders. "Bloody Sunday," as the event was ever after known, discredited the Tsardom and

almost toppled "Little Father" Nicholas from his throne—for
this throne, seemingly secure behind troops and prison wardens,
rested on the mystic faith of the masses, now disenchanted.

In the sequel, the guardians of Autocracy deemed it expedient to concoct the "October Manifesto" of 1905, promising
civil rights and an elective "Imperial Duma," with powers of
legislation and control over the budget and the Ministry. These
concessions were later negated, as the agents of the Tsardom, by
force, fraud, and favors, succeeded in suppressing their foes.
During the course of these disorders sundry disciples of revolt,
many of them Marxists, established Councils or *Soviets* of revolutionary Workers' Deputies in several cities. The Soviet in St.
Petersburg was, at the end, headed by Trotsky—who was soon
arrested, with his colleagues. The Moscow Soviet unleashed
armed rebellion and was smashed by the Tsar's soldiers. A thousand died in street battles.

Revolution failed. The Tsar and his aides made a mockery
of the "October Manifesto" and gave no authority whatever over
national decision-making to the Imperial Duma, soon "rigged"
by electoral devices into a reactionary body of landowners and
wealthy merchants. Two new "political parties" emerged, if
such a term is applicable to public activities in an Autocracy still
unlimited: the "Octobrists," or conservatives content with the
"October Manifesto," despite its negation; and the "Constitutional Democrats" or "Kadets," led by Paul Miliukov, aspiring
toward Western parliamentary democracy.

The role of the Marxists amid these upheavals was ambiguous and finally futile. The Mensheviks were frustrated by their
own assumptions. Lenin, in his pamphleteering, speculated on
the possibilities of a proletarian-peasant "alliance" to complete
the "bourgeois revolution" or perhaps to effect, somehow, a "socialist revolution" *if* "the European Socialist proletariat comes
to the help of the Russian proletariat." Amid such fantasies the
leaders of the RSDLP gathered in conference in Tammerfors,
Finland, in December, 1905. "Koba" (Stalin) met Lenin for the
first time and later confessed his disappointment that "the mountain eagle of our Party" was "a most ordinary-looking man." The
delegates were certain of the imminent overthrow of the Autocracy. They therefore voted to boycott elections to the Duma,
although Lenin urged participation. They adjourned on New
Years' Eve (by the Western calendar). The Tsar's troops in Moscow, having shattered the barricades and bombarded the workers'
district, were hunting down the last defenders of the Soviet.

With reaction triumphant, the Marxists descended into a slough of despond and wallowed helpless therein through dismal years. Congress IV of the Party met in Stockholm in April, 1906, with Bolsheviks and Mensheviks seemingly reunited among the 111 delegates. Congress V, with 336 delegates, convened in a London church in May, 1907, with Stalin, abroad for the first time, sitting silent and Trotsky trying to found a middle faction to reconcile the factions. The confident speeches rang hollow. Ten years were to elapse before another Congress. Lenin and Krupskaya, living secretly in Finland, sensed the police on their trail and fled to Switzerland and then to France. They were not to return to Russia until 1917. Lenin wrote to his mother that he was miserable in "this damned Geneva" and found Paris "a rotten hole." When Laura Marx and her husband killed themselves in 1909, Lenin opined to his wife that suicide might be the best solution to their problems. Trotsky, after 15 months in prison, escaped from Siberian exile, settled in Vienna, and published a journal, *Pravda* (Truth), dedicated to "permanent revolution"—i.e., the destruction of capitalism everywhere in the world. Stalin, arrested in March, 1908, fled exile, was rearrested, again escaped, was once more arrested, escaped anew, and by 1913 was in Siberian exile under a four-year sentence.

During a dreary decade the Party was bankrupt, demoralized, and moribund—without prospects and yet not quite dead. A few episodes of time lost in the wastelands are, nevertheless, noteworthy in the light of things to come. On June 26, 1907, in Tiflis, bank-robbers, wielding guns and bombs, stole 341,000 rubles. The director of the raid was an Armenian Marxist known as "Kamo," colleague and neighbor of "Koba" (Stalin) who organized the enterprise. Lenin later welcomed Kamo in Paris and praised him as "the Caucasian brigand." Such anticipatory "expropriations of the *bourgeoisie*," along with counterfeiting, supplied the Party with funds during the dark years. Such crimes were "un-Marxist" and were solemnly denounced by the leaders of Russian Marxism—who, nevertheless, used the money thus acquired. The Transcaucasian Committee of the Party secretly excommunicated Koba for his part in the Tiflis raid. (He later had everybody shot who took part in his condemnation.) In December, 1912, he conferred with Lenin in Cracow and wrote an article, signed "Stalin," on "The National Question and Social Democracy," espousing "self-determination" and "cultural autonomy" for the national minorities of Russia. Wrote Lenin to

Maxim Gorky: "We have a wonderful Georgian here who is writing a great article."

Such activities could not conceal failure and frustration. The Party had no future. Its leaders quibbled and quarreled and insulted one another. Its followers dropped away. Lenin sought refuge in the writing of a philosophical essay, *Materialism and Empirio-Criticism* (1909), assailing the Marxists who had veered toward Neo-Kantianism and philosophical "positivism." Other Marxists—e.g., Parvus, Rosa Luxemburg, and Angelica Balabanov—pursued political careers in Germany and Italy. Trotsky became a journalist. Stalin got himself exiled (again) to Siberia—where he and many other Marxists long remained, thanks to the machinations of a Tsarist police spy, Roman V. Malinovsky, who won Lenin's confidence and got himself named to the Party's Central Committee. Bolsheviks and Mensheviks in exile launched journals against one another, with other journals reflecting factional division within each camp. A Party "Conference" in Prague in January, 1912, boycotted by the Mensheviks, "excommunicated" them from the party, a decision which they ignored.

In brief, the Russian Marxists between 1907 and 1917 starved and stole and struggled with one another in meaningless ideological disputations. Most of the leading converts in Russia were in jail or in Siberian exile. Most of the converts abroad were more concerned with denouncing one another than with the problem of how best to initiate revolution in the Russia of Nicholas II. Nothing was less likely in the triumphantly reactionary regime of the last of the Romanovs. Nothing of the kind could possibly have occurred save for the fateful decision of the last Tsar and his advisers in the summer of 1914 to wage war on Austria-Hungary and Germany. Given the alliance with France and the intervention of Britain, the calculation was "rational." The consequences were catastrophic. By virtue of the catastrophe, the Russian Marxists whose cause was otherwise hopeless were to find their chance to come to power.

Few among them were aware of the opportunities offered by the decision of the rulers of the nation-states to embark upon World War. Lenin in Switzerland had some inkling of pending prospects. But even Lenin told a Swiss audience as late as January, 1917, that it was doubtful whether "we, the old [Lenin was 46] will live to see the decisive battles of the coming revolution." Six weeks later Nicholas II abdicated his throne.

Victory

The "October Revolution" of 1917 presents the superficial appearance, carefully cultivated by the Marxists themselves, of heroic Bolshevik leadership of the downtrodden masses whose many-millioned members rose in wrath against their betrayers and established the Soviet State—thus offering a new dawn of hope for Russia and the world. A closer approximation to reality would depict the followers of Lenin as fortuitous receivers-in-bankruptcy for a society and a polity whose incompetent custodians had arrived in their folly at total insolvency. The bankruptcy was a double one. The rulers of the Tsardom plunged the nation into a disaster for which they could find no remedy and from which they could devise no escape. Their successors in the short-lived "Provisional Government" of March-November, 1917, compounded the disaster and could also find no cure and no means of flight. The Bolsheviks seized control of a national establishment already in disintegration. Their fumbling efforts to salvage the wreckage led to further disintegration and to more disaster. If something new under the sun finally emerged, this was no product of a prior plan or design but rather of groping attempts to restore some tolerable semblance of order in a Russia which had once more fallen into intolerable anarchy under the impact of alien invasion.

The turmoil of 1917 has been dissected a thousand times by a thousand participants, observers, and historians in East and West alike. Nothing new can here be added to the record. Our purpose is more limited: to understand, as best we can, the government and politics of the USSR yesterday, today, and to-morrow. Such understanding is impossible without some knowledge of 1917. But a bare summary of developments will suffice.

For decades prior to 1914 all Marxists were loosely organized in the "Second International," established at a Socialist Congress in Paris in 1889, following the demise (1876) of the First "International Workingmen's Association" founded by Marx and Engels. As "revolutionary internationalists," all Marxists were convinced of their will and ability, by way of general strikes, sabotage, and revolution in the name of "proletarian solidarity," to halt any war which the bourgeois ruling classes might seek to unleash. With the crack of doom most Marxists discovered to their own astonishment that they were national patriots who rallied to the support of their warring governments against the foreign foe. Among the exceptions were the Bolshevist deputies in the Duma, who were promptly arrested for opposing the war and sent to Siberia.

Lenin in neutral Switzerland was in no doubt as to what Marxists should do in the face of the cataclysm. In No. 33 (November 1, 1914) of *Social Democrat,* another Russian Marxist journal in exile, he summoned the "working masses," pledged to peace and a "republican United States of Europe," to create a revolutionary Third International. "Turning the present imperialist war into civil war is the only correct proletarian slogan. . . . Long live the international brotherhood of the workers united against the chauvinism and patriotism of the *bourgeoisie* of all countries! Long live a proletarian International, free from opportunism!"

With the workers of the world patriotically engaged in mass murder, such appeals fell on deaf ears. Anti-war Marxists met in Zimmerwald, near Berne, in September, 1915, and again in Kienthal in April, 1916, but only to quarrel among themselves with no "Third International" emerging. Lenin's hopes were deferred. He wrote another book: *Imperialism: The Highest Stage of Capitalism* (1916); and then still another, never quite completed: *The State and Revolution* (1917).

Meanwhile the Romanov Autocracy collapsed under the blows of the formidable armies of the Central Powers in 1915–16. The rulers of the Tsardom could neither win victory nor make peace. Millions died. Other millions faced starvation and demanded reform or revolution to save the Motherland. Amid mutinies, strikes, and riots, Nicholas II suddenly made the astounding discovery, on the Ides of March, 1917, that no one was any longer paying the slightest attention to his orders and decrees. Since an Autocrat whom nobody obeys is a contradiction in terms, the Tsar gave up his throne. This "February Revolution" (by the old Russian calendar) eventuated in the formation by a committee of the Duma of a "Provisional Government"— pending the election of a Constituent Assembly to fashion a democratic Constitution for a free Russia, as advocated by all parties. The first Premier of the transitional regime was Prince George E. Lvov. Its Foreign Minister was Paul Miliukov, leader of the Kadets. The Minister of Justice was Alexander Kerensky, an SR and leader of the faction of his party called *Trudoviki* or "Populist Socialists." Other new figures were liberals or mild socialists, all resolved to continue the war and to postpone, until the convening of a Constituent Assembly, all questions of foreign policy, land reform, and nationalization of industry.

This first post-Tsarist regime never solved its problem. War-weary soldiers and civilians demanded peace. Peasants demanded land. Workers demanded bread and socialism. Many aristocrats and some wealthy merchants and industrialists hoped for a Romanov restoration. The middle-class liberals temporarily in power, caught in a cross-fire of mutually contradictory expectations, equivocated, delayed, and compromised. Their position as "rulers" of a new Russia was made untenable by the emergence, as in 1905, of new revolutionary Councils or Soviets of Workers', Soldiers', and Peasants' Deputies whose leaders, while ostensibly supporting the "Provisional Government," soon assumed the tasks of local administration throughout the nation and presently established a "Central Executive Committee" and periodical "Congresses" of Soviet Deputies. The spokesmen of the Soviets came closer to expressing popular aspirations than did the new Ministers in the Winter Palace in Petrograd.

This curious confrontation of a "government" without authority to command obedience and of a non-government, possessed of such authority but not desirous of becoming a government, was to prove fatal to the new Russian democracy. Early in May Miliukov's note to the Allies, pledging continued war, precipitated mob demonstrations which led to his resignation and a reshuffle of posts. Further demonstrations in July led to further reshuffles which brought Alexander Kerensky to the head of the doomed regime. When, in September, the regime was threatened by an abortive rebellion of reactionaries, led by Gen. Lavr G. Kornilov, Kerensky authorized the arming of the workers of Petrograd—and thereby sealed his own fate.

The role of the Marxists in these stirring events of a popular revolution was at first tangential and finally decisive. Lenin and his wife, along with other comrades in exile, availed themselves of the offer of the German General Staff, whose members shrewdly calculated that the more revolutionists were returned to Russia the sooner would the Russian war effort collapse. The exiles returned to the homeland via a "sealed train" across Germany to Denmark and Sweden. Lenin arrived in Petrograd's Finland station shortly before midnight of April 16, 1917, and proceeded amid cheering crowds to the mansion of the ballerina Kshesinskaya, favorite and mistress of the last Tsar, whose home the Bolsheviks had seized and made their temporary HQ. (The building later became the residence and office of Sergei Kirov, Leningrad Party boss, and is now the "Kirov Museum.") Here, from the balcony to mobs in the street and to assembled Marxists within the mansion, Lenin expounded a strange creed, soon to be elaborated into his "April Theses."

Lenin's argument was simple, albeit paradoxical. He contended that the Soviets should repudiate the "Provisional Government" and take over the rulership of revolutionary Russia. Since the Soviet leaders at the time were SR's and Mensheviks, totally lacking in any such ambition, Lenin's prescription seemed fatuous even to his own comrades. "Deliriums," wrote Plekhanov, "are occasionally interesting." Other returning Marxists found Lenin's view equally ridiculous—at first. Stalin came back from Siberia, along with Molotov, Sverdlov, and Kamenev; Maxim Gorky from Italy; Bukharin, Volodarsky, and Pyatakov from USA; Trotsky from the Bronx and from a British jail in Halifax where he was briefly detained in April. All were agreed, save Molotov, that Lenin's view in the spring of 1917 made no sense.

That this view was finally to prevail and to lead to the founding of the Soviet State is evidence of Lenin's political genius— and also of growing anarchy in the Russia of 1917. In endless speeches and articles, Lenin continued his argument:

"The masses must be warned. Revolution is a difficult thing. Errors are unavoidable. . . . The art of government cannot be gotten out of books. Try, make mistakes, learn how to govern. . . . Outside of Socialism, there is no deliverance of humanity from wars, from hunger, from the destruction of millions and millions of human beings. . . . There is no other way out except a proletarian revolution. We want to end this imperialist World War. We want to rebuild the world . . ."

Slowly and ambivalently, Lenin's view came to be accepted by his colleagues and by thousands and millions of non-Marxists, many of whom later regretted their "conversion." The Party had only 23,000 registered members in January, 1917. By April it had 40,000. By the time of its May "Conference," membership approached 80,000. By the time of Congress VI, meeting secretly in Petrograd in August, members totaled 240,000. After the "July Days," interpreted by the Provisional Government as a Bolshevik attempt to seize power, Lenin (accused of being a German "agent") and most of his fellows went into hiding to escape arrest—but won more and more popular support with their slogans of "Peace, Land, Bread" and "All power to the Soviets!"

Kerensky faltered and fumbled and got no meaningful support from his allies in Paris, London, and Washington where policy-makers persisted in invincible ignorance of what was going on in Russia. In early autumn Bolsheviks won control of the Soviets in Petrograd, Moscow, and other urban centers. In late October Lenin secretly met with the other members of the Central Committee of the Party in the tenement apartment of Marguerita Fofanova in Petrograd's Viborg district. His appeal for immediate revolution was voted down. He stormed and raged. A few days later the same leaders met in Sukhanov's apartment and finally voted, 10 to 2, after much wrangling relieved by sandwiches and tea, that "armed insurrection is inevitable and the time is ripe." A "Political Bureau" of the Central Committee was chosen. Its members were Kamenev, Zinoviev, Bubnov, Sokolnikov, Trotsky, Stalin, and Lenin. The two negative votes were cast by Kamenev and Zinoviev.

Thus buttressed by "togetherness," the Marxist comrades of Bolshevik persuasion proceeded to organize an armed seizure of power. The Second All-Russian Congress of Soviets of Workers' and Soldiers' Deputies was scheduled to meet on November 7—or October 25 by the old calendar. Despite doubts among colleagues, Lenin fixed this as the day for the overthrow of the Provisional Government, whose defenders had by now made themselves helpless by their follies. On the appointed day the "Military Revolutionary Committee" of the Petrograd Soviet ordered the armed workers of the capital to storm the Winter Palace. Casualties were few. Kerensky fled. His Ministers were arrested but soon released. The most momentous revolution of the 20th Century unrolled at the outset with little violence or disorder. Other Soviet bodies in other cities now assumed governmental functions—again with little violence save in Moscow where fighting for control of the Kremlin cost several hundred lives.

Lenin spoke to the Second Congress of Soviets at Smolny Institute in Petrograd late in the evening on November 8. Dissenters came and went. To those who remained his message was deceptively simple: We will make peace; we will give the land to the peasants; we will give industry to the workers. "World revolution will soon break out in all the belligerent countries." All delegates of all parties agreed. All sang the "International." Soon afterward Lenin read a "Decree on Land," transferring all estates to the peasant Soviets "until the constituent assembly meets." Other decrees on peace and industry were approved by large majorities.

At Trotsky's suggestion the new Cabinet was called the "Soviet of Peoples' Commissars." Posts were allotted as follows: President of the Council, Lenin; Foreign Affairs, Trotsky; Nationalities, Stalin; Interior, Rykov; Agriculture, Miliutin; Labor, Schliapnikov; Military and Naval Affairs, a committee composed of Antonov-Ovseenko, Krylenko, and Dybenko; Commerce and Industry, Nogin; Education, Lunacharsky; Finance, Skvortsev; Justice, Oppokov; Supplies, Teodorovitch; Posts and Telegraph, Avilov. Said Lenin: "We shall now proceed to construct the socialist order . . ."

3 - Dilemmas of the Oligarchs

The Genesis of Totalitarianism

How to construct the "socialist order" was a riddle which Lenin and his successors were not to solve for ten years and more. The Marxist scriptures offered no formula, least of all for an agrarian, industrially primitive, and now disorganized and demoralized Russia afflicted with the age-old evils of invasion from abroad and incipient anarchy at home. The final answer was to be found in the invention of the first "totalitarian police-state" of the 20th Century—later imitated, for quite other purposes, by Mussolini's Fascists, Hitler's Nazis, Franco's Falangists, and the warlords of Japan. This new and appalling form of polity was not planned or designed by the Bolsheviks who seized control of Russia in 1917. All would have been horrified at any such prospect. Many among them were later to perish at the hands of the monster they had unwittingly created. How then did a new Autocracy of the modern mode and model emerge out of the high hopes for freedom which inspired the Russian masses to support the October Revolution?

The Soviet regime, be it noted, was in no sense a "totalitarian police state" during the first ten months of its existence. The Council of Peoples' Commissars or *Sovnarkom* (in Russian abbreviation) became in late November of 1917 a coalition of Bolsheviks and Left SR's. Civil liberties were not suppressed, despite the establishment in December, 1917, of the "Ex-traordinary Commission to Combat Counter-Revolution, Spec-ulation, and Sabotage" under Felix Djerzhinsky—whose new political police became known in Russian abbreviation as the *Cheka*. Djerzhinsky's policemen did little during the winter and spring of 1917–18, there being little organized opposition to the new order. Other political parties, including Kadets, Mensheviks, SR's, and even anarchists, monarchists, and reactionaries were free to pursue their purposes. The election of delegates to the Constituent Assembly was held without coercion, on November 25, 1917. The one arbitrary act of the new Marxist rulers during their first phase of power was the suppression of this body, on which all Russian political groups had pinned their hopes for many years.

The delegates met in Tauride Palace in Petrograd on Jan-uary 18, 1918, after sundry delays and threats generated by Bolshevik fears of the outcome. Among the 707 seats filled in Russia's first and last "free election," the Bolsheviks won 175; their allies, the Left SR's, 40; the Kadets, 17; the Mensheviks, 16; and the Right SR's, 370, with the balance scattered among splin-ter parties. The deputies chose Victor Chernov, leader of the Right SR's, as their chairman and endorsed many of the new decrees of the Soviet regime. The crucial issue was whether the Constituent Assembly would agree to base the new constitution on the Soviets or seek some alternative basis of authority.

With Lenin in the gallery, the delegates, 237 to 136, rejected the Soviets as units of government in the new free Russia they hoped to bring into being. Bolsheviks and Left SR's walked out. The meeting adjourned at 5:00 A.M. Next morning (January 19) the *Sovnarkom,* on Lenin's motion, decreed the dissolution of the Constituent Assembly. The deputies went home. Two were murdered by mobsters, an act which *Izvestia* denounced as "a blot on the honor of the Revolution." Several other lives were lost when demonstrators, defending the Constituent Assembly, were fired upon by Red Guards.

Maxim Gorky compared the incident to "Bloody Sunday" of 1905. His comparison was inept. Most Russians in 1918 wanted other things far more than they wanted the perpetuation of the now defunct Constituent Assembly. They wanted "peace"—i.e., a cessation of hopeless warfare against the Central Powers; they wanted "land," as peasants everywhere and always have wanted land; they wanted "bread" and "socialism" and a vision of a good life free of exploitation and oppression.

In their groping efforts to fulfill these mass aspirations, Lenin and his comrades—who were by no means (as yet) dictators or oligarchs—provoked internal rebellion and external invasion, neither of which, needless to say, they had any desire to invite. Their response to this double challenge was the creation of the first "totalitarian police-state" of our time. They had anticipated, but discounted, the assault, confident by the canons of their faith that all their problems would be solved by the early advent of the proletarian "World Revolution." They had neither foreseen nor planned their own solution to the problem of their political survival.

The process of response to challenge here exemplified is worthy of the careful attention of all who seek to understand government and politics in the USSR today. The new form of power which was here to emerge, and to give rise to monstrous abuses and to amazing accomplishments, bore little resemblance to the Soviet State during its first phase. What we have come to call a "totalitarian police-state," as imitated elsewhere later, is characterized by one-party rule; arbitrary powers of arrest, imprisonment, or execution by a political police; suppression of all dissent through denial of civil rights; executive domination of legislative and judicial organs of government; and refusal of power-holders to permit free elections in which rival candidates of competing parties appeal for public support.

This is what the Soviet State was soon to become in 1918-19 and thereafter. But these were not at all the attributes of the new regime in 1917-18. The Government was a coalition of two parties. Others were tolerated. The new political police was inactive. Dissent was permitted. Civil liberties were respected. Courts and judges were uncoerced. An elected legislature, the All-Russian Congress of Soviets, met frequently, debated freely on questions of public policy, and reached decisions by majority vote. The new rulers defined their foggy concept of "the dictatorship of the proletariat" in terms of the "expropriation" and "suppression" of the *"bourgeoisie,"* but even these directives of the Marxist creed meant little at the time. Lenin, well aware of the increasingly desperate condition of the Russian economy, appealed naïvely to the owners and managers of Russian industry to cooperate with the new regime. Land-hungry peasants were appeased by the partition of the estates of the landlords. Factory workers were granted "control" of their factories.

The result was a further breakdown of production, distribution, and exchange of goods. But few of the victims of the disintegration of the economy were disposed to offer active opposition to the new order. Apart from the western regions under German military occupation, there was no organized resistance to the Soviets during these months—save at Rostov-on-the-Don where, in December, 1917, Generals Kornilov, Kaledin, and Alexiev set up an anti-Soviet "United Government" and a "Volunteer Army." Despite their monarchist sympathies, they gained the endorsement of such anti-Bolshevik leaders as Paul Miliukov, Boris Savinkov, and George Plekhanov. Policy-makers in London, Paris, and Washington gave support in the hope of ousting the Bolshevik "madmen" and keeping Russia in the war. The British and French Governments granted loans to the rebels and, by secret agreements, sought to partition southern Russia into Anglo-French "spheres of influence."

This enterprise was without significance save as a portent of things to come. Red Guards easily suppressed the rebellion in February, 1918. Kornilov was killed. Kaledin committed suicide. Alexiev fled after naming Anton Denikin as his "successor." Everywhere else throughout the Russian land the authority of the Soviets was peaceably accepted. The masses of peasants and workers hoped against hope that government by Soviets, under Bolshevik leadership, would somehow find the way to salvation.

What that way, if any, might have been and how chaos might have been reduced to order in some quasi-democratic fashion we shall never know. The Soviet regime was soon assailed by foreign foes and domestic enemies, both bent upon its destruction. Its leaders, as the price of survival, evolved a new form of despotism in the name of freedom. The uses and abuses, accomplishments and failures, promises and prospects of this pattern of power are of the essence of government and politics in the USSR during the middle decades of the 20th Century.

The motives and calculations of those at home and abroad who dedicated themselves to the "extermination of Bolshevism" were mixed and mingled, as in all human conduct. At home the consecration of the new Marxist rulers to the "expropriation of the *bourgeoisie*" and of the aristocracy caused all property-owners to hope for, and if possible work for, an early overthrow of the expropriators. Abroad, policy-makers in Washington, London, and Paris, absorbed in desperate combat with the formidable armies of Imperial Germany and invincibly ignorant of what was happening in Russia, continued to hope that an Eastern Front could somehow be maintained or restored. The outrageous words and deeds of the Commissars—in particular, their publication of the inter-Allied "secret treaties" of 1914–17, their repudiation of the Tsarist and Kerensky state debts, their confiscation of all foreign-owned properties in Russia, and in their incessant appeals for "proletarian revolution" to destroy all "bourgeois Governments"—led Western leaders to the conclusion that aid to the Russian enemies of the Soviet regime could readily bring about the liquidation of the lunatics and their replacement by sane, respectable, and responsible power-holders.

The result was a tragedy of errors. Most Russians were unable to accept Western definitions of responsibility, respectability, and sanity. Their prime need was peace, almost at any price, since Russia was defeated and exhausted. The soldiers of the mass armies of the Tsardom, still functioning feebly under the Provisional Government, "voted for peace with their feet," as Lenin put it, by mass desertions from the front. Russia's Marxist rulers—who moved their capital from Petrograd to Moscow in March, 1918—had no choice but to make peace since they had no means of waging war. The rejection by the Western Allies of all Soviet proposals for a general peace left Lenin and his colleagues with no option save a "separate peace." In concluding such a peace, they paradoxically unleashed a new war of annihilation waged against them by all their enemies.

The story of this war, well known to all Russians and still unknown to most Americans, cannot here be recounted. Only a few highlights will be noted. Negotiations with the Central Powers began at Brest-Litovsk on December 3, 1917. An armistice was signed on December 15. When the German emissaries insisted on "conquerors" terms, Trotsky broke off negotiations and espoused a fatuous formula of "no peace, no war." German divisions seized Dvinsk, pushed forward their invasion of the Ukraine, and moved on Petrograd. A hastily organized militia offered feeble resistance and was proclaimed an "army" on February 23, 1918—ever since celebrated in the USSR as the "founding day" of the Red Army. But Lenin was without illusions: "To carry on a revolutionary war, we need an army which we do not have." On March 3, 1918, signatures were attached to the Treaty of Brest-Litovsk whereby a helpless Russia yielded to the victors more than a million-and-a-quarter square miles, inhabited by 62,000,000 people, and containing three-quarters of Russia's available coal and iron, half of her factories, and a third of her best farming lands.

Lenin saw no alternative to surrender save one, to be noted

in a moment. He regarded the capitulation as transitory and unimportant—not because he foresaw the military defeat of the Central Powers on the Western Front in the summer of 1918 but because, bewitched by Marxist postulates, he anticipated imminent revolution in all of the warring nation-states. At Party Congress VII in Petrograd (March 6–8, 1918), 46 delegates representing 145,000 members appeared, although the Party now had 270,000 members. After lively debate, the delegates voted 30 to 12, with 4 abstaining, to support Lenin's approval of the Treaty.

Lenin and Trotsky still hoped somehow to avoid surrender to Berlin and Vienna. Their hope hinged upon massive aid from the Western Allies. All of the Western governments refused to recognize the Bolshevik regime. But London maintained contacts through Bruce Lockhart and Washington through Col. Raymond Robins, head of the U.S. Red Cross Mission to Moscow. Both urged aid to the Soviets to defeat the Treaty and "keep Russia in the war." Their advice was ignored. Wilson sent greetings but no aid. Lloyd George did likewise. Both assumed that the Soviet regime would soon collapse. When Lenin ascertained from Lockhart and Robins that no Allied aid would be forthcoming, he persuaded the Congress of Soviets to ratify the Treaty (March 16, 1918).

The Russia thus granted peace was a Russia soon to be at war with a formidable coalition of foes. Unlike Lenin, most people are incapable of a rational weighing of available options in politics. Even though no alternative was at hand, the "shameful surrender" of Brest-Litovsk aroused patriotic resentment against the regime, even among Communists. Among non-Communists and anti-Communists, resentment took the form of a series of SR assassinations during the spring and summer of 1918, culminating in the shooting of Lenin (who painfully recovered from his wounds) on August 30 by Fanya Kaplan-Roid, an agent of terrorist Boris Savinkov. The Left SR's had meanwhile withdrawn from the *Sovnarkom* in protest against the Treaty and joined the Right SR's in violent opposition to the regime.

The chaotic, far-flung, and savage hostilities which ensued began almost by accident. Some 45,000 Czechoslovak Legionnaires, bent upon national independence, had joined the Tsarist armies in fighting the Hapsburg Empire. Stranded by the Revolution, they sought with Soviet approval to reach the Western Front by way of Siberia, the Pacific, America, and the Atlantic.

When one of their units clashed at Chelyabinsk, May 14, 1918, with returning German and Austrian war prisoners, Trotsky, with no means of enforcing his order, foolishly ordered all the Czechs disarmed. They rebelled, overthrew Soviet authority throughout western Siberia, and, with Allied encouragement, protected local regimes of anti-Soviet Russians. When Czech forces advanced on Ekaterinburg (Sverdlovsk), where Nicholas II and his family were confined, Red Guards, rather than permit the royal family to fall into hostile hands, shot all the Romanovs along with their servants and doctor and burned all the bodies (July 16–17, 1918).

By autumn, despite the Armistice of November 11 which ended World War I, British, French, and American troops were invading Russia from Archangel, Anglo-French forces were penetrating the Caucasus and Ukraine, and Japanese and American expeditions were pushing into Siberia from Vladivostok. Meanwhile scattered anti-Soviet "governments," initially liberal but ultimately dominated by monarchist reactionaries, came into being with Allied protection and mobilized "White Armies" which were largely armed, supplied, and financed by Paris, London, and Washington. The largest of these forces were commanded by Admiral Alexander Kolchak in Siberia and the Urals; Gen. Anton Denikin in the Caucasus and the Ukraine; and Gen. Nicholas Yudenitch in the Baltic. The first of these reached Kazan on the Volga in May, 1919, and was there defeated and soon disintegrated. The second pushed toward Moscow from the south and by October, 1919, reached Orel, Kursk, and Voronezh before suffering a like fate. The third, also in October, 1919, reached the suburbs of Petrograd before being crushed and scattered.

The failure of Allied and White armies to suppress the Red regime—or, in the words of Winston Churchill, a prime mover in the enterprise, to "strangle Bolshevism at birth"—brought no peace to Soviet Russia, thus blockaded and assaulted from all sides. In May of 1920 Josef Pilsudski led the armies of the new Poland in a massive invasion of the Ukraine and Byelorussia aimed at restoring the frontiers of 1772. By early August a Russian counter-offensive reached the outskirts of Warsaw, where it was beaten back by Polish forces under French Gen. Weygand. An armistice of October 11, 1920, signed at Riga ended these new hostilities and left Soviet forces free to turn against the last of the White Armies, led by Baron Peter

Wrangel—whose regime in the Crimea and the Kuban was granted formal diplomatic recognition by France as the "government of Russia" on August 10, 1920. By November Wrangel's troops were vanquished and driven into the Black Sea. The survivors fled abroad in Allied warships. Civil war ended in February, 1921, with the suppression of a Menshevik regime in Georgia and the final abandonment of the Allied military intervention and blockade.

The Soviet State which emerged from this ordeal by fire was a State transformed. A large, albeit ragged and ill-equipped, Red Army was conscripted and brilliantly organized and led by Trotsky. Its triumph over the Whites and the interventionists was due less to superior power than to popular support. During the summer of 1918 the dread *Cheka* became the weapon of "Red Terror," whereby uncounted thousands were shot without trial and the aristocracy and *bourgeoisie* were alike decimated. Comparable atrocities, including *pogroms* against Jews, were perpetrated by the "White Terror," but with less effect since landlords and businessmen supporting the Whites were greatly outnumbered by peasants and workers sympathetic with the Reds. By the close of the war the Communist Party had achieved a "monopoly of legality," suppressed all other parties, expelled their representatives from all Soviet bodies, and abolished all liberty of speech, press, assembly, or political action.

During hostilities the Marxist oligarchs essayed their first desperate attempt at "total socialism" and "total planning" in the name of "War Communism." All industry was nationalized under the "Supreme Soviet of National Economy." Strikes were outlawed. Forced labor was introduced. Banks were socialized. Private trade was abolished. All goods were rationed. Money was reduced to worthlessness by a printing press inflation. In the countryside, in the name of a "State monopoly of grain trading" and "class war in the villages," so-called "Committees of the Village Poor" cooperated with agents of the Commissariat of Food in requisitioning (i.e., stealing) grain from the middle peasants and kulaks to feed the cities and the Red Army.

By such devices the Muscovite Marxists survived and defeated their foes. By such devices they brought into being the first totalitarian police-state of our era—with its "totalitarian" character persisting to the present day and its "police-state" attributes, as we shall see, abandoned only since 1953. And by such devices, despite "victory," they reduced all Russia to such poverty and ruin as to make the building of the "socialist order" more remote than ever.

Socialism in One Country?

By the grim winter of 1920–21 the Kremlin oligarchs found themselves faced with a series of contradictions of such magnitude and complexity as, seemingly, to defy all efforts at solution. At no point did expectation and reality coincide. "World Revolution," deemed by all Bolsheviks to be the pre-condition of their own retention of power in backward Russia, had indeed appeared possible in 1918–19. A "Third" or "Communist" International was founded in Moscow in March, 1919, in the midst of civil war—with Lenin telling Party Congress VIII that "It is inconceivable that the Soviet Republic should continue to exist for a long period side by side with imperialist States. Ultimately one or the other must conquer." In the spring of 1919, while Wilson, Lloyd George, Orlando, and Clemenceau at the Paris Peace Conference rejected all Soviet overtures for peace in the hope that Kolchak's White Army would soon take Moscow, Red rebels brought Soviet regimes to power in Munich and Budapest. But the besieged Commissars in the Kremlin could give no aid. The Bavarian and Hungarian Soviets were soon drowned in blood by the forces of "law and order." In Germany Rosa Luxemburg and Karl Liebknecht, leaders of the "Spartacists" (Communists), were slain by the police and their movement crushed. "Proletarian revolution" everywhere beyond the Russian frontiers—including Finland, Poland, and the Baltic states, all now independent—either failed to materialize or was swiftly suppressed.

Within the Soviet frontiers mass misery had reached a point which beggared description. Industrial production was 15% of its 1914 level, and down to 7% in iron and steel. With money valueless and no goods available, peasants stopped sowing and reaping beyond their own needs. Half of the pre-war farmlands lay fallow. Cities were empty shells. Mass famine swept the Volga valley. Starving farmers revolted. Hungry workers went on strike. Early in March, 1921, the heroic Red sailors of the Kronstadt naval base rose in rebellion to demand civil rights, "Soviets without Communists," and a "Third Revolution." Trotsky's troops crawled across the ice of the Gulf of Finland to assault the citadel. The last of the rebels were slaughtered on March 10—the 50th anniversary of the proclamation of the Paris Commune, which Marx had regarded as the political prototype of the "Worker's Paradise."

What to do? What had to be done was a far cry from what the oligarchs desired to do, but after a fashion it offered a way out of an intolerable situation. A pattern of "coexistence" was negotiated with the Western Powers, whose leaders had beaten down the "World Revolution" but had failed to destroy Soviet rule in Russia. In March, 1921, Britain granted *de facto* recognition and resumed trade. In the same month the final Treaty of Riga was signed with Poland and a trade accord negotiated with Germany—to be followed by the Treaty of Rapallo of April 16, 1922 (negotiated by Georgi Chicherin and Walter Rathenau at the otherwise abortive Genoa Conference), whereby full diplomatic and commercial relations were renewed between Berlin and Moscow and all financial claims were canceled. The USA sternly refused recognition, but granted generous aid to victims of the Volga famine. Russia and the West thus established a "peace" of sorts which was to endure for many years.

At home, Lenin—here as always a pragmatist, not a dogmatist—realized that his dreams of a "socialist order" must be long-deferred. In March, 1920, before Party Congress IX, he had preached electrification as the road to socialism. In February, 1921, the "State Commission for Electrification" (*Goelro*) was converted into a "State Planning Commission" (*Gosplan*). Meanwhile people died of hunger in the face of a total breakdown in production compared to which the worst of "capitalistic crises" were mild indeed. How to "electrify" or "plan" an economy which had ceased to function was a task beyond the capacities of Marxists or even miracle-men. At Congress X of the Party in late March, 1921, Lenin proposed and won support for a "New Economic Policy" (NEP) involving a "strategic retreat" toward capitalism as the only possible means of restoring the output and exchange of goods and services. Its point of departure was the abandonment of the State monopoly in grain trading, the end of rural requisitions in favor of fixed taxes in kind or in a new and stable currency, and the restoration of a "free market" in which peasants could sell their produce for profit at prices fixed by supply and demand rather than by governmental decree.

The NEP, as a substitute for "War Communism," carried with it dangerous implications (for Marxists) and significant reservations. "This capitalism," said Lenin, "is not dangerous to us

because we will decide in what measure we shall grant concessions. . . . The extent of ruin and destitution caused by War
and Civil War condemns us for long to mere healing of our
wounds." Small entrepreneurs in manufacturing and retail trade
(Nepmen) were permitted to resume private business for gain.
The "commanding heights" of heavy industry, transport, and
foreign trade remained socialized. Foreign capital was invited to
invest in the Soviet economy on a contract basis. The response
was meager. Economic concessions to "capitalism" were not
matched by any political concessions to "democracy." The replacement of the *Cheka* in February, 1922, by the "State Political Administration" (GPU) in the Commissariat of Internal
Affairs left the Soviet State as much a police-state as before. In
the words of an old witticism, all parties were tolerated on condition that one be in power and all others be in jail. The Party's
principle of "democratic centralism" now meant less democracy
and more centralism. A quarter of the 733,000 members in 1921
were expelled for "unworthiness" in the first *chistka* or mass
purge.

The All-Russian Congress of Soviets and its Central Executive Committee ceased to be decision-making agencies. Major
resolves in public policy were increasingly determined by the
Party and, within the Party, less by the membership or the
Congresses than by the Central Committee, and less by these
bodies than by the Political Bureau (Politburo) and Secretariat
of the Central Committee. Such resolves began to be announced
jointly in the name of the Party Central Committee and the
Sovnarkom ("Council of Peoples' Commissars," 1917–46, and
"Council of Ministers" since 1946), a practice persisting into the
1960's.

The political results of the NEP was the perpetuation of the
oligarchy of the leaders of the Party, culminating after much
factionalism and wrangling in a new absolutism or personal
dictatorship marked by hideous abuses and injustices. The economic result of the NEP was a slow and painful restoration of
agricultural and industrial productivity by 1927–28 to, roughly,
the level of 1914 in a community still desperately poor and still
wholly ignorant of the devices whereby it was later to raise itself "by its bootstraps" to the stature of the second industrial
power of the world. All of this in the 1920's lay in the future,
to be worked out by trial and error, with error predominating
in the equation. But the recovery of production and exchange

to pre-war levels offered an opportunity for a resumption of the "socialist offensive." These, however, are anticipations.

In the midst of the NEP, Lenin died at the age of fifty-four—in his *dacha* in the Moscow suburb of Gorki during the bitter winter afternoon of January 21, 1924. (Woodrow Wilson died thirteen days later.) During his final illness, which began with the first of a series of paralytic strokes in May, 1922, Lenin offered admonitions to his colleagues in a series of letters collectively known as "Lenin's Testament" and never published in the USSR until 1956. His advice reflected doubts as to the viability of the system of power which he, more than any other man, had brought into being. But his admonitions were largely confined to evaluations of his colleagues. Zinoviev and Kamenev were "weak" but should not be denounced. Pyatakov is a good administrator, but a poor politician. Bukharin is excellent, but less a real Marxist than a "scholastic." Stalin has "concentrated enormous power in his hands, and I am not sure that he always knows how to use that power with sufficient caution. . . . Trotsky is the most able man in the present Central Committee— but [he is also characterized] by his too far-reaching self-confidence and a disposition to be too much attracted by the purely administrative side of affairs." More significantly, in the light of future events, Lenin commented (January 23, 1923):

> Stalin is too rude, and this fault, entirely supportable in relations among us Communists, becomes insupportable in the office of General Secretary. Therefore, I propose to the comrades to find a way to remove Stalin from that position and to appoint another man who in all respects differs from Stalin except in superior ability—namely, more patient, more loyal, more polite, and more attentive to comrades, less capricious, etc. This circumstance may seem an insignificant trifle, but I think that from the point of view of preventing a split and from the point of view of the relations between Stalin and Trotsky . . . it is not a trifle, or it is such a trifle as may acquire decisive significance.

Lenin's last communication, March 5, 1923, was addressed to Stalin, with whom he severed "comradely relations" because of Stalin's "insults" to Krupskaya. Four days later Lenin suffered his third stroke, from which he never recovered.

Along with all political leaders regarded by posterity as "statesmen" rather than as "politicians," Lenin had hindsight, insight, and foresight. He foresaw only dimly—"as through a glass, darkly"—that the oligarchy he had created might lead to a new despotism by a new Autocrat whose defects of vision and character, as in days of old, might lead to stupidities and atrocities of such magnitude as to make a mockery of the liberating vision of the October Revolution. He clearly foresaw the prospect of a socialist Russia and, more immediately, the coming rivalry of Trotsky and Stalin for control of the Party. His advice was ignored by his countrymen, as was the advice of Woodrow Wilson—who once said, as his life was fading: "I would rather fail in an enterprise that will some day succeed than succeed in an enterprise that will some day fail."

Lenin's enterprise was destined some day to succeed. Western judgments of his contribution and that of his colleagues to human fortunes have long remained ambiguous—for they range (1919) from Elihu Root ("a horrid group of cutthroats and assassins"), the American Association for International Conciliation ("degenerates, drunkards, and sex perverts"), and the *New York Times,* November 1, 1919 ("ravening beasts of prey, a large part of them actual criminals, all of them mad"), to *Life* Magazine, early in 1943, captioning a portrait of Lenin: "This is perhaps the greatest man of the 20th Century." Let posterity decide.

The complex course of Soviet politics after Lenin's passing can here only be outlined. Stalin as General Secretary of the Central Committee soon made himself "boss" of the Party machine by outmaneuvering Trotsky—whose intellectual conceit and contempt for the uncouth Georgian ill served his own purposes. The issues of policy between these competitors for power were three: (1) the duration of the NEP; (2) intra-Party "democracy"; and (3) World Revolution.

As for the first, Trotsky urged the early liquidation of the Nepmen and kulaks, the swift collectivization of agriculture, and speedy inauguration of a totally socialized economy. Stalin held that such measures would be feasible only when production had recovered to its pre-war levels. As for the second, Trotsky contended that Stalin, in quest of personal power, was perverting the Party and pushing it into policies which the mass of its members would have repudiated if given an opportunity to express their views. Stalin, who soon condemned "Trotskyism" as a "petty bourgeois deviation from Marxism," insisted—with much justification in the late 1920's, although not in the 1930's —that his policies accurately reflected the will of the rank and file. Trotsky ultimately held that "Stalinism" was a "betrayal" of the Revolution"—which had passed its "Thermidor" and moved into "Bonapartism," from which it could be rescued only by assassination and a new revolution. In retrospect, there is no reason to believe that had Trotsky rather than Stalin become Party "boss" or *Vozhd* he would have been in the end any less despotic, dictatorial, and intolerant than his rival was to become.

The third issue was crucial. Congress XIV in December, 1925, resolved that "in the sphere of economic development, the Congress holds that in our land, the land of the dictatorship of the proletariat, there is 'every requisite for the building of a complete socialist society' (Lenin). The Congress considers that the main task of our Party is to fight for the victory of socialist construction in the USSR." Trotsky, while inconsistently championing the rapid advent of total socialism in the Soviet Union, adhered to the original Bolshevik position that Russan backwardness rendered the enterprise hopeless without "proletarian revolution" in the advanced "capitalist" countries—where, after all, the revolution should have first matured according to the Marxist scriptures. Therefore, in Trotsky's view, the prime objective of the Marxist masters of Russia should be the promotion of World Revolution through the Communist International—or, as Trotsky later argued in exile, through a "Fourth International," since the "Third" had become a Stalinist instrument for betrayal of the cause. Stalin maintained conversely that the post-war "stabilization of capitalism" meant the inevitable postponement of World Revolution—not to the Greek Kalends, but to the next "crisis of capitalism" or to the next "imperialist war."

In June, 1926, Trotsky joined his ex-enemies, Zinoviev and Kamenev, in forming an anti-Stalin bloc within the Party. In 1927 this group of "Left Oppositionists" (in Party jargon) tentatively joined the "Right Deviationists," led by Nikolai Bukharin and Alexei Rykov (Lenin's successor as Premier of the USSR) in common opposition to Stalin. The latter group, in flat contradiction to the Trotskyites, favored a prolongation of the NEP and feared that Stalin's emerging program of collectivization and industrialization would prove disastrous. But here, as always, politics makes strange bedfellows and bedfellows make strange politics.

The efforts of the "Oppositionists," Left and Right, were in vain. When, during 1927, Britain's Conservative Government severed diplomatic relations with the USSR (May 26); Soviet Minister, Peter Voikov, was assassinated in Warsaw (also on May 26); and Chiang Kai-shek's Kuomintang in China simul-

taneously broke with its Communist allies and embarked upon
their forcible suppression, Trotsky and his supporters launched
an all-out propaganda assault on Stalin's leadership of the Party,
marked by riotous street demonstrations in Moscow and Leningrad on the tenth anniversary of the October Revolution.

In the aftermath the Central Committee (November 14,
1927) voted to expel Trotsky and Zinoviev from the Party. Congress XV (December, 1927) expelled all the leading "Oppositionists," ruled that adherence to Trotsky's views was incompatible
with Party membership, and endorsed the pending "Five Year
Plan" of collectivization and industrialization. All the "heretics"
recanted and were later readmitted to the Party on probation.
Only one refused to submit: Trotsky. He was exiled to Alma
Ata in Turkestan in January, 1928. Here he carried on clande-
stine correspondence, contending in his final letter of defiance to
warnings from Moscow that Stalin's supporters were "creatively
impotent, false, contradictory, unreliable, blind, cowardly,
inept" and devoted to "executing the orders of the enemy
classes." The GPU (January 20, 1929) ordered his deportation as
a "counter-revolutionary."

Trotsky went to Istanbul, then to France, thence to Norway, and finally to Mexico City—where, after years of agitation
for a "new Russian revolution" against Stalinism, he was murdered, August 21, 1940, by a mystery man of many aliases, including "Frank Jackson," who said that he had killed Trotsky
for "betraying Trotskyism," but who was regarded throughout
the Western world as a Stalinist agent sent by Stalin to liquidate his arch-enemy. "Jackson" was sentenced by a Mexican
court to twenty years in jail. In the spring of 1960 he was released and spirited away to Prague, still a man of mystery.

Whatever may be the facts, this tragic denouement did not
alter the meaning of Stalin's triumph over Trotsky in the USSR
of the 1920's. Without renouncing their Messianic goal, the
Marxists who ruled Russia would devote their energies not to
the visionary dream of World Revolution, but to the practical
business of "building socialism in one country."

The Police-state

The task which Stalin and his followers set for themselves
in 1928 and thereafter was a task without precedent in past
human experience. The immediate goal was the creation, for
the first time in history, of a totally socialized and consciously

planned economy in which the labor of each would promote the welfare of all in a context precluding the exploitation of man by man. The ultimate goal, beyond socialism, was "communism" in which all would lead free and happy lives in an affluent society with each rewarded according to his "needs" and contributing his talents to the cooperative commonwealth.

This cloudy Utopia—which, incredibly, was to come to some semblance of realization in the Russia of the 1960's—was paradoxically the product of one of the most atrocious tyrannies in all the annals of man's inhumanity to man. The totalitarian police-state which emerged from civil war became more "totalitarian" and more a "police-state" with the inauguration of the first Five Year Plan (1928–33), aimed at rapid industrialization and the collectivization of agriculture. The economics of "building socialism" we shall consider elsewhere in due course (see pp. 131–36). The politics of "building socialism" is our present concern, despite the artificiality of such a distinction in a totally socialist system of government and business.

Various other distinctions are in order if the course of Soviet politics during the decade before World War II is to be made meaningful. The abuses and horrors of the first *Piatiletka* or Five Year Plan were for the most part not the fruits of malice and fear on the part of the Stalinist oligarchs who were whip-lashing a reluctant people into a gigantic national effort at "modernization." They were rather the results of miscalculations and mistakes, engendering mass misery despite much mass enthusiasm and self-sacrifice, in pursuit of a pioneer enterprise for which no guidance was available either in the Marxist scriptures or in the human record. Muddles and blunders were manifold and doubtless inevitable. Conversely, the far more monstrous horrors and abuses of the mid-1930's—when the people of the USSR were beginning to enjoy a promise of ultimate prosperity as their rulers painfully learned the new arts of managing and expanding a socialist economy—were precisely attributable, as we shall see, to fear and malice on the part of policy-holders. Contrary to contemporary and still persisting Western impressions, these first two chapters of Stalin's despotism were not "all of a piece," but were quite different in causes and consequences.

To return to the beginning, socialist industrialization was impossible without more food from the farms. Under the NEP, total agricultural production by 1927–28 had recovered to its 1914 level, but marketable grain available for urban use or export was only 30% of the 1914 level. By partitioning the landed estates, the peasants had transformed the rural economy from a pre-revolutionary aggregate of some 16,000,000 units to a NEP pattern of some 25,000,000 individual farms. All farmers were eating better than ever before, particularly the *kulaki* or most productive and prosperous peasants and the *seredniaki* or middle peasants, in contrast to the *bedniaki* or poorest peasants. Industrialization required either a major increase of farm output or pressure on the peasantry to consume less and market more of their produce.

For non-Marxists the obvious solution would have been to encourage the *kulaki* and *seredniaki* to produce more by higher prices, subsidies, tax exemptions, and other incentives. For Marxists this solution was inconceivable since it would have eventuated in the emergence of a new class of profit-seeking farmers committed to "bourgeois" attitudes and values. Lenin, followed by Stalin, urged the consolidation of small farms into large cooperative "collectives" (*kolkhozi*) as the only permissible Marxist means of extracting more food from the countryside. The Communist rulers of China were to demonstrate in the 1950's, through their rural "communes," that such a transformation could be achieved, with striking results in terms of productivity, with a minimum of coercion and dislocation. The Communist rulers of Russia in the 1930's had no such knowledge. Their blundering efforts to solve the problem, albeit ultimately successful, were proximately disastrous.

Congress XV "declared war" on the kulaks, espoused the old slogan of "class war in the villages," and proposed to "socialize" Russian agriculture by encouraging the poorest (i.e., least productive) peasants to expropriate the richest (i.e., most productive) peasants in the process of collectivization. The new agrarian revolution reduced 25,000,000 individual farms to some 250,000 *kolkhozi*. The method was calamitous. The Party slogan of 1929 was: "Liquidate the kulaks as a class!" The most efficient of Russian farmers, faced with the loss of all their property through forcible incorporation in the collectives, resisted as best they could by refusing to sow and reap, burning barns and crops, killing livestock, and sabotaging the program of collectivization.

This blind resentment and resistance led to a reduction, between 1928 and 1933, of horses from 30,000,000 to 15,000,000; of horned cattle from 70,000,000 to 38,000,000; of sheep and goats from 147,000,000 to 50,000,000; and of hogs from 20,-

000,000 to 12,000,000. Soviet agriculture had not recovered from this appalling loss by 1941 or even by 1953. Stalin in *Pravda*, March 2, 1930, sought to call a halt by rebuking comrades for "Dizziness with Success" and by urging that collectivization must be voluntary. "Collective farms cannot be set up by force." Houses, gardens, orchards, livestock, and poultry should not be collectivized by "distortionists . . . blockheads!" A halt was called, but the appeal was too late. Even a tyrant cannot always control the momentum of a movement he has once unleashed, least of all when its agents gain personal profit from continuing the course already embarked upon.

The disaster here involved was almost, but not quite, complete—as the "Right Deviationists" within the Party feared that it might well be. Hundreds of thousands of kulaks were arrested by the GPU and deported to forced labor camps in Siberia and the far north. Other hundreds of thousands, totally disoriented by persecution, sank into apathy throughout the Russian countryside and assumed that the regime would somehow feed them. The assumption was false. Hundreds of thousands and perhaps millions of demoralized kulaks in the Ukraine and central Russia were left to starve to death, not because of the shortage of food but because they were "class enemies."

This catastrophe in its initial stages led the "Right Deviationists," as already noted, to seek common cause against Stalinism with the "Left Oppositionists"—all to no purpose, since the first Five Year Plan, despite appalling errors and frightful human and material costs, was clearly achieving its major objectives by the early 1930's. What followed was of a wholly different order and is intelligible, if at all, only in terms of new and well-warranted fears of foreign attack on the part of the decision-makers in the Kremlin. In addressing the First All-Union Conference of Managers of Socialist Industry on February 4, 1931, a decade after the end of the Allied and American intervention and a decade before the Nazi invasion of 1941, Stalin asserted:

Those who fall behind get beaten. But we do not want to be beaten. No, we refuse to be beaten! . . . Old Russia was beaten by the Mongol Khans, she was beaten by the Turkish beys. She was beaten by the Swedish feudal lords. She was beaten by the Polish and Lithuanian gentry. She was beaten by the British and French capitalists. She was beaten by the Japanese barons. All beat her—for her backwardness, for military backwardness, for cultural backwardness, for political backwardness, for industrial backwardness, for agricultural backwardness. She was beaten because it was profitable and could be done with impunity. Do you remember the words of the pre-Revolutionary poet: "You are poor and abundant, mighty and impotent, Mother Russia." These words of the old poet were well learned by those gentlemen. They beat her. . . . Such is the law of the exploiters—to beat the backward and the weak. . . . That is why we must no longer lag behind. . . . You must put an end to backwardness in the shortest possible time and develop genuine Bolshevik tempo in building up the socialist system of economy. There is no other way. . . . Either we do it, or they crush us.

These words of the tyrant were spoken eight months before the seizure of Manchuria by the Japanese warlords and two years before the conspiratorial Nazi conquest of power in the German Reich. These Fascist responses of the *"bourgeoisie"* to the challenge of the Great Depression precluded the "proletarian revolution" which all Communists took for granted in the new "crisis of capitalism." They likewise threatened a military assault upon the Soviet Union. During the period of the Second and Third Five Year Plans the Kremlin oligarchs vastly expanded the armed forces, built a huge war industry, and sought allies abroad.

But Stalin's most dramatic and shocking response to the expectation of war was the "Great Purge"—compared to which all earlier excesses and brutalities of the Soviet police-state paled into insignificance. There was no hint of future horrors at Congress XVII (1934) or the "Congress of Victors," where 1,225 delegates represented 1,874,000 members. In 1933–34 large numbers of Party members were dropped for unworthiness, but here as before "purge" meant no more than expulsion. The political police was renamed in July, 1934, the "Commissariat of Internal Affairs" (NKVD) and headed by the sinister Henry Yagoda, who at Stalin's behest was soon to organize a reign of terror to which, like most terrorists, he himself fell victim in the end.

The nightmare to come began with murder. On December 1, 1934, in Smolny Institute, Sergei M. Kirov, Party leader No. 2 after Stalin, was shot to death by a young CP member, Leonid Nikolayev. The killer's motives may have been private rather than political. The matter is still shrouded in mystery. Stalin's response was doubtless influenced by a series of other assassinations perpetrated by Fascist and Nazi agents (Rumanian Premier Ion Duca, December 19, 1933; Austrian Chancellor Engelbert Dollfuss, July 25, 1934; French Foreign Minister Louis Barthou and Yugoslav's King Alexander, October 9, 1934), despite the absence of credible evidence of any link between these killings and the murder of Kirov. Within a few weeks Stalin, without even consulting the Politburo or the *Sovnarkom* and acting through the NKVD and the Military Collegium of the Supreme Court of the USSR, ordered the execution of scores of people as "terrorists," "White Guards," and "Trotskyites"—many of them already in jail on December 1 and thus incapable of having had any hand in Kirov's death.

In the grisly sequel a far-flung plot was allegedly disclosed to slay Stalin and other leaders and to overthrow the Soviet State through sabotage, treason, and foreign intervention. In January, 1935, there began a series of highly publicized "trials" before the Military Collegium of the Supreme Court under Judge V. V. Ulrich with A. Y. Vyshinsky as State Prosecutor. In the first of these dramas Zinoviev was sentenced to 10 years in jail and Kamenev to 5 for having "known" of the plot against Kirov and failing to act. In the second (August, 1936) both "Old Bolsheviks," along with 14 others, were found "guilty" of far worse crimes and sentenced to death. In the third (January, 1937) 13 other "Old Bolsheviks" suffered a like fate, with Karl Radek, Gregory Sokolnikov, V. V. Arnold, and S. M. Stroilov given prison terms (none was ever heard of again), while Trotsky and his son, Lev, were held liable to "immediate arrest and trial" for treason "in the event of their being discovered on the territory of the USSR." In the fourth of this series (March, 1938) Rykov, Bukharin, Yagoda, and 15 others were ordered shot.

Meanwhile, in secret trials in 1937 Marshal Tukhazhevsky and 7 other high-ranking officers of the Red Army were court-martialed and executed. The diplomatic service, the managerial bureaucracy, the trade union leadership, and other cadres of the elite was similarly decimated to the tune of numerous suicides among prominent public personalities. The leadership of the NKVD passed in September, 1936, from Yagoda (shot) to N. I. Yezhov (disappeared) and then to Lavrenty Beria in December, 1938. The enormous police apparatus of oppression, functioning at Stalin's orders under these sadists and masochists, herded millions of little people into forced labor camps, which became a major industry in the 1930's. To return to the top, of the 1,966 delegates and alternates to Party Congress XVII, 1,108 were arrested and many shot, with 55 of the 71 members of the Central Committee and 60 of the 68 candidate numbers vanishing without a trace.

What political purpose, if any, in Stalin's twisted mind was

sought to be served by this orgy of persecution and death? No
final answer is available. None may ever be arrived at, since
Man, who has come to understand Nature all too well—perhaps
as a means to his own self-destruction—still has little understanding of human nature (despite the contributions of Pavlov
and Freud), particularly as regards his own "shadow-side" or
unconscious drives toward incest, murder, and suicide. Still less
can we always see clearly, despite a long and honorable tradition
of "Political Science," how and why people in politics behave
as they do.

Any attempt to answer the question here posed can only be
tentative. All the defendants in the public trials openly confessed to acts of treason against the Soviet State—which all of
them had helped to build. That the "Left Oppositionists" and
"Right Deviationists" had vaguely and obscurely conspired in
feckless fashion to dethrone Stalin is not in doubt. Why then
did they "confess" not to what they did but to what they were
accused of doing? Khrushchev's later answer (torture) is inadequate. Most of the "confessors," like Rubashov in Koestler's
Darkness at Noon, undoubtedly confessed out of a sense of final,
albeit fatal, obligation to the only thing in which they believed
—i.e., the Party.

All human beings must believe in something beyond themselves or else languish in loneliness or go mad. This spiritual
need of the psyche is often more clamant than the biological
urge to preserve life and postpone death—and more compulsive
than the moral imperatives of honesty, honor, and integrity.
The abject victims of the "purge trials" were clinging to the
only thing in which they had faith. They willingly gave their
lives to its service. That the Party they worshipped had been
converted by Stalin into a machine of personal despotism they
could not grasp, for to concede such a possibility would be a
self-denial of their own identity.

As for Stalin's motivations in instigating and planning the
"Blood Purge," our best evidence, even though it leaves many
questions obscure, is Khrushchev's memorable indictment of the
"Crimes of Stalinism" in the final "secret" session of Congress
XX, February 24–25, 1956. His arraignment of the dead dictator
has never, to date, been published in the USSR. But in the
spring of 1956 it was read in thousands of meetings to millions
of Soviet citizens throughout the land. This curious procedure
also admits of no satisfactory explanation.

Khrushchev's exposé was couched in quite un-Marxist

terms of defects of character. He noted, quite correctly, that the "Right Deviationists" and "Left Oppositionists" had suffered total political defeat long before the "Blood Purge." Why then the horror which followed? Khrushchev's answer was simple—undoubtedly too simple: Lenin broke with Stalin in 1923 because of the latter's "rude outbursts, vile invectives, and threats" to Krupskaya. Stalin was addicted to "brutal violence" and committed to the "moral and physical annihilation" of all who refused "absolute submission" to his will. Many "innocent people" and "honest Communists" were thus forced by "barbaric tortures" to sign false confessions as "enemies of the people" and to suffer death in violation of all precepts of human justice and "socialist legality." Stalin was "sickly suspicious" and distrustful of all his colleagues, many of whom never knew when they conferred with him whether, in the sequel, they would be promoted or shot. "In the past Stalin doubtless performed great services. . . . We cannot say that these were the deeds of a giddy despot. He considered that this should be done in the interest of the Party, of the working masses, in the name of the defense of the gains of the revolution. In this lies the whole tragedy!"

In retrospect, Stalin's madness in the 1930's, which was to prove almost fatal to the Soviet State in the 1940's, had a twisted "logic," albeit mistaken, immoral, perverted, and psychopathic. The "logic," never acknowledged, proceeded as follows: Russia sooner or later will be assaulted by a formidable coalition of foes; alliances with other Powers against common enemies, while essential, will prove futile; the USSR will long be left alone to combat the Fascist Triplice; despite boastings of Soviet "invulnerability" and "invincibility," the result at worst will be lethal and at best calamitous to the Soviet State; amid disaster, anti-Stalinists or potential anti-Stalinists will seek to depose Stalin and "come to terms" with the enemy out of their conviction that only such a course, as in 1918, could "save the Revolution." For Stalin such a course could only mean the "betrayal" of the Revolution, along with the end of his own Autocracy.

From these semi-insane but half-plausible premises, sundry half-mad conclusions followed. In the service of the Motherland and of the cause of Communism, all possible successors to Stalin's dictatorship must be liquidated in advance by charging them with crimes which they had not committed but might commit during the coming "time of troubles." Stalin, anticipating war, thus disposed of all prospective competitors for power by ingenious processes of torture, "brain-washing," "confessions," and quasi-voluntary immolations on the altar of the Party.

This phantasmagoria of deception and violence, reminiscent of Ivan the Terrible, spelled defeat for the USSR in the opening phases of World War II. Final triumph was achieved not because of, but in spite of, Stalin's conception of how his country should prepare for combat. In spite of himself, he emerged as the "organizer of victory"—purchased at the price of millions of lives, many of which could have been saved if Stalin in the 1930's had perceived more sanely the prerequisites of national defense. The Stalinist police-state persisted until Stalin's demise in 1953. The later liberalization of the Soviet polity (see pp. 147–51 below) is best left for subsequent consideration in another context of paradox. For, in fact, Stalinism, which effected the monstrous liquidation of scores of thousands, was itself a self-liquidating political phenomenon—for reasons to be examined in due course.

4 - The Practice of Politics

The Ghost of Plato

People who fear tyranny and love freedom have ever been concerned with dividing, restricting, and diffusing the power of those who act in the name of the State. In the modern democracies of the West, libertarians have often come close to their goal through such devices, despite the disposition of democracy in sharply stratified societies to degenerate into plutocracy. People who fear anarchy and love order have ever sought to maximize political power and to concentrate it in the hands of the few. Through many centuries and over vast areas in all the civilizations of mankind, the favored few have been hereditary dynasts and aristocrats. Authoritarians who have championed such arrangements have frequently found their ideal, as in the old Russia, corrupted into arbitrary absolutism and dim-witted despotism.

The new Russia is ruled by the Party. This novel pattern of power has long puzzled Western observers and even Russian participants, for it cannot be apprehended in terms of customary categories of governmental forms—apart from asserting what is true but unenlightening; that it is a new type of oligarchy, best described by such new terms as "totalitarianism" and the "one-party State." Between the World Wars of the 20th Century the outer structure, but not the inner essence, of this political novelty was copied with local variations by Mussolini's Fascists, Hitler's Nazis, Chiang Kai-shek's Kuomintang, Japan's warlords, and other converts to one-party dictatorship—all to no purpose save final failure and tragedy, compared to which the record of the Party in the new Russia is a "success story." All inventions, including political inventions, can be borrowed and used by others for ends having nothing in common with the original purpose of the inventors. The Fascist "totalitarians" of our Century borrowed the political devices invented by the Russian Marxists and used them for anti-egalitarian and anti-libertarian purposes designed to protect old elites of land and money. The Russian inventors of "totalitarianism," in the inner essence of their faith, were dedicated to building an egalitarian and libertarian society—to be achieved, paradoxically, by authoritarian and totalitarian methods designed to smash old elites of land and money and to create a socialist order.

Despite the horrors of Stalinism, it is too early to assert in the 1960's, after almost half a century of the "Soviet experiment," that such an enterprise is self-defeating and can eventuate only in tyranny and ultimate breakdown. This is possible but improbable, for reasons to be explored later in our inquiry. We are here confronted with something new under the sun which cannot be depicted in the old clichés of the language of politics, least of all by analogy to "parties" in the Western democracies.

So much granted, it is still useful to note that some precedents exist, however shadowy, for the political innovations of the Russian Marxists—which, as we have seen, were not anticipated by Marx nor planned by Lenin but came to pass, almost unwittingly, by virtue of the exigencies of civil and foreign war in 1918–21. Who shall rule? Since the many in all human societies cannot rule but can only choose the few to rule, or obey or defy the few who rule, a central question of all politics is: Who shall be the few to rule?

The age-old answer—kings and nobles—is unacceptable to most citizens in the "modern" phase of the Western Civiliza-

tion and of many of its precursors. China long ago evolved a
rulership of scholars whose authority served the Middle Kingdom well until Western pressures in the 19th Century rendered
old ways obsolete. Twenty-four centuries ago in ancient Athens
Plato grappled with the same problem. In the *Republic* he urged
government by a small, carefully chosen, and highly educated
elite of "guardians" to manage affairs of state under the rulership of philosopher-kings. Men have ever since debated to little
purpose as to whether Plato was a champion of egalitarianism
and libertarianism or of authoritarianism and totalitarianism.

Ambivalently, he was both. Because he was both, his dream
of a new aristocracy (of which the corrupt form is "oligarchy"
in Artistotle's science of politics) curiously parallels the vision
of the Russian Marxists as to what their Party was intended
to be. Since all philosophical idealists, Plato included, are
anathema to Marxists, the parallel is not a product of mimesis
but of coincidence. It is, nonetheless, striking. Plato's guardians,
as he describes them in words he attributes to his beloved
teacher, Socrates, were to rule not because of birth or wealth
but because of talent, self-discipline, dedication to the common-
weal, and elaborate training in dialectics and statecraft. Their
ranks, open equally to men and women, were to be recruited
from "the surest and the bravest and, if possible, the fairest," all
alike devoted to the public virtues of wisdom, courage, and
temperance. All would share property in common (from which
injunction it is arguable that Plato was indeed the first "Communist") and even spouses and children. In a polity so ordered
and so ruled, freedom and authority would allegedly be reconciled in the final attainment of the supreme goal of Justice.

Plato's dream-state was, of course, never achieved. His fel-
low-Greeks preferred to destroy their civilization, under the
delusion that they were "saving" it, through recurrent wars
among City-States, "Great Powers," and "Empires," all of which
brought them all alike to ruin. The comparable dreams of the
Russian Marxists have also, thus far, eluded realization. In the
human condition aspirations and accomplishments commonly
remain far apart, with deeds often negating hopes and sometimes reducing them to a mockery in a topsy-turvy world of trial-
and-error. Yet the march of Man from primordial darkness
toward ultimate light, and from primitive anarchy and tyranny
toward a free and open society, is always the work of dreamers
and visionaries, aspiring to the unattainable but capable of

moving their fellows to pursue the quest. Such, amid tragedies and triumphs, has been the mission of the Party which rules the USSR.

The Party's "monopoly of legality" was initially a response to the civil and foreign war of 1918–21, after which no revival of other parties was permitted by the Communist victors. The Marxist-Leninist rationalization of one-party rule originally equated this species of oligarchy with the "dictatorship of the proletariat." A long accepted formulation now holds that rival political parties are expressions of class antagonisms; that there are no antagonistic classes in Soviet society; and that a multiplicity of parties would therefore be an absurdity. That this formula is demonstrably false both in the USSR and the Western democracies does not deprive it of sanctity in the eyes of the Marxist rulers of Russia.

The role of the Party has been variously assessed by Western observers and by its own spokesmen. Foreign judgments have ranged from "the Vocation of Leadership" (Sidney and Beatrice Webb in 1936) and the "hope of the world" to "control by terror" and a monstrous machine of oppression. Every such evaluation is "true" in reflecting incontrovertible aspects of the oligarchy. Every such evaluation is "false" in neglecting other and equally incontrovertible facets of rulership. To choose among these alien verdicts would be to deny the protean and paradoxical character of the Party's function in Soviet society and thus to ignore reality—granting, as we must, that "reality" is always hard to come by since, more often than not, it exists only in the vision of the observer.

Official Soviet definitions of the Party's function are scarcely more helpful, for they are inevitably couched in the jargon of Marxism-Leninism which, in matters such as these, is obfuscating rather than illuminating. In Soviet constitutional documents prior to 1936 (see pp. 93–99 below), the Party was never mentioned. In the USSR Constitution of 1936, which, as amended, remains the basic law of the land, the Party is mentioned only twice: it is referred to (Art. 141) among the organizations entitled to nominate candidates for public office, and it is characterized as follows (Art. 126) among the groups which Soviet citizens are entitled to join: "and the most active and politically conscious citizens in the ranks of the working class, working peasants, and working intelligentsia voluntarily unite in the Communist Party of the Soviet Union, which is the vanguard of

the working people in their struggle to build a communist
society and is the leading core of all organizations of the working people, both public and State."

The Charter of the Party in force in the late 1950's and
early 1960's describes the Party thus:

> The Communist Party of the Soviet Union is a voluntary militant
> union of like-minded people, Communists, consisting of members of
> the working class, working peasants, and working intellectuals.
>
> The Communist Party of the Soviet Union, having organized an
> alliance of the working class and the laboring peasantry, achieved, as
> a result of the Great October Socialist Revolution of 1917, the over-
> throw of the power of the capitalists and landlords, the establishment
> of the dictatorship of the proletariat, the elimination of capitalism and
> the abolition of the exploitation of man by man, and ensured the build-
> ing of a socialist society.
>
> The principal objects of the Communist Party of the Soviet Union
> today are to build a communist society through gradual transition from
> socialism to communism, continuously to raise the living and cultural
> standards of society, to educate the members of society in a spirit of
> internationalism and fraternal ties with the working people of all
> countries, and to strengthen to the utmost the active defense of the
> Soviet Motherland against aggressive actions on the part of its enemies.

Such formulations, albeit interesting as statements of purpose, tell us little about the actual role of the Party—which
consists, after all, of human beings emotionally identified with
common symbols of shared objectives and prepared to work hard
for the achievement of goals which they (or their leaders) regard as the highest values of life. Membership in this comradeship of devotees has varied widely, although ever increasing
despite Lenin's insistence on selectivity and on quality rather
than quantity. Members have varied even more widely in background through the five decades of the Soviet State.

During the early 1900's when the Party was an underground
conspiracy of revolutionists, its members numbered fewer than
10,000. Early in 1917 the members numbered c. 24,000—a
figure which expanded to 240,000 by September. (Commented
Lenin: "240,000 Bolsheviks can rule Russia as readily as 240,000
land-owners.") Membership did not reach the million mark
until 1926. Subsequent expansion of the rolls of the sacred
brotherhood, in spite of periodical contractions through purges,
expulsions, executions, and war deaths, brought membership to
almost 7,000,000 at the end of World War II and to almost
8,000,000 when Stalin died. At Congress XIX (October, 1952)
full members numbered 6,013,259 and candidate members 868,-

886. The corresponding figures at the time of Congress XX (February, 1956) were 6,795,896 and 419,609; and at Congress XXI (January, 1959), 7,622,356 and 616,775 candidates. By the early 1960's members and candidates totaled almost 9,000,000.

Who are these dedicated souls and how are they recruited? Without trying to survey the many detailed studies that have been made of these matters, we may venture a few generalizations (supported by reams of statistics in sundry scholarly monographs) which will hold for the post-Stalin years. The Party has long ceased to be, if indeed it ever was, a comradeship of workers and peasants, nor is it any longer in any meaningful sense the "vanguard of the proletariat." Most members are now well-educated technicians, engineers, managers, scientists, teachers, and other professional people of the new "intelligentsia" or "socialist middle class" brought into being by the massive industrialization and urbanization. Perhaps a quarter of a million members (exact figures are unavailable) are full-time Party workers (*Apparatchiki*), paid by the Party as local secretaries or as specialists in the Party's complex bureaucracy of agitators, propagandists, educators, supervisors, etc. All the rest have full-time jobs of their own and serve the Party on their jobs as well as evenings, week-ends, and vacations. In comparison with the Soviet population as a whole, the composition of the Party greatly over-represents males (only a fifth of the members are women), appreciably over-represents urbanites at the expense of country-dwellers, and slightly over-represents Great Russians as against the non-Russian nationalities of the USSR.

But the Party was never intended to be a cross-section of Soviet society. It is an elite of talent in which membership is a privilege and an honor, to be earned and retained by service, and not a sinecure or a duty. Many prominent scientists, artists, and writers (e.g., Ilya Ehrenburg) prefer to remain outside the ranks so that they may devote all their time and energy to their professional work rather than to burdensome Party activities. An applicant must be recommended by three Party members of three years' standing and must be approved not only by a general meeting of the "primary Party organization" (i.e., local unit) to which he is applying but also by the district or city Party committee—with similar arrangements regarding expulsions for unworthiness. All applicants must serve a probationary period as "candidates" for at least a year, during which they have a voice but no vote in their local unit. Candidates and full members alike pay monthly dues ranging from $\frac{1}{2}\%$ on earnings under

500 rubles up to 3% on earnings over 2,000 rubles. All are subject to expulsion if in arrears for three months. Three-quarters
of the Party's revenues come from dues and the balance from
income-producing Party enterprises, chiefly publishing.

Payment of dues is the least of the duties of a Party member. He has "rights" carefully safeguarded in the Party statutes—
in Stalin's time more often honored in the breach than in the
observance. But a member's obligations are far more meaningful in terms of his mission. On the negative side, he must keep
out of church and remain sober, honest, respectable, and "cul-
tured." On the affirmative side, he must participate energetically
in all Party work, observe the duties of criticism and "self-
criticism," help formulate Party policies, obey and carry out
Party orders once a decision has been made, and gladly volunteer for special assignments, even those involving long sojourns
at arduous tasks in some far-off wilderness. His rewards are
pride, honor, a sense of service, political preferment, and often
access to opportunities for vocational advancement less likely to
be opened to non-Party members.

Lest it be thought, as many Westerners appear to think,
that Russia is ruled by a self-selected aristocracy comprising only
4% of the population, it is needful to note that the Party is supplemented by, and in a large part recruited from, a hierarchy
of mass organizations of the young. The Young Communist
League (*Komsomol*), now officially known as the "All-Union
Leninist Communist League of Youth," was founded in 1918
with 20,000 members. By the early 1960's it had 20,000,000 members, aged 14 to 27, comprising a third of all youths in these
age brackets and two-thirds of those with higher education. Although designated as a "non-Party" organization, it closely
parallels the Party in structure and function and admittedly
"does all its work under the direct guidance of the Party."

Young people aged 9 to 15 are encouraged to join the
"Young Pioneers," also with 20,000,000 members in the early
1960's. This Soviet equivalent of Boy Scouts and Girl Scouts,
directed by the *Komsomols,* maintains summer camps, museums,
and clubhouses and engages in a vast variety of educational and
recreational activities, all directed, needless to say, to inculcating
the Soviet equivalent of "Americanism"—i.e., Marxism-Leninism
and the Communist ethos. Guided groups of Young Pioneers,
identified by red kerchiefs, are to be seen in all Soviet cities in
all seasons on their way to libraries, museums, planetariums,
art galleries, or sporting events. Finally, children between 7 and

9 may join the "Little Octobrists," also numbering many millions, although recent membership figures are unavailable.

The Party hierarchy with its junior auxiliaries thus embraces not 4% but almost 25% of the peoples of Sovietland—few of whom, to be sure, have any decisive voice in the determination of public policies. This circumstance does not differentiate Soviet society from other human societies of the past and present, whether "democratic" or "totalitarian." The distinction to be noted is that in "democratic" societies all citizens are free in theory to dissent from, and criticize, official views and policies and to agitate and organize to effect changes in the *status quo,* whereas in the USSR all citizens are expected to conform to the "Party line," with only a limited voice for Party members, and a neglible voice for non-Party members, to bring about by word or deed any major change in the current "line" through discussion or agitation. Political organization and activity outside of the Party is forbidden.

The Soviet scheme of things never functions perfectly and often functions badly, as in all human affairs. But when it functions well, as often it does, it approximates Plato's plan for the careful and progressive selection of an aristocracy of skill, embodying the best virtues of a richly talented community and elevating the best to leadership. An able and ambitious boy or girl in the USSR will begin as a Little Octobrist and ascend, if found worthy, into the Young Pioneers. Further testing, if the tests are passed, will gain admission to the *Komsomols*—and beyond that, with many falling by the wayside, into the Party itself, within whose ranks capacity for leadership can lead to fame and fortune. Along the way, thanks to mistaken judgments or to the unpredictability of the human equation, even the highest ranks may be permeated by careerists, self-seekers, and thieves—again as in all societies. Not even Plato, nor anyone since, has ever found a foolproof answer to the ancient question: Who shall guard the guardians? The answer of the Russian Marxists is in some respects far worse than other answers which have been attempted, in other respects better, and on balance impressive in terms of creative achievements by the rulers of the new Russia.

Apart from *Komsomols,* Young Pioneers, and Little Octobrists, contemporary Soviet society, like its highly industrialized counterparts in the West, displays a bewildering variety of adult organizations whose many millions of members have organized themselves for shared purposes: trade unionism, cooperatives, art, literature, science, sports, drama, ballet, philately, chess, and thousands of other interests. All such organizations in the Atlantic democracies are in principle voluntary and autonomous groupings of people with common concerns having no necessary relationship to the common goals, if any, of the community as a whole. All such organizations in the USSR are in principle segments of shared community purposes and all are guided or directed or controlled, with more or less success, by the corresponding unit of the Party.

Such guidance is, indeed, the function of the Party in a polity which is not "pluralistic" but "monolithic." This is the meaning of "totalitarianism." For Western liberals who cherish a maximization of individual and group freedom, this is an evil concept. Yet, apart from the word, it is a noble ideal for the "togetherness" which characterizes a society dedicated to common purposes. If we add to the Party and its junior auxiliaries all the other organizations which the Party "advises" or bends to its own ends, we should be obliged to conclude that the Party embraces, or at least permeates and controls, all aspects of the Soviet community. This, indeed, is the case and is the avowed purpose of the Party.

How then shall we describe these rulers? What they are not is much clearer than what they are. They are not landed aristocrats nor merchant princes nor private industrialists nor speculating capitalists nor demagogue-dictators nor militarists nor feudalists. They combine policies and purposes hitherto divided in past human experience among separate segments of those aspiring to rule mankind. They constitute a secular priesthood, devoted to a theology and dedicated to public service. They comprise a militant army marching forth as if to war. They include scoundrels, saints, and martyrs. The best among them are selflessly sanctified in their tasks and are capable of inspiring millions to heroic accomplishments. The worst are sycophants, grafters, and sadists. The mass of members, as in most human organizations, range from simple souls, inspired by idealism or greed, to sophisticates, thirsty for the pleasures of power or generously consecrated to the realization of a dream. Those most respected and influential among them include executives and bureaucrats, frequently dull-witted but oftentimes capable of great achievements.

In short, the rulers of the USSR are *sui generis* and thus unique, for good or ill, among all previous aspirants to the governance of men. Their uniqueness is neither a vice nor a virtue, despite Western judgments of their viciousness. Such judgments are always subjective, never objective. Posterity will judge some decades hence, if mankind does not meanwhile commit thermonuclear suicide. Let judgment wait, while we go on to examine how public policy-making proceeds within the context of the rulership of the Party.

The Party Machine

Most priesthoods and all armies are organized into hierarchies, or "chains of command," whereby those at the base of the pyramid are answerable to, and carry out the orders of, those at the top. Most political parties in democratic states are in theory, if not always in practice, so structured as to make those at the apex of leadership representative of, and responsible to, the rank and file membership at the bottom. The USSR is not a democratic State. Its ruling Party, during most of its four decades of rulership, has functioned more as an army or as a priesthood than as a political party in the Western sense. Lenin's organizational principle of "democratic centralism" (see p. 34 above) sought to reconcile two antithetical concepts in a new synthesis in which leaders would be chosen by followers and followers would obey leaders. The problem he sought to solve is an eternal problem of all politics: how to combine effective authority by leaders with meaningful freedom for followers. His solution, albeit temporarily successful, was to prove a total failure during the thirty years following his death. Whether in the post-Stalin era it still offers possibilities or prospects of new success is a question best deferred until we strive to grasp the complicated organizational architecture of the Party which Lenin founded and brought to power.

The task is formidable and confusing. Few groups of power-holders have excelled the Russian Marxists in confusing shadow with substance, solemnly proclaiming "rules" which are subsequently ignored, devising procedures on paper which are widely at variance with human realities, and revising, reshuffling, renouncing, and renovating all sorts of agencies of Party and Government alike at a dizzy tempo. Even the official name of the Party has thrice been changed: from "Russian Social Democratic Labor Party (Bolsheviks)" to (1918) "All-Russian Communist Party (Bolsheviks)" to (1925) "All-Union Communist Party (Bolsheviks)" to (1952) "Communist Party of the Soviet Union." Structure has been as protean as terminology. It is

nevertheless possible, without becoming lost in details, to outline the Party apparatus as it emerged from a long past into the
1960's.

Members are grouped into almost half a million "primary
organizations," formally called "cells." These local units, ranging
in size from a handful to several hundred members, are with
few exceptions based not on territorial areas, such as precincts,
wards, election districts, etc., but on economic entities such as
factories, offices, farms, and schools. Each has a Bureau, a Secretary, and a General Meeting which is expected to convene at
least once a month. As one ascends the hierarchy, higher bodies
correspond to major political and administrative subdivisions
culminating in the 15 Union Republics, all of which have their
own Parties save the largest of the Republics, the RSFSR,
where each *Krai* or territorial unit has its separate Party structure.

The primary organizations elect delegates to City Conferences or District Conferences, each of which has a Bureau and a
Committee. These in turn elect delegates to Regional (*Oblast*)
Conferences, each again with its Bureau and Committee, which
elect delegates to the Party Congresses of the Republics or the
Krais of the RSFSR. The Republican Party Congresses, meeting
at least every two years by the terms of the current rules, choose
Central Committees which choose Bureaus. They likewise choose
delegates to the All-Union Party Congress in which the mass
membership is indirectly represented—formerly by one delegate
for each 1,000 members; in 1952 and 1956 one for each 5,000
members; and in 1959 one for each 6,000 members.

Before considering what in principle is meant to be the
highest decision-making organ of the Party, it is well to note
that until recently the Congress was supplemented by a Party
Conference, consisting of a somewhat smaller number of delegates elected by lower bodies and meeting more informally between Congresses. The first and second such Conferences met in
Tammerfors, Finland, in December, 1905, and in November,
1906. The eighteenth and in fact the last Conference gathered
in February, 1941. This institution was abolished in 1934, revived in 1939, and finally done away with as unnecessary in
1952.

The Party Congress met annually between 1917 and 1925,
then biannually, later once every three years—on paper but not
in practice. Under the rules adopted at Congress XIX in 1952 a
Congress is expected to convene at least once in every four years.

Almost half the delegates at recent Congresses have been full-time Party functionaries or Governmental officials. Most delegates are local or national leaders who have attended institutions of higher learning and in many instances have received prizes or honors for distinguished service. The Congress is thus an assembly not of typical or representative Party members but a select body of the Party elite. Under the Party statutes the Congress revises the rules and the Program, lays down the "line" on the major questions of current policy, and chooses the members of, as well as hears reports from, the Central Auditing Commission and the Central Committee of the CPSU.

Between Congresses the Central Committee "directs the entire work of the Party." This body, which in intent is chosen by, and answerable to, the Congress, grew from 15 full members and 8 candidate members in 1918 to 71 members and 68 candidates in 1927. At Congresses XIX, XX, and XXI (1952–59) its size was finally fixed at 133 members and 122 candidates or alternates, scheduled under recent rules to meet in plenary session at least every six months. The Central Committee names the three top-level bodies in the hierarchy: (1) the Party Control Committee, charged with enforcing discipline; (2) the Secretariat, consisting in recent years of a First Secretary and 10 Assistant Secretaries, entrusted with the direction of the entire Party apparatus throughout the country and functioning through a dozen or so "Sections"—Foreign Affairs, Military Affairs, Agriculture, Heavy Industry, Light Industry, Building and Planning, Education, Women's Affairs, Cadres, Culture and Science, Propaganda and Agitation, Trade Unions and Komsomols, etc.; and (3) the Party Presidium, established in 1952 by the merging of the former Organization Bureau and Political Bureau (Politburo) into a single "directing center" or "supreme organ" of the Party.

The members of the Presidium, as of the earlier Politburo, are all holders of the highest posts in Party and Government alike. Its membership was enlarged to 25 full members and 10 candidate members at Congress XIX, but was again reduced after Stalin's death to 10 full members and 4 alternates—with minor subsequent fluctuations below or above these figures. Here is perhaps the most powerful single body of rulers in the contemporary world.

As for the inescapable question—where does effective influence upon decision-making actually reside?—no single answer is applicable to the whole period of the Party's rule nor is any

simple answer fixed and final. To be sure, in giving concrete
application to "democratic centralism," the Party thus far has
sacrificed democracy to centralism. In the days of Lenin, however, the Central Committee was actually responsible to the
Party Congress—which then met frequently, debated issues
actively, and reached major decisions by majority vote. Stalin,
as Secretary of the Central Committee, subsequently made himself Party boss (*Vozhd*) on his way to becoming a new Autocrat.
Congresses became less and less frequent. None was held between 1939 and 1952.

Meetings of the Central Committee likewise became fewer
and degenerated into exercises in unanimity. Even the Politburo
was often ignored. These bodies expelled old members and
"co-opted" (self-selected) new members with no regard to the
Party Congress ostensibly charged with such tasks. The vast
machine of the apparatus became a vehicle whereby one man at
the center manipulated his colleagues and subordinates like
puppets, terrorized and destroyed all potential critics and dissidents, and reduced the rank and file to robots.

Has the post-Stalin Party recovered from its Stalinist degeneration and corruption? Has intra-Party "democracy" been
restored to any significant degree? The best current answer to
both questions would seem to be: not quite. Yet the direction
of change is unmistakable. Since 1953 Congresses meet again
on schedule, albeit still without meaningful debates or votes.
Proceedings of the Presidium and the Central Committee remain secret, but there is ample evidence, as we shall see, of
decision-making in both bodies through lively debating and
voting. Local Party units choose officers and delegates by secret
ballot and sometimes overrule "suggestions" from above. New
light and new air have penetrated rooms long stifling in darkness. The light is still dim and the air not always fresh. Yet
there are reasonable prospects of a further liberalization and
democratization of the formidable machine of power which continues to rule the USSR.

Patterns of Leadership

Much Western writing about the CPSU emphasizes practices and patterns of behavior which are in no way distinctive of
politics in the Soviet Union but are common to all political
parties and all politicians everywhere and always. Through the
decades and years of the Red oligarchy, Communist bosses have

held high posts in both Party and Government. They have used patronage to reward their friends, punish their enemies, and bring into being little or large bureaucracies of "organization men" upon whose support they have relied for the furtherance of their own ambition. They have "packed" or "rigged" Party agencies and Governmental bodies to serve their purposes. They have made a fine art of the familiar precepts of "divide and rule" and "steal the opposition's thunder." They have played rivals off against one another. They have intrigued, connived, and conspired against each other. They have rationalized inter-personal feuds for power into quarrels about "principles." They have converted controversies over public policies into inter-personal feuds for power. They have cheated, lied to, and deceived their fellow citizens; and educated, exalted, and inspired them. Any such enumeration of the ways of *Homo politicus* could be extended almost indefinitely.

These attributes and habits, as all careful students of comparative government and politics should know, are in no way peculiar to the CPSU. They are shared by all who seek to win friends and influence people by participating in politics. Graphic accounts of these practices and of their practitioners in times long gone are to be found in the writings of Machiavelli, Plutarch, Pliny, Suetonius, Herodotus, Thucydides, Isaiah, Jeremiah, and of other commentators on politics in ancient China, India, Sumeria, and Egypt. In our own time all politicians do likewise— from Krasnoyarsk to Keokuk, Leningrad to Los Angeles, Oman to Omaha, Peking to Pittsburgh. These are the brands of the breed, ubiquitous and eternal. To dwell upon them in the CPSU tells us nothing about what is unique in Soviet politics but only that Russians are human and that Soviet politicians are much like their counterparts elsewhere.

What then differentiates politics in the USSR from politics in other lands? Since the Party tolerates no competitors, clashes of views and interests in public policy, and rivalries for ascendancy in the conduct of public affairs, all take place within the Party and not in competition between parties. In a regime of total socialism, moreover, there is no distinction between "public" and "private" enterprise and, therefore, no meaningful difference between "politics" and "economics."

Here, as always and everywhere, rulers command obedience through force, fraud, and favors. But "favors" in the USSR do not involve, as is often the case in the Western democracies, a process whereby "public officials" strive for pelf and power by sponsoring Governmental policies designed to enrich "private interests," lobbies, or pressure groups. No such entities exist in the USSR. If they exist potentially, they have no means of political action and therefore no practical ways in politics to further their purposes. Few, if any, of the Red oligarchs have been "spoilsmen" or "grafters," amassing private fortunes at public expense. The wise or unwise allocation of material benefits and deprivations by those who wield political power is, in the Soviet Union, not a matter of "public" servants acting as brokers among "private" interests, but a matter of economic planners, always under the direction of the leaders of the Party, reconciling as best they can the hopes and expectations of competitors for favors in such a way as to promote the supreme national objective of maximizing the production of goods and services.

By "fraud" as a tool of power is here meant not conscious dishonesty or deceit but merely the systematic manipulation of symbols for the purpose of eliciting mass obedience, approbation, and, if possible, enthusiasm in the pursuit of aims set by rulers. Here the Marxist masters of Muscovy have done wondrously well. Their elaborately organized techniques of "agitation" and "propaganda" have put Madison Avenue to shame and inspired the masses of Sovietland to extraordinary sacrifices and exertions to achieve the objectives set by the Party.

Force is always the crudest and often the least effective means of commanding obedience. Napoleon once commented: "You can do anything with bayonets except sit on them." Force has, nevertheless, been the ultimate weapon of the Marxist oligarchs, ever since the initiation of the Red Terror of 1918, and was frequently the chief weapon during the reign of Stalin. Its modalities are familiar enough to Western readers, since most Western commentators on Soviet rule have relished the task of depicting its horrors in detail: the knock on the door in the small hours, the cells and torture chambers of the Political Police, the extraction of confessions, the forced labor camps, the bullet in the back of the head, the miasma of mutual distrust and universal fear. These odious devices of the Soviet polity, to be sure, have been largely abandoned since 1953. They cannot be deemed irrevocable and permanent features of the regime, as some Western writers have contended.

It is nonetheless true that the leaders of the Party ruling Russia since 1917 have, during the most of the intervening years, relied heavily upon coercion as a means of enlisting loyalty and suppressing dissent. The victims, as we have seen, have included hundreds of Party bosses and thousands of Party members along with millions of non-Party "class enemies" or "traitors." All must conform to the official ideology and "Party line." Political success depends upon agility in making "correct" adjustments to changes of creed and program decreed by the Party's high priests. No one enjoys freedom of speech, press, assembly, and public action as known in the Western democracies. These things may change in the USSR, and are indeed changing, as all things change in all human affairs. But these are the enduring attributes of "totalitarianism," in the USSR as elsewhere. So long as "totalitarianism" endures, there can be no "loyal opposition," as in the democracies. All opposition to Party directives and all criticism of Governmental policies tend to be equated by power-holders with "treason" toward the State. And treason, by the age-old imperatives of sovereignty, must be crushed by force.

The trends of change in these matters we shall consider in due course. Meanwhile, what can be said of the quality and caliber of the leaders brought to power in this strange context of rulership by "guardians"? And what can be said—since all men are mortal, including politicians—of the problem of succession? In hereditary monarchies, when functioning as planned, the problem solves itself through accepted rules of inheritance. In bi-party or multi-party democracies, whether parliamentary or presidential, the problem also solves itself, through popular elections. In one-party oligarchies, such as the USSR, Red China, the "satellites" of Eastern Europe, Outer Mongolia, North Korea, and North Vietnam, the problem is more complex. Lenin's plan was simple and plausible. Party members elect delegates to a Party Congress which chooses a Central Committee whose members in turn determine the composition of the Politburo or Party Presidium and Secretariat as repositories of ultimate authority in decision-making. But here as elsewhere, and here more than elsewhere, systems of succession sometimes fail to function as planned, since politicians are often prone to regard their own purposes as more important than the plans of their predecessors.

Let us defer for the moment the problem of succession in Soviet political leadership and return to the initial question of what manner of men have in fact attained to the highest levels of the hierarchy. To identify them is not difficult. They comprise the full members of the Politburo or Presidium of the Party's Central Committee. Between 1917 and 1961 some 50 individuals have been members of this body. Of these, 6 were executed, 2 were murdered, 4 vanished, 1 killed himself, 7 died, and 9 were dismissed and demoted. Among the rest continuity, rather than change, was the rule. In 1952, the last year of Stalin's reign, the members of the Party's Politburo (Presidium) included one (Stalin) who had been "on the board" for 35 years; two (Molotov and Voroshilov) for 27 years; one (Kaganovich) for 22 years; another (Andreyev) for 20 years; and yet others whose lesser years of service were still impressive: Mikoyan (17); Khrushchev (13); Malenkov and Beria (6).

Who were these leaders? Who are their younger successors? An adequate answer would require biographical sketches of each of them, for which space is here lacking. Such biographies are readily available in Soviet and Western publications, although Soviet sources on principle, reveal nothing of the "private lives" of leaders. An "objective" outside observer, viewing the surface of the Soviet political scene in the late 1930's and beyond, might well have concluded that the Communist system of elite recruitment brought to power only psychopaths, sadists, masochists, and martyrs. Other observers, more concerned with Soviet science, technology, industry, art, and mass education, might equally well have concluded that the Communist system of recruiting leaders had brought to power, or at least to prominence and influence, an extraordinary aristocracy of talent capable of phenomenal achievement. Each interpretation of the Soviet paradox may be deemed half-true and half-false.

Any effort to present a composite portrait of "typical" leaders of the CPSU would depict a figure possessed of fanatical dedication, soaring ambition, acute intelligence, indomitable energy, and much experience in obeying and giving orders in the armed forces or in Party service or in economic enterprises— or, more commonly, in some combination of managerial roles. As regards social background, the waning generation of older leaders who joined the Party before 1917 consisted, more often than not, of intellectuals raised in middle-class or upper-class families. Far more of the intermediate generation of more recent leaders are of peasant or proletarian origin, always an asset in a group which rules in the name of "the dictatorship of the proletariat." The youngest and currently emerging leaders are more frequently children of "white-collar" workers, executives, or professional people.

Since one concrete case is worth a dozen generalizations, let us recall the well-known facts in the life of the best known of the leaders in the late 1950's and early 60's. Leader No. 1, to be sure, is not "typical" of lesser lights, but his career is fairly

representative of many others in the top echelons. Nikita Sergey-
evich Khrushchev was born April 17, 1894, in Kalinovka, then
a poor and petty village and mining camp near Kursk, close to
the Ukrainian frontier. His father was a coal miner. The son grew
up in poverty and ignorance, toiling at times as a herdsman, a
miner, and a locksmith. Still only semi-literate at 23, he joined
the Bolsheviks in 1918 and fought in the Civil War. He worked
by day, went to school at night, and in 1929 was sent by the
Party to the Moscow Industrial Academy to complete his education. Loquacious, earthy, clownish, shrewd, he won the respect
of his fellows and by the mid-1930's was a local Party leader in
Moscow, where he shared credit with Kaganovich and Bulganin
for directing construction of the subway. By 1934 he was a
member of the Central Committee and an alternate member of
the Politburo. Another four years found him a full member of
the Politburo and First Secretary of the Party in the Ukraine.
Here, in what was then the chief granary and major industrial
center of the USSR, he completed the reorganization of the Party
in the aftermath of Stalin's "Blood Purge." The extent of his
complicity, apart from customary public eulogies of the *Vozhd,*
in what he was later to denounce as Stalin's atrocities is not a
matter of public record—for reasons all too obvious in the Communist system of power. In all times of troubles history is written
by the survivors.

During the years of disaster, when the Nazi *Wehrmacht*
ravaged the Ukraine with fire and sword, Khrushchev was still
there directing resistance and organizing guerrilla warfare against
the invaders. By 1944, when he was awarded the Order of Lenin
on his fiftieth birthday, he had served as a deputy to the Supreme
Soviet and a member of its Presidium, and as a deputy to the
Supreme Soviet of the Ukraine and ultimately as Ukrainian
Premier. He had also been named a Lieutenant General and
been granted the Order of Suvorov. After 1945 he played a leading managerial role in famine relief and reconstruction, in smash-
ing guerrilla bands of Ukrainian "separatists" or "nationalists,"
and in collectivizing and "Sovietizing" the recovered "lost provinces" to the west. This homely man of the "grass-roots"—soon to
be known to all the world as the blunt, ebullient, and vivacious
leader of the Soviet State—was unknown to the world and even
half unknown in Moscow where, unlike his peers and rivals, he
spent little time and avoided close contact with Stalin—who
nevertheless appreciated and rewarded his peculiar talents. Not
until 1950 did he begin to play a national role—first in the suc-

cessful consolidation of the collective farms into a much smaller number of far larger units and then in his abortive scheme to abolish the old villages of the peasantry in favor of *agrogorods* or apartment-cities for farmers. Failure or success in specific projects of social engineering did not alter Khrushchev's image in the eyes of Party and public. The image was that of a "self-made" man of humble origins who had served his country well. A similar aura surrounds most other leaders of the Party who have risen to prominence.

Comrade Khrushchev's "private life" is also comparable to the private lives of other leaders of the oligarchy. Here is no sequence of juvenile delinquency, repeated "affairs," marriages, divorces, remarriages, neurotic breakdowns, and other evidences of social and psychic disorder, but rather a conventional "bourgeois" family constellation. Following the early death of his first wife, who bore two children, Khrushchev married Nina Petrovna in 1924, who bore three more. Of the five younger Khrushchevs, an elder son, Leonid, was killed during World War II. Son Sergei is married. Daughters Yulia and Yelena were unwed at the time their parents brought all the family along on their American tour in 1959. Daughter Rada is the wife of Alexei I. Adzhubei, editor of *Izvestia*. As of 1960 Nikita and Nina had four grandchildren: Yulia, daughter of Leonid, and Nikita, Alexei, and Ivan, children of the Adzhubeis.

The Parade of the Power-holders

The larger issues of selection of leaders and of succession to leadership can best be explored and in part explained by surveying, with a minimum of hypothesizing about matters unknown, the top-level circulation of the political elite since World War II. The bare record of known events is in any case a pre-requisite for understanding changing trends of elite recruitment in the CPSU. These events are seldom, if ever, the objects of critical discussion in the USSR, where the infallibility of the Party leadership is still, despite disillusionment, an article of faith. These events have fostered widely divergent interpretations among Western commentators. For present purposes let us limit ourselves to the public facts of succession to leadership and avoid speculation regarding secret intrigues among the oligarchs— about which nothing can be known with certainty.

The first point to be made is that the outstanding politicians in the Party remained in fear of their lives at the hands of the

Georgian despot long beyond the years of the "Blood Purge." Despite the hideous trauma of World War II and the amazing accomplishments of rapid reconstruction in its aftermath, Stalin's addiction to "brutal violence" and his insistence on "absolute submission" (to use Khrushchev's words of 1956) continued to manifest themselves in sundry ways. During the war years supreme power was concentrated in the State Committee of Defense, consisting of Stalin as Chairman, Molotov as Vice-Chairman, Voroshilov, Beria, and Malenkov. The latter two became members of the Politburo in March, 1946. Two other top leaders died: Alexander Shcherbakov in 1945 and Andrei Zhdanov in 1948. The passing of Zhdanov was followed by the still unexplained "Leningrad Case" in which, obviously at Stalin's orders, Zhdanov's followers were purged and the brilliant young economist Nikolai Voznesensky, head of the *Gosplan* and an alternate member of the Politburo, was secretly liquidated. Also in 1949–50 several Jewish writers were done to death and the rich Yiddish culture of the USSR was virtually suppressed in the name of combating "Zionism" and "cosmopolitanism."

Party Congress XIX (October, 1952), the first in 13 years, reflected the aging dictator's choice of Georgi M. Malenkov as his probable successor-designate, qualified in the direction of "collective leadership" by way of the enlargement (temporary, as it turned out) of the Politburo, now renamed "Presidium," to 25 members and 11 alternates. But Stalin, "sickly suspicious" and paranoid, was soon contemplating a new "Blood Purge." In mid-January, 1953, the press announced the "discovery" of a vile plot wherein the chief Kremlin physicians, most of them Jewish, had "confessed" to conspiring with "imperialist and Zionist spies." They had allegedly caused the deaths of Zhdanov and Shcherbakov and were planning the murder of various high military leaders. The MVD (Beria) was accused of "laxity." What new horrors were to ensue will never be known. All that was clear, with spine-chilling clarity, was that once again no one, however high in the hierarchy, was safe against vindictive accusations on the part of the son of a Georgian cobbler who ruled as Autocrat in the Kremlin.

In this macabre context the Party Central Committee and the Council of Ministers jointly declared on March 4 that Stalin, aged 74, had suffered a stroke two nights previously. Further medical bulletins ended with the news that Stalin had died at 9:50 P.M., March 5, 1953. Malenkov, Molotov, and Beria delivered the eulogies at the State funeral. On March 6 the Central

Committee, the Council of Ministers, and the Presidium of the Supreme Soviet jointly named Malenkov, aged 51, as Premier and Beria, Molotov, Bulganin, and Kaganovich as Vice-Premiers. The Party Presidium was reduced to 10 members. The "Jewish doctors plot" was repudiated as a "fraud," with the accused released and restored to their posts. An amnesty freed many prisoners from labor camps and jails. "Unity," "Calm," "Vigilance," "Peace," "Collective Leadership," and future avoidance of "Hero-worship" and the "Cult of Personality" were enjoined upon Party and public.

As in 1924, when Lenin died, an orderly transition from the death of the Leader to a new regime was apparently achieved by the oligarchs. Yet the new "collective leadership" proved unstable. Some aspired to perpetuate the Stalinist system of power. Others deemed Stalinism obsolete and hoped to "liberalize" Party and Government in response to the expectations of a vast populace which was now industrialized, urbanized, and educated and could no longer be safely governed, as in the dark days of old, by rulers committed to economic austerity and police-state terrorism. Among the reformers was Khrushchev, who succeeded Malenkov as First Secretary of the Central Committee in mid-March—in which post he was officially confirmed in September. For less than a fortnight had the erudite, affable, and unfortunate Malenkov held simultaneously the two highest political posts in Sovietland. This new bifurcation of power was a portent of things to come. So also was Beria's determination, in the face of his colleagues' resolve to end the Stalinist police-state, to perpetuate the authority of his Political Police and thereby perhaps make himself Stalin's successor.

Stalinist means of disposing of Stalinists were still employed during the first year of the post-Stalin regime. On July 10, 1953, the collective oligarchs announced that Beria had been arrested on June 26 as an "enemy of the people" and would be tried for treason, since he had striven to make his MVD "superior to Party and Government" and had become an "agent of international imperialism"—a role he was absurdly said to have assumed in 1919. What followed was in the best Stalinist style, save that the MVD was downgraded and deprived of its arbitrary powers of arrest, imprisonment, and execution. Following a secret "trial" before a military tribunal, Beria and his "accomplices" were said to have been shot in December, 1953, thus suffering the fate of most of their precursors as chiefs of the Political Police. Other aides of Beria were seized and slain in the months that followed. The police-state was thus abolished by recourse to the methods of the police-state—a circumstance which outsiders may attribute, as they choose, to "poetic justice" or "cultural lag." Such methods, as we shall see, were not henceforth to be used in resolving rivalries for power among Stalin's successors.

These rivalries soon became acute, less because of interpersonal jealousies than because of honest difference of views regarding the best course of Russia's rulers in domestic and foreign affairs. The substance of these differences is touched upon elsewhere in these pages. Here we may usefully limit our attention to the fluctuating interplay of Communist politicians within the peculiar and unique post-Stalin procedures for resolving the conflicts among prospective leaders. These procedures, thus far, have little in common with those practiced in the Western democracies. But they constitute an advance toward humanism and tolerance when weighed against Stalin's methods of rulership.

On February 8, 1955, Malenkov resigned as Premier, pleading inadequate experience and responsibility for agricultural difficulties. (Both pleas were specious, since Malenkov had vast managerial experience while agrarian policy was not Malenkov's specialty but Khrushchev's.) Marshal Nikolai A. Bulganin was named Premier, Malenkov Vice-Premier and Minister of Electric Power Stations, while Marshal Georgi K. Zhukov—brilliant strategist and war-hero relegated to obscurity by the jealous Stalin—became Minister of Defense. These changes were not unrelated to West German rearmament, which had become a certainty by early 1955 and was to be countered by the men of Moscow through new measures of defense, including the Warsaw Pact of May 14, 1955, and through an all-out and world-wide propaganda and diplomatic drive designed to end the Cold War. Khrushchev emerged as Party leader No. 1 and accompanied Bulganin in 1955–57 in far-flung State visits throughout Eurasia. Molotov had apparently opposed the Austrian treaty of May 15, 1955, and was anathema to Yugoslavia's Tito, whom Bulganin and Khrushchev were courting in hopes of reconciliation. On June 1, 1956, as Tito arrived in Moscow, Molotov was replaced as Foreign Minister by Dmitri Shepilov, who in turn gave way to Andrei Gromyko on February 15, 1957.

The "crisis of leadership" which boiled up to a climax in 1957 and the subsequent shifting of personalities among major posts in Party and Government cannot accurately be reduced to any simple formula. In Soviet politics, as in all politics, motives are mixed and the webs of intrigue are tangled skeins. Yet this much may safely be said: Khrushchev and his supporters embraced bold new policies which his critics in the hierarchy deemed dangerous or unworkable. These included "de-Stalinization," symbolized by Khrushchev's "secret" indictment of the dead dictator at Congress XX (February, 1956); the assiduous pursuit of "peaceful coexistence" with the Western powers and efforts to negotiate a reduction of armaments; the opening to cultivation of vast virgin lands beyond the Urals; the consolidation of some 250,000 collective farms into 80,000 large units; the transfer of the machine-tractor to the farms themselves; the provision of agriculture incentives as a means of trying to match the USA in per-capita output of meat and dairy products; and a nation-wide decentralization of industrial management.

Among Khrushchev's opponents were those who clung to bureaucratic centralization of the economy; who favored continued expansion of heavy industry to the neglect of consumer's goods; who resisted change in the agrarian *status quo* and held the eastern areas to be too arid to prove productive; who deemed disarmament hazardous and permanent peace with the "imperialists" impossible; and who blamed the "de-Stalinization" campaign for Sino-Soviet friction, for the dissolution of the Cominform in April, 1956, at Tito's insistence, for a weakening of the Communist bloc, and for Poland's peaceful revolution and Hungary's violent revolt, bloodily suppressed by Soviet troops, in the autumn of 1956. Obviously, not all oppositionists shared all these views. But enough were shared by enough to generate an opposition—which, however, was far too fluid and elusive to be labeled "Stalinist" or "neo-Stalinist" or anything else at all save, perhaps, anti-Khrushchev.

Following Congress XX the Central Committee was enlarged from 125 to 133 full members and from 110 to 112 candidate members. Thanks to these new places and to numerous removals of members from the previous Central Committee, Khrushchev, through his control of the Secretariat, was able to add some 50 new full members, most of them, needless to say, supporters of his policies. The new Presidium of 1956 consisted of veterans Voroshilov, Molotov, Mikoyan, Kaganovich, Bulganin, and Malenkov plus Kirichenko and Suslov (added in July, 1955) in addition to Pervukhin and Saburov along, of course, with Khrushchev himself. The candidate members were Shvernik, Shepilov, Zhukov, Leonid Brezhnev, N. A. Mukhitdinov, and Ekaterina A. Furtseva, the first woman to attain such heights.

Reports from Warsaw alleged that Khrushchev had won a bare majority in the Central Committee in December, 1956, against a motion to replace him as First Secretary by Malenkov. In June, 1957, he was outvoted in the Party Presidium, but convoked a plenary session of the Central Committee (June 22–29) where he was supported after full and free, albeit non-public, debate. The unanimous decision of the Central Committee (with Molotov abstaining) was announced on July 3: Molotov, Malenkov, Kaganovich, and Shepilov were ousted from their Party and Government posts; Pervukhin and Saburov were demoted to lesser posts from their First Deputy Premierships. Khrushchev, visiting Czechoslovakia with Bulganin, said four days later: "We had some black sheep in a good flock. They thought they would seize power. We took them by the tail and threw them out. . . . It is not bad if, in improving the theory of Marx, one throws in also a piece of bacon and a piece of butter. . . . Nothing can stop the birth of a new social order." In late October Zhukov was replaced by Marshal Rodion V. Malinovsky as Minister of Defense and on November 2, by order of the Central Committee, deprived of his Party posts on charges of resisting Party control of the Army, fostering his own "cult of personality," and "political unsoundness, inclining to adventurism" in foreign policy.

In these and subsequent demotions, procedures and penalties differed markedly from those invoked in Stalin's day. The losers were not branded as "enemies of the people," but as members of an "anti-Party" group. Decisions were not made by the *Vozhd* or the Politburo or the Secretariat, but by the Central Committee after debates and votes. The vanquished were not deprived of their lives nor of their liberty nor even of their Party memberships, but only of their positions in the Presidium and Central Committee. Zhukov was assigned to "new duties." Shepilov was sent to teach school in Central Asia and later returned to Moscow to work in the Institute of Economics. Kaganovich became director of a cement plant in the Urals. Malenkov was appointed manager of a hydro-electric station in East Kazakhstan. Molotov was named Ambassador to Outer Mongolia and later (August, 1960) Soviet representative to the International Atomic Energy Agency in Vienna.

Meanwhile, the new Supreme Soviet met on March 27, 1958, and unanimously re-elected Voroshilov, aged 77, as Chief of State (Chairman of the Presidium of the Supreme Soviet). He at once proposed that Khrushchev replace Bulganin as Premier. All concurred, including Bulganin who resumed his old post as head of

the State Bank and in August was named director of the Stavro-
pol Economic Council. The miner's son from Kursk in 1958, like
the cobbler's son from Gori in 1941, thus combined in his own
hands the Premiership in the Government with the First Secre-
taryship and the Chairmanship of the Presidium of the Party—
but with no such sinister prelude or postlude. Khrushchev later
denounced Bulganin, who in December abjectly confessed his
"sins" before the Central Committee, for having shared the views
of the "anti-Party" group.

During 1959–60 further shifts of leaders close to the apex
of the Party pyramid were due not to sharp cleavages over policies but to incessant search for new talent to achieve maximum
success in carrying out policies already adopted. Promotion was
swift for those skilled in performing the impossible. Demotion
was equally swift for those who failed to fulfill expectations.
Thus, in January, 1960, demotion was the lot of Alexei I. Kirichenko and Nicolai I. Belyaev, both Khrushchev's right-hand
men—the former for failing to reduce "bureaucracy" in Party
and State in the Ukraine, and the latter for not making the most
of the "virgin lands" program in Kazakhstan. Between May 4
and 7, 1960, Frol R. Kozlov was transferred to the Party Secretariat and replaced as a First Deputy Premier by Alexei N. Kosygin, head of the *Gosplan;* Nicolai G. Ignatiev and Vladimir N.
Novikov were named Deputy Premiers; Ekaterina A. Furtseva
replaced Nikolai A. Mikhailov as Minister of Culture; Kirichenko and Belyaev were dropped from the Party Presidium, in
which Kosygin, Nicolai V. Podgorny, and Dmitri S. Polyansky
became new members; and Voroshilov was succeeded by Leonid
I. Brezhnev as Chief of State.

In mid-summer of 1960 the 15 full members (plus 9 alternates) of the Party Presidium comprised 5 veterans of the "Old
Guard" (Khrushchev, Mikoyan, Shvernik, Voroshilov, and Otto
Kuusinen, a Finnish Communist long in Muscovite exile) and
10 relatively new figures: Polyansky, Podgorny, Kosygin, Ignatiev,
Brezhnev, Kozlov, Furtseva, Averky Aristov, Nuritalin Mukhitdinov, and Mikhail Suslov—with all the members of the Secretariat for the first time also in the Presidium. From these newer
figures and from others still largely unknown will be recruited
the top leadership of the years to come. They and their colleagues
do not much resemble Plato's "Philosopher Kings" or "Guardians." Neither are they mediocrities or spoilsmen or mere manip-
ulators of patronage. The Party has come close to attaining that

with which no modern state can safely dispense: a managerial elite of tested capacity, devotedly dedicated to public service.

5 - The Process of Governance

The Image of Constitutionalism

The Soviet Union is ruled by the Party. What then is the need for a complex structure of formal "government," paralleling the structure of the Party, inextricably intermingled with the Party hierarchy, and at all levels controlled and directed by the Party? For students of comparative government and politics who are accustomed to think in functional and operational terms, the question is not naïve. In parliamentary or presidential democracies, where rival parties or coalitions of parties compete with one another for public favor in free elections and alternate in occupancy of public offices, "party" and "government" are two discrete modes of human organization for public purposes, with the distinction between them evident by the very nature of their relationship. But in a one-party oligarchy, what purpose is served by maintaining an elaborate administrative, legislative, and judicial apparatus apart from the Party itself?

Possible answers to our question may emerge as we proceed to examine the external machinery of government in the USSR. By way of anticipation we may reasonably assume that among Russians, as among other peoples, "purpose" or "need" is seldom the prime determinant of the institutions through which, and within which, men and women seek to order their lives. Custom and habit invariably play a part, along with honored traditions and cherished aspirations. So also do borrowings from strangers in that universal process of cultural mimesis and diffusion which marks all living civilizations. Arrangements for government, as for other human affairs, are seldom models of logic, rationality, and necessity. More often they are accretions of old ways of doing things overlaid with new ways adopted from abroad because they are deemed good or hopeful or "progressive" or because they serve to lend seemliness, dignity, and authority to patterns of power which, in fact, may have nothing in common with alien practices. Such is surely the case with the formalized structure of "government" in the Soviet Union. The ultimate outcome of truth and consequences in such matters, insofar as anyone can now foresee it, is a question best postponed to a later point in our quest. For the present we can best begin by noting the peculiar role of "constitutionalism" in the Soviet polity.

The modern concept of a "constitution" as a basic law for the ordering of public business was a product, despite a few earlier analogues and precedents, of the "social contract" theory of society and of the State which came to be widely accepted among the Atlantic middle classes in the 17th and 18th Centuries. The history of the concept is not germane to our current concern. It is enough to note that more than two hundred years ago most "liberals" of the Western world had persuaded themselves that written constitutions, as contracts between rulers and ruled, were significant as symbols of "liberty" by virtue of imposing legal restraints on the arbitrary action of rulers and affording legal protection for the rights of the ruled.

This formula for freedom had no counterpart, as we have seen, in the Russia of ancient days nor even, despite pretenses and muddled imitations of Western models, during the last years of the Tsarist Autocracy. Yet the formula, however ill-understood, captivated the imaginations of almost all Russian liberals, reformers, radicals, and revolutionaries during the 19th Century and beyond, from the simple-minded "Decembrists" of 1825 to the Kadets, SR's, and SD's of the early 1900's (see p. 47 above). All seekers after liberation from a dark heritage took it for granted that, once the Revolution had cast down or at least restricted the Tsardom, the people would freely elect a "Constituent Assembly" whose members would draft a Constitution as a basic law for an emancipated Muscovy fashioned after the Western democracies. Marxists had doubts, since their dogmas taught them that all "bourgeois" constitutions were shams and frauds. But even the Marxists, as converts to a creed which emerged within the context of Western liberalism, had no doubts regarding the desirability of a solemn charter of freedom and a structure of "constitutional government" wholly distinct from the oligarchy of the Party and the cloudy imperatives of the "dictatorship of the proletariat."

Given these directives in the minds of the men who ruled Russia after the October Revolution, their forcible suppression of the original Constituent Assembly on January 19, 1918 (see pp. 18–19 above), left an emptiness crying to be filled, for the Soviet regime, thus far, was lacking in any semblance of a constitution. They turned to the Third All-Russian Congress of Soviets, then in session. The deputies drafted a "Declaration of the Rights of the Laboring and Exploited People" and a resolution on the "Federal Institutions of the Russian Republic" and then established a committee, including Sverdlov, Bukharin, and Stalin, to formulate a basic law for the "Russian Socialist Federated Soviet Republic" (RSFSR). The result was the first Soviet Constitution, ratified by the Fifth Congress of Soviets on July 10, 1918. This document of 90 articles, echoing the original *Communist Manifesto,* was perforce limited to Russia minor and not applicable to Russia major, all of whose outlying provinces were either under German occupation or in burgeoning rebellion against Bolshevik control from Moscow.

The Constitution of 1918 put on paper, and thus legitimized in law, the Governmental arrangements which had developed haphazardly and by trial-and-error out of the turmoil of Revolution. "Supreme power" was vested in the All-Russian Congress of Soviets, meeting semi-annually and consisting of one delegate of urban Soviets for every 25,000 voters and one delegate of rural Congresses of Soviets for every 125,000 inhabitants (Art. 25). The Congress at the pinnacle of the pyramid appointed a Central Executive Committee (CEC) of not more than 200 members as "the Supreme Legislative, Administrative, and controlling organ of the RSFSR" (Art. 31). The CEC in turn appointed a Cabinet or *Sovnarkom* (Council of Peoples Commissars), composed of chiefs of 18 Commissariats. The right to vote was extended to all citizens over 18, "irrespective of sex, religion, or nationality," if engaged in productive work or military service, and expressly denied to private businessmen and employers, capitalists, clergymen, members of the deposed dynasty or of the Tsarist police, imbeciles, lunatics, and criminals (Arts. 64 and 65). All voting was open and oral, and not by secret ballot. Voters, moreover, could directly elect only members of city and village Soviets, and this often on the basis of vocational, instead of geographical, representation. All other deputies to Soviet bodies were indirectly elected, with city Soviets choosing delegates to the Congress of Soviets and a hierarchy of rural Congresses of Soviets in districts (*Volosts*), counties (*Uezeds*), and provinces (*Gubernias*) each in turn selecting delegates to higher bodies. All deputies were ostensibly subject to recall (Art. 78). The Party was nowhere mentioned in the document, nor was any sanction given to rival parties.

The first Soviet Constitution thus "legalized" a governmental structure marked by a discriminatory franchise; occupational elections on a local level; urban overrepresentation; indirect election of the national legislature; no clear "separation of powers" among legislative, executive, and judicial functions; a pretense of "division of powers" in an allegedly federal system; and an unacknowledged perpetuation of the oligarchy of the Party, slightly disguised by the verbal and procedural devices noted above.

This Constitution of the RSFSR became the model for the first Constitution of the USSR. By 1921, with Red victory in the Civil War, other "Soviet Republics" had been created in peripheral areas previously controlled by anti-Communists. All entered into "treaty relationships" with the RSFSR in accordance with the formula that each was "sovereign" and "independent," although all in fact were ruled by the Party. In December, 1922, Stalin proposed to the Tenth All-Russian Congress of Soviets the establishment of a "Union of Soviet Socialist Republics." A committee of delegates (December 30, 1922) drafted a "Treaty of Union" among the RSFSR, the Ukrainian SSR, the Byelorussian SSR, and the Transcaucasian SFSR (Armenia, Georgia, and Azerbaijan). By simple semantic legerdemain, the Tenth Congress of the RSFSR, with deputies added from the other Republics, became the First Congress of the USSR—although a distinct and comparable local congress for the RSFSR was soon brought into being. On July 6, 1923, the new CEC of the USSR voted a Union Constitution, finally ratified by the Second Congress of Soviets of the USSR on January 31, 1924. The new Union grew from 4 to 6 units in 1925 with the emergence of the Uzbek and Turkmen Republics; to 7 with similar status for Tadjikistan; and to 11 by 1936 with the elevation of Azerbaijan, Georgia, Armenia, Kazakhstan, and Kirgizia to "Union Republics." The member states of the USSR waxed to 16 during World War II with the forcible incorporation into the Soviet empire of Latvia, Estonia, and Lithuania and with the creation, respectively on the frontiers of Finland and Rumania, of the Karelo-Finnish Republic and the Moldavian Republic. The incorporation of the Karelo-Finnish Republic into the RSFSR in July, 1956, reduced the members of the USSR to 15, at which figure the total remained at the time of writing.

Whether this "Union" deserves to be termed a "Federation,"

as this term is generally understood in the West, is a problem best deferred to the next section of the present chapter. Here let us note that the first Union Constitution of 1922–24, a document of 72 articles, closely followed the pattern of the 1918 Constitution of the RSFSR, albeit proclaiming the "equality" of all the Union Republics and granting them a "right of free withdrawal from the Union," providing all the other Republics should agree to secession. The new Congress of Soviets of the USSR was declared to be the supreme organ of federal authority, possessed of enumerated and limited powers of government with all "residual" powers remaining in the member Republics. The federal Congress, indirectly elected like its Russian precursor, named a Union CEC consisting of two chambers: a Soviet of the Union, chosen in proportion to population (by 1936 consisting of 451 members, with 300 from the RSFSR, 75 from the Ukraine, 30 from Transcaucasia, 13 from Byelorussia, etc.), and a Soviet of Nationalities of 136 members, including 5 delegates from each Union Republic, 1 delegate from each "Autonomous Region" within each Republic, plus other complex arrangements for federal representation.

Provision was made, on the previous model, for a federal *Sovnarkom* or Cabinet and for a "Presidium" of 27 members, chosen by the two chambers of the CEC as (Art. 29) "the supreme legislative, executive, and administrative organ of authority of the USSR" in the intervals between sessions of the CEC, to which Cabinet and Presidium alike were declared to be "responsible." The *Sovnarkom,* described (Art. 37) as "the executive organ of the CEC of the USSR," initially comprised 5 All-Union Commissariats (Foreign Affairs, War and Marine, Foreign Trade, Communications, Posts and Telegraphs), each operating through its own federal bureaucracy, plus 5 "United" or joint "Union-Republican" Commissariats (National Economy, Food, Labor, Finance, and Workers' and Peasants' Inspection), each operating locally through officials of the parallel Commissariats of the Union Republics. Any resemblance in practice between these devices and the British parliamentary principle of executive responsibility to the legislature or the American presidential principle of "separation of powers" was purely coincidental. Then, as now, the complex bureaucratic machinery of formal government in the USSR functioned effectively only by virtue of being controlled and directed at all crucial points by the Party—which, during the 1930's and 1940's, became the operating tool of Stalin's new Autocracy.

All men, being by nature more anarchic than orderly, yield obedience to their rulers only when they are convinced, or at least half-persuaded, that the salvation of their souls or the survival of their bodies demands such obedience. Submission to authority is most readily rendered when rulers are envisaged as incarnations of the Godhead or as "representative" of the will or welfare of their subjects. Thus, in the ever-changing *credenda* and *miranda* of power, ancient Oriental despots and the Emperors of Rome, as of China and Japan, pictured themselves as deities; modern monarchs robed themselves in the dogma of the "divine right of kings"; and contemporary politicians govern by "the consent of the governed" or for the "good" of the governed. Not even the most arbitrary of absolutisms, whether beneficent or malevolent, is ever exempt from these timeless imperatives of politics. Such was the case in the USSR, as elsewhere, during the years—at once grim and exciting, brutal and exhilarating—of the early "Five Year Plans," the "Second Revolution," and the "Great Purge." Out of such exigencies emerged a new Soviet Constitution which, as amended, is still the Constitution of the USSR today (see pp. 168–87 below).

The drastic transformation of Soviet society between 1929 and 1935 under the impact of forced collectivization and industrialization led the Party leadership (i.e., Stalin and his devout or frightened supporters) to the conclusion that a new basic law and a new pattern of governance were called for by the needs of a new time. On February 6, 1935, the Seventh All-Union Congress of Soviets approved the naming of a Constitution Commission to draft a new charter providing for equal suffrage, direct election, secret ballot, and due cognizance of "the present relation of class forces." The CEC, a day later, appointed a Commission of 31, with Stalin as Chairman. Its final draft was widely distributed throughout the land in June, 1936, as a basis for nation-wide public discussion—which gathered headway in more than half a million meetings attended by 36 million people. Thousands of proposed changes were sorted out; 150 were given careful consideration; 43 were finally adopted. Whether this process was "democratic" in the Western sense, or fraudulent by Western standards (since the proceedings were at all times supervised by the Party oligarchs), is less important than the fact that the Soviet public was afforded an opportunity, even if illusory, to participate in the drafting of a new national charter.

The result was praised by Stalin, in orthodox Marxist terminology, as "the only thoroughly democratic constitution in the world" (cf. his address of November 25, 1936, before the Extraordinary Eighth Congress of Soviets). The deputies on December 1, 1936, unanimously resolved to approve the draft and named an Editorial Commission of 220 distinguished members (including sundry notables soon to be purged) to put it into final form. Khrushchev (*Izvestia*, December 2, 1936) ridiculed Fascist claims of "triumph" over Marxism, eulogized the new Constitution as a "victory of Marxism-Leninism-Stalinism, a victory that is not only ours but is also that of toilers the world over," and predicted that "in the Stalin epoch, the epoch of victorious socialism, the working class under the leadership of our great *Vozhd* will conduct a far-reaching battle for the final victory of communism" throughout the world. On December 5, 1936, the Congress unanimously adopted the final version of the new charter amid nation-wide festivities.

The "Stalin Constitution," as it was called until the passing of the *Vozhd* in 1953, radically altered the outer forms, if not the inner essence, of governmental authority. In place of indirect elections by a show of hands on the basis of a discriminatory franchise, provision was made (Arts. 134–42) for "universal, direct, and equal suffrage by secret ballot," open to all men and women over 18 (save lunatics and convicted criminals) "irrespective of race or nationality, religion, educational and residential qualifications, social origin, property status, or past activities." All vestiges of vocational representation vanished. All Soviet deputies—Union, Republican, and local—would be chosen by direct election in single-member districts, with all subject to recall. Candidates would be nominated by "public organizations and societies of working people: CP organizations, trade unions, cooperatives, youth organizations, and cultural societies" (Art. 141). The Party was defined (Art. 126) as "the vanguard of the working people in their struggle to build communist society and is the leading core of all organizations of the working people, both public and state."

In acknowledging for the first time in Soviet Constitutional documents the hegemony of the Party, the framers of the new charter were innovators. In the provisions noted above they were also innovators or at least imitators of Western formulas for governance. Such also was their role in the major changes they proposed in the formal structure of public authority. The old Congress of Soviets, with its bicameral CEC, was abolished in favor of a "Supreme Soviet of the USSR," elected for 4 years and comprising 2 houses: the Soviet of the Union, consisting of

deputies elected in districts of 300,000 inhabitants and numbering
at the outset 569; and the Soviet of Nationalities, numbering 574
at the outset and composed of deputies elected on the basis of
25 for each Union Republic, 11 for each Autonomous Republic,
5 for each Autonomous Region, and 1 for each National District.
All federal legislation requires approval by a majority of both
houses. Both together appoint a Presidium of 1 Vice-President
from each of the Union Republics and 1 President who, in law
and diplomatic protocol, is "Chief of State." The Supreme Soviet
also names, and may remove, the *Sovnarkom* (or "Council of
Ministers" since 1946), embracing at the outset the chiefs of 25
Union Commissariats and 15 Union-Republic Commissariats
(i.e., "Ministries") and headed by a Chairman who is "Prime Minister" or "Premier," again in imitation of Western parliamentary
democracies.

How this new scheme of things was applied in practice and
reconciled with the continuing oligarchy of the Party will become apparent as we proceed with our analysis of form and fact,
image and reality, shadow and substance, in the Soviet polity.
Here it is worth noting that the new design for power provided
on paper for a completely democratic pattern of national and
local government—with Republican and local constitutions
revised to accord with the fresh dispensation on the federal
level—and for an "independent" judiciary as well as for executive
responsibility to the legislature. Indeed, the Government of the
USSR could become tomorrow a perfect exemplar of parliamentary democracy without changing a line or a word of its Constitution.

This circumstance poses a puzzle of semantics and of human
nature in politics. Political scientists are constantly confronted
with such puzzles and are never quite able to solve them, since
their "science" thus far is inadequate to the task. Yet the paradox here posed may be clarified, if not fully explained, if we
bear in mind the inevitable contradiction of "theory" and "practice" in all the affairs of men—who are, for better or worse, ambivalent creatures. Western democracy in theory postulates the
equality and dignity and civic responsibility of all citizens, out
of whose rational deliberations regarding the public interest will
emerge, via the vehicle of free elections, able leadership, and wise
public policies. Western democracy in practice often exhibits the
distressing spectacle of public apathy or anomie; the reduction
of "universal suffrage" to an empty concept by virtue of gross
inequalities of wealth and income and of persisting patterns of

racial and national discrimination; rulership by plutocrats, pressure groups, spoilsmen, or intolerant demagogues who exploit the irrationalities of the human animal; and, all too frequently in our time, the degeneration of democracy into total irresponsibility, threatening the very survival of the State and even of civilization itself. Such contradictions are many times multiplied in the emergent polities of Asia, Africa, and Latin America, where a colonial legacy of mass illiteracy, poverty, and frustration tends to render impossible any meaningful realization of the democratic dream.

"Soviet democracy" is rich in comparable paradoxes. The "most democratic constitution in the world" at once became, and will long remain, a pattern of words and procedures whereby an oligarchy commands obedience from a mass—alternately indifferent, hostile, or enthusiastic regarding the purposes of their rulers—whose members, despite the prevailing theory of public power, have no genuine choice in the selection of rulers or the determination of public policies. But the ultimate test of any system of power is not the test of inevitable discrepancies between theory and practice. The ultimate test is purely pragmatic. Does the system, whatever its contradictions, serve human needs and aspirations? By this test (see pp. 128–51 below), the Soviet scheme of authority, for all of its incongruities, bears favorable comparison with other schemes elsewhere.

The Façade of Federalism

The USSR inherited from the Tsardom a far-flung empire of polygot peoples, only half of whom were "Great Russians" in language and in other components of their culture. The rest —ranging from many-millioned masses of Ukranians, Byelorussians, Jews, Transcaucasians, and Central Asian Moslems to tiny historical curiosities and thinly scattered tribes of primitive nomads—retained their identities despite, or perhaps because of, efforts at "Russification." The "nationality problem" troubled all reformers and revolutionists of all schools in their revulsion against Tsarist discrimination, oppression, and *pogroms* and in their visions of a free Russia founded upon the brotherhood of peoples of all races and tongues. What response this challenge might have evoked had the Kadets or SR's or some other group come to power in the Revolution of 1917 we can never know, nor is the question a fruitful subject for speculation save among antiquarians. How the challenge was sought to be met by the

Marxists of Bolshevik persuasion who in fact came to power is our present concern, for their "solution," by way of a peculiar form of "federalism," has long since been embodied in successive Soviet Constitutions and reflected in all Soviet schemes of national and local government.

If we may by permission make a long story short: the first publication signed "Stalin" was prepared in Cracow and Vienna in 1912 and printed in *Prosvyeshchenye* (Enlightenment). Its title was "The National Question and Social Democracy." Its theme was the necessity of providing for the autonomy, self-determination, and equality of all racial and national groups in the revolutionary Russia of days to come. During the next five years Lenin alternately embraced and denounced "federalism" as the answer to the riddle, without ever clearly defining the term. In the first *Sovnarkom* of 1917 Stalin became chief of the short-lived "Commissariat of Nationalities." In the sequel the leaders of the Party, albeit frequently debasing, degrading, or betraying their own expressed convictions under the pressure of real or imagined necessities, arrived at a formula to be incorporated into basic law and governmental practice: each nationality, whether majority or minority, was to be free and equal and entitled to its own language and folkways, subject to the proviso that its culture was to be "national in form, but proletarian (i.e., Marxist or Communist) in content"; all were to be united in a Federation of Union Republics, within each of which lesser groups would enjoy local autonomy within a framework of a federation of federations.

Before we undertake to assess the meaning of the formula in practice, it will be well to take cognizance of the major political and administrative segments into which the peoples of the USSR have been divided (or united) by virtue of the efforts of their rulers to give content to the formula. Here a detailed atlas is indispensable for knowledge of who lives where and under what legal status. But even the best of maps, however recent, is likely to be misleading because of rapid rearrangements in a swiftly growing society. Thus, for example, during the 20 years between 1939 and 1959, Soviet citizens living east of the Urals waxed from 48,000,000 to 63,000,000, while cities of more than 200,000 inhabitants east of Tashkent increased, 1926 to 1959, from 0 to 72, with frequent governmental reorganizations mirroring the expansion of population and of the economy. Any detailed effort to pin-point Soviet political areas may be obsolete before it appears in print because of the fluid and protean pattern of local administration. Yet the over-all design may be sketched, since it exists in fact and is likely to persist for years to come.

On the eve of World War II (1941) the RSFSR, by far the largest Union Republic in area and population, included within its confines 15 "Autonomous Soviet Socialist Republics," 6 "Autonomous Regions," and 10 "National Districts," each with its own local soviet, *Sovnarkom,* and other agencies of Soviet rule. Place and language names are strange to Western ears. They include, among the ASSR's, the Bashkir, Buriat-Mongolian, Chechen-Ingush, Chuvash, Kabardino-Balkarian, Kalmyk, Mordovian, etc.; among the "Autonomous Regions," the Adygei, Cherkess, Jewish (Birobidjan), Karachi, Khakass, and Oirot; and among the "National Districts," the Chukot, Komi-Permiatsk, Koriak, Taimyr, Yamalo-Nenets, etc. Among other Union Republics, Georgia embraces the Abkhazian and Adzhar Autonomous Soviet Socialist Republics and the South Ossetian Autonomous Region; Azerbaijan, the Nakhichevan ASSR and the Nagorno-Karabakh AR; Uzbekistan, the Kara-Kalpak ASSR; and Tadjikistan, the Gorno-Badakshan AR—all, to be sure, subject to change without notice.

These complexities and confusions are not unique to the USSR, as anyone knows who has ever studied political geography elsewhere in any nation-state engaged in rapid industrialization or already enjoying its fruits. The USA, where the modern concept of federalism had its birth, is a symmetrical federation of 50 states—within each of which, however, local government is a jumble of townships, counties, parishes, municipalities, port authorities, metropolitan districts, etc., none of which is "logical" but all of which serve community needs. Mankind thus far has devised no better way to reconcile neighborhood and regional requirements for public services with the imperatives of national unity. Such is also the case in the cumbersome and ever-changing pattern of area administration in the USSR, despite the oft-expressed view of Soviet commentators that in the Soviet scheme of rulership there is no meaningful difference between "national," "Republican," and "local" government.

Amid numerous and frequent shifts and reshuffles certain continuities nonetheless admit of delineation. Just as the USA will long endure as a federation of 50 states, each cherishing its identity and its own traditions, so the USSR will long remain a Union of 15 Republics, each unique by virtue of deep roots in a long past. Since no knowledge of Soviet government is possible without awareness of the distribution of population, let us consider briefly the problem here posed. That the issue is in part a "problem" is due to Soviet official secrecy regarding vital statistics, inspired by suspicion, insecurity, and official desires to conceal from a hostile world the appalling death toll of World War II. Despite this barrier, some more or less accurate estimates are possible, thanks to pre-war and post-war census figures released by the appropriate authorities in Moscow. The census of December 17, 1926, reported a national total of 147,-028,000 people. The census of January 17, 1939, registered 170,468,000 inhabitants of the USSR. Thereafter all was silence until the Central Statistical Board of the Council of Ministers issued, in July, 1956, a handbook on *The National Economy of the USSR* (*Narodnoye Khozyaistvo SSSR*) estimating total population at 191,700,000 in 1940 (including the annexations of Western Marchlands in 1939–40) and 200,200,000 in April, 1956. The most recent census of January, 1959, calculated the total population of the USSR at the time as 208,826,000. If we may assume the substantial accuracy of these estimates and enumerations, we can tabulate the approximate populations of the 15 Union Republics for the dates indicated:

	Census of 1939	Est. of 1956	Census of 1959
RSFSR	108,369,000	112,600,000	117,494,000
Ukrainian SSR	40,469,000	40,600,000	41,893,000
Byelorussian SSR	8,910,000	8,000,000	8,060,000
Uzbek SSR	6,336,000	8,500,000	8,113,000
Kazakh SSR	6,094,000	8,500,000	9,301,000
Georgian SSR	3,540,000	4,000,000	4,049,000
Azerbaijan SSR	3,205,000	3,400,000	3,700,000
Lithuanian SSR	2,880,000	2,700,000	2,713,000
Moldavian SSR	2,452,000	2,700,000	2,880,000
Latvian SSR	1,885,000	2,000,000	2,094,000
Kirghiz SSR	1,458,000	1,900,000	2,063,000
Tadjik SSR	1,484,000	1,800,000	1,982,000
Armenian SSR	1,282,000	1,600,000	1,768,000
Turkmen SSR	1,252,000	1,400,000	1,520,000
Estonian SSR	1,052,000	1,100,000	1,196,000
Karelo-Finnish SSR	600,000	—	—

These figures pose as many problems as they solve. The decline of population in Byelorussia and Lithuania and the slow rate of increase in the Ukraine, Moldavia, Estonia, and Latvia can readily enough be explained in terms of deportations of dissidents, flights of refugees, and Nazi massacres of war prisoners and civilians. Cruelty and tragedy fail to explain the figures for Uzbekstan and Georgia. But these are matters beyond our present purview. The question with which we are here concerned is this: In what sense, if any, can the formal structure of governmental power in a Soviet Union of 15 Union Republics be described as a "federation"?

The term needs defining, even for those Western peoples (e.g., Canadians, North Americans, Mexicans, Brazilians, Australians, South Africans, Swiss, West Germans, Austrians, et al.) who live under "federal" governments. All government in any community larger than a village or small town presupposes some "division of powers" between central and local authorities. In the process of patching together local units into larger polities, modern statesmanship has devised three ways of achieving this allocation. The most widespread in contemporary nation-states involves a sovereign power of decision in central or national agencies as to what powers of governance may lawfully be exercised by local officials. This arrangement is commonly described as "unitary government"—e.g., the United Kingdom, France, Italy, Indonesia, Japan, and each of the 50 states of the USA. At the opposite end of the range of possibilities is a design for power wherein local units, each preserving full "sovereignty," decide by agreement among themselves what authority shall be vested in common or central agencies. The usual name for such a scheme is "confederation." Examples: the USA, 1781–89, the Confederate States of America, 1861–65; the League of Nations; the United Nations.

"Federalism," as understood in the West, is a half-way house between these extremes. A truly "federal" government is best defined as one in which governmental powers are distributed between central and local agencies by means of a written constitution which cannot be amended by either the local units or by the central or federal government acting alone, but only by some process in which both participate and give their assent to change (see Art. V of the Constitution of the USA). Federal governments, moreover, possess two crucial powers never vested in the central organs of confederations or alliances: the power to levy taxes on individuals and the power to pass laws enforceable on individuals. The essence of federalism is agreement among the member states, provinces, cantons, or republics to entrust to those who act in the name of the

Federation or Union such limited but adequate powers of law-making as all deem needful for the common interest and the general welfare of all of the member units and of all of their inhabitants—and, *ipso facto,* of all the citizenry of a broader polity contrived on the precept: *E Pluribus Unum.* The laws thus enacted are the "supreme law of the land" if held to be "constitutional" by appropriate judicial authorities charged with interpreting the proper meaning of grants of power to federal legislators. They therefore prevail, in case of conflict, over local laws. And they are enforced not by the coercion of states by states or by federal power but by their application to all citizens of all states of the union on the part of local policemen and judges, all of whom are pledged to uphold and enforce the federal Constitution and federal laws (cf. Art. VI of the U.S. Constitution). Federalism further postulates, in most modern instances, double citizenship and a postal, customs, and monetary union among the member states.

The Soviet Constitution (see pp. 168–87 below) provides on paper for many of these attributes of federalism as defined in Western practice. Interested readers can readily confirm the fact by perusing Arts. 13, 14, 15, 19, 20, 105, 123, and 130 of the document. Amendments (cf. Art. 146)—always inserted at the proper place in the text rather than being attached in numbered order at the end as in the U.S. Constitution—require a two-thirds vote of each chamber of the Supreme Soviet, with no provision for "ratification" by state legislatures (USA)—i.e., by the Supreme Soviets of the Union Republics. But since the latter are represented equally in the upper house or Soviet of Nationalities, it can be argued that the federal principle of joint participation of national and local governments in the process of constitutional amendment is still preserved.

An anomaly of Soviet federalism is the right of the Republics, by an amendment of 1946, not only to maintain their "own Republican military formation" (analogous to "state militias"), but to enter into diplomatic and consular relations and to negotiate agreements with foreign sovereignties (cf. Arts. 18-A and 18-B). The latter privilege, unknown in most other federal governments, has in practice been limited to the Ukraine and Byelorussia, both of which are "independent" members of the United Nations and have exchanged envoys and concluded accords on matters of local interest with some of the "satellite" States of the Communist bloc.

A more striking paradox in the Soviet scheme of things is

the "right" of secession (cf. Art. 17) granted to the Union Republics. No other federal government has ever granted any such right to its member states. The matter was moot in the USA between 1789 and 1860 and was tragically but definitively settled through trial by battle, 1861–65, in what Northerners call the "Civil War" and what Southerners call the "War between the States" or the "War for Southern Independence." American devotion to the principle of "self-determination" of peoples, so often invoked in condemnation of the USSR, was not deemed applicable a century ago by the Union government of the Lincoln Administration to the aspirations of Southerners to achieve the sovereignty of the "Confederate States of America." The right of secession of the Union Republics of the USSR has, of course, remained meaningless within the context of the governance of the Union and of all of its members by the monolithic and highly centralized Communist Party.

Yet this provision of the Soviet Constitution, however empty in practice, need not be interpreted by Western critics as hypocrisy. It symbolizes a vague idea—doubtless wholly impracticable and incapable of realization in any framework of human affairs now imaginable—that in an allegedly free association of free peoples each major grouping of such peoples should ideally enjoy freedom to abandon its association with its partners. Nothing has ever come of this right in Soviet politics, nor is anything ever likely to come of it—short of some catastrophic disintegration of the Soviet Union in a national disaster. Said Stalin (November 25, 1936), in a masterpiece of understatement: "Of course none of our Republics would actually raise the question of seceding from the USSR."

As for the rest, Communist political practice, in contrast to Soviet constitutional theory, has over the years made of Soviet "federalism" something so different from its Western parallels, precursors, and models as to render dubious the applicability of the same term to patterns of power which have little in common. Soviet "federalism," to be sure, has promoted a large measure of inter-racial and inter-national tolerance, understanding, and cooperation and brought the boons of mass literacy, industrialization, and urbanization to sundry "backward" peoples. Yet devotion to the pluralistic and humanistic ideal of federalism by Party and Government did not preclude the recrudescence in the last years of Stalin's reign, and beyond his reign, of an atavistic anti-Semitism—rationalized in terms of "anti-Zionism" and "anti-cosmopolitanism"—which virtually destroyed the rich Yiddish culture of the Jewish communities of the USSR and doomed to death, jail, or exile many of its ablest artists. Age-old habits of intolerance, discrimination, and segregation persist in the USSR as in the USA, and indeed in all human societies, with all pots calling all kettles black. At worst the men of Moscow have fallen short, as most men do, of fulfilling their highest aspirations. At best the Marxist masters of Muscovy have brought education and "culture" and higher living standards to most of the minority peoples of the Soviet Empire.

But if we pose the question of whether Soviet practice conforms to Soviet theory and to Western conceptions of federalism, the answer from the record can only be in the negative. Federalism (Western-style) presupposes local autonomy and local consent for all changes in the existing distribution of authority. Soviet annexation of Estonia, Latvia, Lithuania, Eastern Poland, Bessarabia, and Northern Bukovina in 1939–40 involved no meaningful procedures of consent for the peoples concerned. The same is true of Stalin's deportation to Siberia during World War II of the entire populations, under suspicion via "guilt by association" of sympathizing with the enemy, of the "autonomous" areas of the Volga Germans, the Crimean Tartars, the Kalmyks, the Karachais, the Chechen-Ingush, and the Kabardino-Balkarians. Some, although not all, of these peoples were later returned to their homelands. Said Khrushchev in his indictment of Stalin (February, 1956, at Congress XX):

> The Ukrainians avoided meeting this fate only because there were too many of them and there was no place to which to deport them. . . . Not only a Marxist-Leninist but also no man of common sense can grasp how it is possible to make whole nations responsible for inimical activity, including women, children, old people, Communists, and *Komsomols,* to use mass repression against them, and to expose them to misery and suffering for the hostile acts of individual persons or groups of persons.

Khrushchev's Russia has condemned Stalin's crime and made partial reparation. But no approximation to Western notions of federalism has yet been achieved. On February 26, 1954, the Crimea was transferred from the RSFSR to the Ukraine. In July, 1956, the Karelo-Finnish Republic was abolished and annexed to the RSFSR. No record is available of any meaningful consultation on these matters by power-holders in Moscow with local authorities or with the peoples thus transferred from one jurisdiction to another. The decisions were announced jointly, as is customary for all major decisions, by the Party Central Committee and the federal Council of Ministers. Soviet federalism, like much else in the polity put together by the Muscovite Marxists, is a unique contribution to the arts of governance. In dialectical terms, it is a strange "synthesis" of Western pluralism as "thesis" and Communist monism as "antithesis." Whether, if ever, this contribution will evolve into a new solution, or come more closely to resemble an old solution, of the ancient and ubiquitous problem of reconciling the unity of the whole with the liberty of the parts in political commonwealths composed of diverse peoples is a question which admits of no clear answer in the decade of the 1960's.

The Managers

In the world of the West, and often elsewhere, all recent and contemporary descriptions of national governments postulate, implicitly or explicitly, that the functions and agencies of rulership are more or less neatly divisible or trifurcated into "executive," "legislative" and "judicial." This familiar triad is attributable, in part, to John Locke's (1632–1704) *Treatise on Government* and to Montesquieu's (1689–1755) misinterpretation of the secret of English liberty in his *L'Esprit des Lois*. Both writers were influential in persuading the Founding Fathers of the USA that freedom under authority and liberty under law could best be achieved by a "separation of powers" among three coordinate but independent branches of government. Each would act autonomously and checkmate the other two in such fashion as to keep governmental powers within tolerable limits, preserve individual rights, and insure caution and prudence in public policy-making.

This formula, widely copied in other lands, does, in fact, reflect an inevitable and necessary division of labor in all governments through all time in the urbanized and literate cultures of mankind, regardless of whether it is clearly perceived or given peculiarly American juridical twists. In all States certain people, however chosen, are authorized by common consent to prepare and promulgate rules of law binding upon the whole community. Certain people (usually other people, designated as "executives" or "administrators") are charged with translating the laws thus made into the public projects or controls of private conduct expressed in the purposes of the legislators. And certain people (again, usually other people, designated as "judges") are empowered to interpret and apply the law in civil and criminal litigation arising out of disputes regarding the rights and duties of citizens. Each of these activities impinges upon, and overlaps, the other two, even where a "separation of powers" is most strictly enforced. Yet the distinctions among them are everywhere recognized and observed.

This universal allocation of functions in all States is as characteristic a feature of the government of the USSR as it has always been in other times and climes. Our immediate concern is with the "executives," "administrators," or "bureaucrats" of the Soviet Union—with the law-makers and judges to be dealt with in the two following sections. In his groping quest for Utopia, Lenin toyed with the thought that in the Heavenly City of days to come any ordinary citizen could, somehow, be law-maker, administrator, and judge all rolled into one. In his search for effective mechanisms of tyranny, Stalin (like other tyrants before and since) combined in his own hands, and in those of his obedient subordinates, the roles of legislator, administrator, judge, and executioner in the spirit of Lewis Carroll's dog who proclaimed to the mouse: "I'll be judge, I'll be jury," said cunning old Fury, "I'll try the whole cause, and condemn you to death." But in an era less hopeful and naive than Lenin's and less grim and brutal than Stalin's, the Marxist rulers of Russia have granted in theory what they long ago conceded in practice—namely, that law-makers, administrators, and judges have quite different tasks which had best be kept as separate and distinct as possible.

What then is to be said, to begin with, about the "executive" branch of government in the USSR and about the "administrators" in the Soviet system of power? The first thing to be said is that all analogies to Western arrangements are misleading, despite superficial similarities, since the polity, economy, and society of the USSR bear little resemblance to Western analogues. "Cultural convergence," to be sure (see pp. 149–51 below), tends in the end to make all industrial States more and more alike in their devices for managing community affairs and in the life-experiences of most of their peoples. But points of departure and ultimate goals are of a wholly different order in the two cases. It follows, therefore, that "public administration" in the USSR is something quite different from the activities which, at first glance, seem to be parallel or comparable in the nation-states of the "Free World" or the "Neutralist" world.

Let us first note resemblances before emphasizing differences. On the executive level, Soviet Government began (see p. 46 above) with the establishment of a baker's dozen of "People's Commissariats," each headed by a Party leader and each charged with maintaining or restoring, amid chaos and breakdown, some traditional governmental function: Foreign Affairs, Interior, Agriculture, Labor, Defense, Commerce, Education, Finance, Justice, etc. Each Commissar, despite Bolshevik contempt for "bureaucracy," was obliged to recruit a staff of central and local subordinates to carry out his tasks and thus, willy-nilly to create a bureaucracy. All bureaucracies proliferate ("Parkinson's Law") and the Soviet bureaucracy more than most. The Council of People's Commissars (*Sovnarkom*) rapidly grew by leaps and bounds, both in the number of its Commissariats and in size of its staffs. By 1946, when it was rechristened the "Council of Ministers" (cf. Arts. 64–77 of the Soviet Constitution), it had become a large body of top-level executives, comprising 15 Chairmen of Committees, 7 heads of All-Union Ministries (operating locally through their own officials), and 10 heads of Union-Republican Ministries (operating locally through the officials of the corresponding Ministry of the Republic). The number of federal Ministries waxed to 60 in Stalin's later days, was reduced to 26 following his death, grew again to more than 50 by 1956, and has since been reduced to a variable smaller number. Each of the Union Republics and all of their local sub-divisions, down to urban and rural Soviets, have experienced comparable contractions and expansions of their "executive" or "administrative" departments.

All of this is normal in all government everywhere. Parallels can also be found elsewhere for the problems posed by "democratic centralism" as a principle of bureaucratic, as well as Party, organization; for procedures of "mass participation," "mass criticism," and "self-criticism"; for issues of "one-man" vs. "collegial" management, with the former the prevailing rule in the USSR; and for all the complex tasks, similar in all bureaucracies and here beyond our purview, of organizational structure and of recruitment, training, salary grading, promotion, and retirement of personnel. What is unique in Soviet administration is its all-embracing scope. In all previously existing States, the human activities designated as "public administration" have been limited to the arts of high politics—e.g., war and diplomacy —and to such public services as could not reasonably be left to private enterprise—e.g., postal communication, tax collection, road building, schooling, and (in Western Europe, although not

yet in the USA), railways, bus lines, airways, telephones, telegraph, medical and dental service, opera, theater, etc. All other
activities designed to serve human wants and needs have been
left to private entrepreneurs seeking profit by selling goods and
services to consumers who pay for what they buy at prices fixed
by the competition of buyers and sellers in a more or less "free
market." All of this is long gone in the USSR.

In a planned economy based on total socialism all business
enterprise which is "private" in most Western countries is
"public" or "Governmental" in the Soviet Union, along with
most non-business activities, including education, science, the
arts, sports, and recreation. "Public administration" in the
USSR is, therefore, not a matter of carrying out public programs
for regulating private actions nor of managing limited Governmental projects designed to serve community purposes. It is, on
the contrary, a matter of organizing, through public agencies,
the entire production and distribution of all goods and services
to serve the needs of all consumers in a vast and far-flung population. Such an enterprise was long deemed fantastic and impossible by most Western commentators. The rulers of contemporary Russia—after much trial-and-error fumbling, costly
mistakes, and brutal tragedies in their groping quest for a new
order—have solved the problem.

The initial solution in the 1930's and 1940's was to bring
into being a large number of federal "Commissariats" or "Ministries," most of them with counterparts in the Union Republics,
with each charged with responsibility for the production of
designated goods and services for the whole economy. The more
recent solution, following the "decentralization" of industrial
and agricultural management in 1957–58, has been to abolish
most of the industrial Ministries in the USSR and the Republics
and to replace them by some 105 Regional Economic Councils
(*Sovnarkhozy*) charged with comparable duties in their local
areas. Each is assisted (or impeded) in its tasks by the cooperation of sundry semi-autonomous organizations of a formally non-
government character: trade unions, cooperatives, professional
associations, cultural societies, etc.—all of which, however, are
guided by the broad directives of the Party.

The resulting pattern of administration has few parallels
in the West, but is to be found, with local variations, throughout Eastern Europe, in North Korea, North Vietnam, and, above
all, in Communist China. The essence of the pattern is the conscious and deliberate organization of the entire population by

the ruling Communist oligarchs for the production and distribution of all goods and services, with everyone exhorted, induced, or coerced into doing his share toward attaining the goals set in successive "Economic Plans." In the USSR these goals, long-range and short-run, are set by the Party Presidium and the federal Council of Ministers on the basis of complex statistical analyses of past production, current capabilities, and future potentialities of increased output in all branches of industry and agriculture. The resulting directives flow from the federal *Gosplan* (State Planning Commission) to the federal Council of Ministers; then to the Republican *Gosplans* and Republican Councils of Ministers; then to the Regional Economic Councils; then to the *Glavks* or "trusts" whereby all economic activity is coordinated and controlled; and finally to individual factories, mines, mills, and collective or state farms—each of which is thus given its production quota by years and quarter-years, with penalties for failing to meet the mark and rewards for exceeding the stipulated targets.

In such a scheme of things as this, almost the entire working population is publicly, rather than privately, employed and is thus included in the State bureaucracy. In principle, albeit scarcely so in practice, the 50,000,000 workers on collective farms, unlike those on State farms, are not Governmental employees but jointly own their agrarian enterprises and share the proceeds. Among others who are nominally outside the Civil Service are the few remaining private farmers, numbering perhaps 200,000 in the early 1960's; private artisans or handicraftsmen (c. 500,000); artisans employed by cooperatives (c. 2,000,000); a small, unreported, but probably declining number of domestic servants; and a few "private" gold prospectors and fur-trappers in the far North and Eastern Siberia. Lawyers do their work as members of cooperative "colleges of advocates" established in each Republic, with a few conducting "private practice" on the side. Doctors and dentists, although State employees, may also practice privately in off-hours, as some among them do. Aside from these exceptions, which are in part debatable, all wage and salary workers in the USSR, numbering 52,400,000 in 1958 and scheduled to increase to 64,000,000 by 1965 under the Seven Year Plan, quite literally "work for the government"—including artists, musicians, actors, writers, and scientists and even street vendors of newspapers, books and periodicals, ice cream, beverages, and stationery.

This huge, multiform, and ubiquitous bureaucratic hierarchy is directed by a managerial elite which includes the executive directors of Ministries, both Union and Republican; of State Planning Commissions, Union and Republican; of the Regional Economic Councils; of the *Glavks* or "Chief Administrations" of industries; and of individual enterprises and factories, numbering well over 200,000 by the early 1960's. The typical Soviet manager is a college graduate, usually with a degree in engineering. He is a Party member. He has completed his training and begun his career with work in production. His income is usually five or six times that of the average factory-worker, but with one-fifth to one-third of it derived from bonuses rather than salary. Demotion for failure is as swift as promotion for success. Responsibility for meeting output targets, utilizing equipment and supplies efficiently, and raising labor productivity is strictly enforced by granting wide discretion to administrators—and by pressures for performance which are probably heavier than those which beat upon the average American corporation executive or factory director.

To the managers of the Soviet economy much is given in the way of incentives and rewards. From them much is asked. In the USA their opposite numbers in private business usually enjoy much larger incomes and greater social prestige than do intellectuals in the arts, sciences, and professions. In most of Western Europe businessmen have less prestige, but make more money, than intellectuals. In the USSR intellectuals and business executives are alike awarded high incomes and universal respect as co-equal members of the "Intelligentsia." The net result is a managerial elite whose members, with few exceptions, are strikingly knowledgeable, imaginative, and competent as well as honest, earnest, and dedicated to their duties. By virtue of their labors, those who direct the Soviet State have succeeded in making Soviet society a "going concern" and in building a socialist economy which is vastly productive and capable of a rate of growth seldom attained in the industrial capitalisms of the North Atlantic communities. But of these matters more anon.

The Law-givers

Public administration as a function of government is, as we have seen, something quite different in the USSR from its apparent counterparts in Western lands. Legislation in the Soviet Union is comparably dissimilar to the law-making process

in the democracies. Confusion is compounded by Russian borrowing of Western procedural forms with no borrowing of the
substance of Western political realities. Meaningful distinctions
cannot be drawn in terms of ethnocentric postulates of Western
"superiority" and Russian "inferiority" or *vice versa*. The
Marxist rulers of Russia have devised procedures of law-making
which have been copied in part from Western models but which,
in their actual function, bear little resemblance to Western
analogues. The selection of law-makers and the processes of
legislation in the USA and in most of Western Europe have
long developed within a political context of democracy and
an economic context of "capitalism" or a "free enterprise"
system of business. Corresponding arrangements have evolved
in the USSR within a political context of oligarchy and an economic context of socialism. Full awareness of these divergencies
of backgrounds will help to explain (amid much else) the
peculiar features, in Western eyes, of law-making in the Soviet
Union.

What, to begin with, is the Soviet method of choosing law-
makers? In the democracies political parties, competing for public support, nominate candidates for seats in legislative bodies
—national, regional, and local—with the partisan composition
and broad policies of such bodies determined in principle by
the free choice of the voters among rival aspirants for office.
This familiar formula of "democracy" and "representative government" is mirrored by mimesis in the Constitution of the
USSR. In practice, the Communist rulers of the country have
devised a wholly different scheme for the selection and for the
work of law-makers.

In preparation for the election of the first Supreme Soviet
under the Constitution of 1936, a Central Electoral Commission
was charged with establishing electoral districts and precincts,
registering voters and candidates, directing propaganda, pre-
paring ballots and ballot boxes, counting the votes, and re-
porting the results. Single-member constituencies were mapped
out for all seats in both the Soviet of the Union and the Soviet
of Nationalities. Within each district candidates were nominated
at public meetings of trade unions, cooperatives, army regiments,
collective farms, and local units of the *Komsomols* and of the
Party. The names of all candidates were published in the local
press 25 days before the election, with ballots printed 15 days
before the election. During these 10 days, however, all candidates
for each seat, save one, withdrew from the race in a kind of in-

formal or extra-legal "primary" supervised by the Party. Thus precisely 569 candidates "ran" for the 569 seats in the Soviet of the Union and 574 for the 574 seats in the Soviet of Nationalities. Of the former group 81% were Party members and of the latter 71%, with the balance composed of what were called "non-Party Bolsheviks." The intensive "campaign" preceding the election was conducted in the name of the "Bloc of Party and Non-Party People."

The choice of deputies was thus made not by the voters at the polls but prior to the polling. In the privacy of his voting booth the voter with his secret ballot was offered no options among candidates. He could register dissent only by crossing out the name of the official candidate and writing in another name of a local district candidate. Should the voter write in the name of someone who was not a local candidate, even though the name was "Stalin," his ballot was invalidated. In the USSR, as in England and in most of the European democracies (unlike the USA), candidates need not be residents of their districts, but may "stand for election" in any district they choose. Party leaders, guided by appropriate Party organs, decide for themselves in what districts they will "run."

The first "election" day under the new Constitution—Sunday, December 12, 1937—was aptly described by Stalin as "a public holiday for our workers, our peasants, and our intellectuals." Private parties and public parades and demonstrations, amid general jollification, marked a civic exercise in unanimity. Every device of propaganda was employed to obtain overwhelming endorsement of the official nominees. The announced results, which were no doubt honestly reported, were heartening to the Party leadership. Soviet voters, whether terrified or indifferent toward the "Great Purge" already well underway (see p. 65 above), were evidently impressed by the manifest achievements of the Second Five Year Plan. They faithfully performed the rites to which they were summoned by their rulers. Of 93,639,458 enfranchised citizens, 90,319,436, or 96%, cast ballots. Among the ballots for deputies to the Soviet of the Union, 636,808 were reported as invalid, with 632,074 having names crossed out. Among the ballots for deputies to the Soviet of Nationalities, 1,487,582 were reported as invalid, with 562,402 having names crossed out. "Protest votes" were thus negligible. The deputies "elected" to the 1,143 seats in the two chambers of the federal Supreme Soviet comprised 855 Party members and 288 non-Party members; 354 workers and peasants;

120 Red Army or Navy men; 78 intellectuals; 51 members of the NKVD or political police; and 184 women.

Since all humans are creatures of habit, from which they seldom deviate save under dire compulsion, the Soviet electoral pattern of 1937 has been followed ever since, up to the time these words are written, and has been copied with only minor variations in all Republican, provincial, and local elections. With the coming of war the second federal election, scheduled for December, 1941, was indefinitely postponed. On February 10, 1946, 101,450,936 Soviet voters (out of a total of eligible voters of 101,717,686) cast ballots, 99% affirmatively, for 682 deputies of the Soviet of the Union and 657 deputies of the Soviet of Nationalities, with Party members numbering 1,085 out of the total of 1,339. The ceremonial was repeated on March 12, 1950; March 14, 1954; and March 16, 1958. In the latter election, with the next scheduled for 1962, 99.7% of all registered voters cast ballots for 1,428 deputies: 788 in the Soviet of the Union and 640 in the Soviet of Nationalities. Of those voting, 99.5% endorsed the official candidates, with the miniscule balance casting blank ballots on crossing out names. Unanimity was again the order of the day.

The Party's "monopoly of legality" has thus been in no way altered by the introduction of universal suffrage, secret ballot, and direct elections. In Communist doctrine, under Stalin and since Stalin, a political party is defined (quite erroneously in the light of the history of most political parties throughout the world) as the instrument of a social class in conflict with other social classes. Since it is a Communist article of faith that in a socialist society there can be no antagonistic social classes, it follows that in the USSR there is neither any need nor any possibility of rival political parties. However plausible or implausible this rationalization may be, it is nonetheless true that even within the confines of a one-party regime it is still possible to offer voters some choice on election day. In the Polish parliamentary elections of 1957 and 1961 the governmental slate of the "National Unity Front" included half again as many names of candidates as there were seats to be filled. The voter could therefore mark his cross before the candidates he preferred among those officially nominated, with those receiving the highest number of votes declared elected. But even this limited form of multiple candidacies has had, thus far, no counterparts in the USSR, where only one name for each office appears on the ballot.

Since these Soviet ceremonials in solidarity have no visible effect on popular representation or national policy-making, most Western commentators have dismissed the procedure as a meaningless ritual or an exercise in hypocrisy. Such a view is true by Western standards of free elections among competing candidates of rival parties. Such a view is false, in the eternal paradox of Muscovy, by Russian or Slavic or Soviet standards of "democracy," whereby unity and unanimity are deemed more important, by virtue of tragic historical experience, than diversity and rivalry among political competitors for public favor. That Soviet "elections" decide nothing is undeniable. That the processes of formal government decide little is also clear, as we shall see. Yet both have functions in the Soviet scheme of things.

Every oligarchy, if it is to remain in power to pursue its purposes, must mobilize public support for its programs. In the long run its success in so doing will usually depend upon its capacity to fulfill its promises. Despite lapses over the years, some of them shockingly horrible and others persistently frustrating, the rulers of Russia in our time have carried out most of their pledges or at least painted a persuasive portrait of future fulfillment. In the short run, every oligarchy must strive to command day-by-day and year-by-year popular support of its policies by cultivating an image of public approval and of public participation in policy-making. This is the prime function of the electoral system and of formal government in the USSR. Soviet legislators do not "represent" the divergent views and interests of Soviet citizens, save tenuously, informally, and indirectly. Neither do they decide major issues of policy. Their role is more modest, albeit necessary: to serve as a link or liaison between Party and people.

The scope of this role is further reflected in the work of Soviet law-makers. Here again appearance and reality are far apart, for the former is a procedural copy of Western democracy while the latter is a substantive incarnation of the oligarchy of the Party. In principle and on paper, the federal Supreme Soviet, like British and Continental parliaments, appoints and removes the Cabinet or Council of Ministers; approves, amends, or disapproves the annual budget proposed by the Ministry; studies, debates, and votes upon legislative proposals submitted by the Prime Minister and his Cabinet colleagues; initiates, discusses, and decides upon projects put forward by its members; and engages in much committee work, common to all legislatures elsewhere, in the way of travel "junkets," hearings, research, reports, investigations, etc., all allegedly necessitated by the need of information as a basis for wise law-making. The unicameral Supreme Soviets of the Union Republics, comparable to state legislatures in the USA, theoretically perform similar functions on the local level.

In fact, Soviet legislators scarcely indulge at all in these normal activities of Western law-makers, although few among them and few among their constituents seem to be aware of the discrepancies between theory and practice which impress Western critics. Federal deputies are not full-time salaried officials as are American Congressmen and Senators and members of most parliaments elsewhere. All have other jobs. The Supreme Soviet ordinarily meets only twice a year in sessions lasting only a week or two. Its members are paid travel expenses and a *per diem* allowance. They choose, and may remove, the Cabinet, but this is a formality since (thus far) they invariably accept the recommendations of the Party leadership. Occasionally they make minor modifications in the State budget proposed by the Council of Ministers, but never engage in independent consideration of revenue measures and appropriation bills as their Western counterparts often do. Nor do they ever, with rare exceptions, initiate legislative proposals of their own. They study the proposals of the Cabinet—which are based upon the directives of the Party Central Committee and the Party Presidium —and sometimes observe the forms of individual suggestions, committee reports, speeches, and debates (always within the limits of the current "Party line"), but never decide any issue by recording "yeas" and "nays." All votes in the Supreme Soviet are unanimous. All of these observations are applicable to the Supreme Soviets of the Republics and, with few qualifications, to local Soviets.

This pattern of legislative subservience to the executive branch of government has come to prevail on all levels of rulership in the USSR. Even in municipal Soviets and rural Soviets, law-makers, with few exceptions, are chosen in the fashion described above and perform their duties in much the same way—i.e., by ratifying unanimously the proposals put before them by executive officials. These proposals, obviously, are not at all a product of deliberation and debate among lawmakers nor even of serious discussion, save as to details, among administrators. Soviet legislation—federal, Republican, and local—is a translation into statutory form, enforceable in the

courts, of decisions on public policy reached not by legislators
as legislators, nor by administrators as administrators, but by
both in their alternative roles as members of the Party.

What has happened here need not be deemed "mysterious"
or "hypocritical" or a "travesty" for those of us familiar with
Soviet political history. In Lenin's time divergent views were
not only threshed out and resolved by majority vote in the
Party Central Committee and Politburo, but were also debated and decided by "yeas" and "nays" in what was then the
national legislature: the All-Russian Congress of Soviets (see
pp. 46–48 above). In Stalin's time, this practice was abandoned
in favor of decisions by the *Vozhd* and his Party *apparatchiki*,
all of which had to be approved by nominal law-makers under
penalty of "purging" for non-cooperation. In Khrushchev's
time, despite the "liberalization" of the regime, old habits have
persisted and have thus far precluded any significant participation by Soviet law-makers in public decision-making. All disputes are debated, voted upon, and resolved in the Presidium
and Central Committee of the Party, and not by legislators or
administrators in their governmental capacities.

The future role of Soviet law-makers poses a problem in
speculation. If Khrushchev and his successors find prevailing
legislative arrangements reasonably satisfactory in maintaining
operational relationships between Party and people, they will
maintain the *status quo*—since they are pragmatists in practice
as well as dogmatists in theory. If, on the contrary, they conclude that new departures are called for, they will move toward
multiple candidacies in elections and toward reviving in legislative bodies the practices of free debate and decision-making by
a majority vote which prevailed in Lenin's Russia. In either
case no amendments of the Soviet Constitution will be needed.
The words of the document admit of a perpetuation of the
current pattern. They also admit of the emergence of a completely democratic system of responsible parliamentary government. Which option the rulers of Russia will ultimately choose
is a secret of times to come.

The Judges

Most human beings throughout all recorded time have been
much given to disputation. In complex societies, where inter-
personal and inter-group relations are based upon contract

rather than upon status, innumerable disputes regarding contractual rights and obligations are inevitable by virtue of
diversities of views and interests between husbands and wives,
parents and children, officials and citizens, employers and employees, landlords and tenants, buyers and sellers, *et cetera ad
infinitum*. In all societies, moreover, some alienated souls are
frequently disposed toward anti-social activities, ranging from
embezzlement and theft to treason and murder. "Private" methods
of dealing with such problems—e.g., dueling, blood-feuds, ven-
dettas, or other individual or family modes of defending honor,
seeking justice, or inflicting punishment—have long since been
frowned upon as intolerable and have been forbidden in all
civilized communities. The preferred alternative, as old as
civilization itself, is the public promulgation of legal rule binding upon all members of the community and the public establishment of judicial tribunals for the trial and restraint of
criminals and for the settlement of civil disputes through litigation.

These prerequisites of decency and order in all the man-
sions of men are no less imperative in the USSR than in other
societies. At the outset of the Soviet regime, it is true, Lenin
and his comrades toyed briefly with the thought of abolishing
all courts and relying upon "popular justice" and "revolutionary legality." And in the cloudy Communist vision of the ultimate "withering away of the State," crime will disappear and
justice will presumably be achieved (in ways unspecified) without policemen or judges. Meanwhile, both have been found to
be necessary, as always and everywhere elsewhere.

The Marxist "philosophy of law" and the structure and development of the Soviet judicial system cannot here be dealt
with in detail. A sketch must serve to complete our survey of
the formal processes of government in the Russia of our time.
A few distinctions deserve preliminary emphasis. All Marxists,
in revolt against "bourgeois illusions," regard law and courts
as weapons of politics, and as "shams" and "frauds" if depicted
in any other light. Some evidence in support of this view can
be found, by diligent searching, in the judicial record of the
Western democracies. But the Western ideal of justice, even if
never perfectly attained in practice, is of a wholly different
order. The peoples of the West—most notably the Romans of
ancient days and the British of the past millennium, with both
becoming models for far-flung imitators on other continents—

long ago concluded that justice could best be served by an "independent judiciary" ideally above and beyond all pressures of politics.

Throughout most of the British Commonwealth, in much of Continental Europe, in the USA, and among emulators in other lands, this ideal has fostered the growth of a system of courts whose judges, while bound to apply and uphold the law as enacted into statutes or embodied in judicial precedents, are carefully safeguarded against domination by legislative or executive officials. The goal of "a government of laws and not of men" has meant that no power-holders or policy-makers are "above the law." All must act within the law and are subject to judicial restraint, correction, or punishment if they fail so to do. In the American formula of "separation of powers," postulating the avoidance of tyranny and the preservation of freedom through "checks-and-balances" among three coordinate branches of government, all legislative and executive decisions are subject to "judicial review" and may be voided if found by the highest court to contravene constitutional limitations imposed by the supreme law of the land.

Such arrangements as these, with their concomitant bodies of constitutional and administrative law, have few precedents in Russian experience and no parallels in the Marxist view of law and the State. The "rule of law" had little meaning in the Autocracy of the Romanovs and even less in the Autocracy of Stalin. Only slowly and recently, as we shall see, has the Soviet legal and judicial system arrived at some approximation to those standards of impartiality and uniformity in the administration of justice to which democratic States have long aspired and often attained.

The peculiarities of justice in the USSR are attributable (if we may re-emphasize the obvious, which is frequently forgotten) to the twin circumstances that the Soviet polity is based upon a one-party oligarchy and the Soviet economy is based upon total socialism. The former fact has meant that policemen and judges have long been charged with duties which have had little to do with "objective" justice or equity and much to do with maintaining the dictatorship of the Party. The latter fact has meant that civil suits among private individuals and corporations over property and over contractual rights and obligations, which constitute the bulk of litigation under "capitalism," are of little importance in Soviet courts and are largely replaced by disputes of a quite different character between public agencies engaged in the socialized production and distribution of goods and services. Since people who survive and endure must somehow adapt themselves to circumstances, particularly if the circumstances are beyond their power to change, rulers and ruled in the USSR have adjusted themselves to these realities in a variety of ways (some sinister, some inspiring, and all novel in Western eyes) whereby disputes among people are resolved in a fashion regarded as normal and acceptable by most of the population.

The most sinister of these ways was long exemplified in the Political Police—the *Cheka,* OGPU, NKVD, MVD, all successive names for the same agency of terror against real or imagined enemies of the regime. This vehicle of intimidation for the enforcement of conformity, functioning as the prime weapon of Stalin's despotism, long operated outside the law and beyond the courts. The "special boards" or groups of three (*troika*) in the Ministry of Internal Affairs could arrest and "try" suspects in secret and sentence their victims to jail, exile, or death with no appeal from their verdicts and no responsibility to any other agency of government—save to Stalin himself in the heyday of hysteria. Thousands were shot and scores of thousands were doomed to forced labor camps during the dark decades of the 1930's and 1940's.

Following Stalin's death the monstrous abuses of this system of "administrative justice" were acknowledged and exposed. Three directors of the system—Menzhinsky, Yagoda, and Yezhov —died by violence in the course of the self-generating "purging" of the "purgers." After Lavrenti Beria suffered the same fate in 1953 (see pp. 88–89 above), the MVD was "down-graded" and deprived of its hitherto arbitrary powers of arrest, trial, and punishment. The "special boards" were abolished in September, 1953, and their functions transferred to military courts whose acts are subject to review by the Supreme Court of the USSR. Khrushchev's Russia, while still a "totalitarian State," was no longer a "police-state" as in Stalin's time. In the late 1950's and early 1960's no Soviet citizen any longer anticipated the knock on the door at 2:00 A.M.; the transit to prison for torture to exact "confessions"; and abrupt dispatch to limbo for alleged "crimes against the State."

On a wholly different level, Soviet experimenters in the subtle arts of settling disputes and penalizing those who violate social norms of conduct have devised a variety of other procedures quite outside the law and the courts. Among them is the

system of *Gozarbitrazh* or "State Arbitration," whereby speci
tribunals—federal, Republican, territorial, regional, and loc
—have functioned since the early 1930's to adjust controversie
usually arising out of contractual agreements for the deliveri
of goods or services, among the socialist enterprises, *Glavk*
Ministries, or Regional Economic Councils which operate tł
Soviet economy. These tribunals do their work informally an
often offer prior advice to avoid formal proceedings. They ar
not "courts," but resemble administrative tribunals elsewhere
As such, although outside of the judicial system, they hav
evolved a respectable body of "administrative law" which serve
them well in the performance of their tasks.

Another instance of Soviet experimentation in extra-lega
and extra-judicial methods of resolving disputes is to be foun
in the "social assemblies" set up in some of the Union Republic
in 1957–60. These are local gatherings of citizens—on collectiv
farms, urban apartment houses, or neighborhood districts—
to "try" individuals charged with "parasitic" or "anti-social"
activities not involving any formal violation of law. Such assem
blies hold hearings, debate the issue, and vote the accused "ir
nocent" or "guilty" by a show of hands. For those found "guilty,
penalties range from reprimand to deportation for five year
to some other area. There is no appeal. The local Soviet mus
be represented at the hearing, however, and must confirm th
sentence. Such a system lends itself to obvious abuses, but i
probably effective in enforcing prevailing norms of social re
sponsibility.

Apart from these informal processes for deciding contro
versies and disciplining dissidents, the rulers of the USSR have
long since found it necessary, as have all rulers elsewhere, to
enact codes of law and to establish courts for application, in
terpretation, and enforcement of the rules. Despite Communis
insistence that the resulting body of jurisprudence and hierarchy
of judicial tribunals are wholly different from (and, of course
better than) their "bourgeois" counterparts, the end-product
are strikingly similar, save in details, to their parallels in othei
modern nation-states.

As in every federation, the courts of the USSR are dividec
into two broad categories of federal or Union tribunals and
local or Republican tribunals. All civil cases and some crimina
cases are tried in Republican courts. Aside from trying suits
brought by one Republic against another, of which none is on
record thus far, federal courts have only criminal jurisdiction—

apart from the theoretical possibility, which seems to be little availed of in practice (unlike the USA), of "appealing" certain cases from Republican to federal courts on points of constitutional and administrative law. The federal judiciary is headed by the Supreme Court of the USSR, currently consisting of a President, two Vice-Presidents, nine Judges, sundry lay "assessors," and, *ex officio*, the Presidents of the Supreme Courts of the fifteen Union Republics—all of whom (save the last named group) are appointed for five-year terms, as are all lower federal judges, by the Supreme Soviet of the USSR.

The Supreme Court formerly had specialized "Collegia," with counterparts on lower levels, to deal with cases of labor discipline on the railroads, in water transport, and in labor camps. Since Stalin's death all of these have been abolished, with their functions transferred to the courts of the Republics, except for the "Military Collegium" of the federal Supreme Court which tries cases in which members of the armed forces are accused of breach of duty or civilians are accused of espionage, sabotage, or related crimes against the State. This "Military Collegium," headed by V. V. Ulrich as Presiding Judge with A. Y. Vyshinsky as State Prosecutor, conducted the public "purge trials" of 1935–38, when the Supreme Court was little more than an instrument of Stalin's will. On August 19, 1960, a new "Military Collegium," now enjoying some independent authority, sentenced Francis Gary Powers, pilot of the ill-fated U-2 spy-flight of May Day, 1960, to ten years "loss of liberty," of which the first three were to be spent in prison.

The Supreme Court of the USSR, as in all federal systems, can "disallow" (or, in the American idiom, hold "unconstitutional") Republican statutes which are judged to be at variance with the federal Constitution. It is further charged (cf. Art. 104) "with the supervision of the judicial activities of all the judicial organs of the USSR and of the Union Republics." This authority, however, is shared by the federal judiciary with the Presidium of the federal Supreme Soviet (cf. Art. 49). Unlike its American counterpart, the Supreme Court has no authority to hold federal statutes unconstitutional. In Soviet, as in British, juridical theory and practice, in contrast to the USA, the national legislature interprets the Constitution and decides what is permitted and forbidden by the supreme law with no "judicial review" of its findings.

As for the Republican and regional hierarchies of courts, each Union Republic and each Autonomous Republic has a

Supreme Court appointed for a five-year term by the corresponding local Supreme Soviet. Courts in Territories, Regions, Autonomous Regions, and Areas are appointed for a similar term by
the local Soviets. At the bottom of the system are the "People's
Courts," with limited civil and criminal jurisdiction. These
local judges, many of them women, are "elected" by the voters
for three-year terms by the usual Soviet mode of election. Since
there are no juries in Soviet courts, popular participation in the
judicial process is sought to be achieved by "lay judges" or
"assessors," with counterparts throughout the judicial hierarchy.
In the People's Courts, each judge is flanked by two "assessors"
who are also "elected" for two-year terms but are not expected
to serve for more than ten days in any one year. These "lay
judges" are not lawyers. They may overrule the professional
judge, but seldom do. They give a democratic illusion, and
often a democratic reality, to the local administration of justice.

The Soviet system of courts is paralleled on all levels by
the "Procuracy" which comprises a hierarchy of quasi-judicial
and quasi-bureaucratic officials who fulfill the functions associated in English-speaking lands with those of "Attorneys General," "State's Attorneys," or "Public Prosecutors." Their task
is to insure observance of law by investigating alleged infractions
and initiating proceedings against those accused, whether high
officials or simple citizens, of violating the law. The Soviet
scheme of "Procuracy" is centralized. The "Procurator-General"
of the USSR is appointed by the Supreme Soviet for a term of
seven years. Republican and regional Procurators are appointed
by the Procurator-General for terms of five years. Local Procurators are named by the Procurators of the Union Republic for
five-year terms, subject to the approval of the Procurator-General of the USSR (see Arts. 113–117 of the Constitution). On the
basis of police reports, Procurators initiate criminal prosecutions;
authorize arrests; protest court verdicts as too lenient or too
severe; appeal court decisions, if they choose, to higher courts;
hear complaints of citizens against bureaucrats; and, in general,
serve as guardians of "socialist legality."

The ultimate test of every system of law and adjudication
is pragmatic. Do people at large regard the legal and judicial
scheme under which they live, and by which they strive to restrain criminality and to settle controversies, as conducive to
"justice" or as arbitrary, capricious, tyrannical, brutal, and unreliable? Definitions of "justice" notoriously differ, even in the
purest of democracies. Yet all men and women in all civilized

societies share a sense of being treated "justly" or "unjustly" by their fellows who act in the name of government. Soviet citizens have long been inhibited by political and social pressures from giving public voice to their views on such matters. Their private views remain debatable. Their judgment of the adequacy of the legal and judicial system admits of no clear measure.

Granting these difficulties of evaluation, it still seems safe to assume that few Soviet citizens had any confidence during the reign of Stalin that the rules of law and the hierarchy of courts which then prevailed offered much hope of "justice," however defined. It seems equally safe to assume that a fair approximation to an opposite conclusion has been attained during the years since 1953. The suppression of the arbitrary powers of the political police; the abolition of the labor camps; the elaboration of new civil and criminal codes in 1957–59; the new stress on safeguarding the legal rights of citizens; the fresh emphasis on the presumption, in fact if not in form, that all accused of crime are innocent until proven guilty; all these and other changes in the post-Stalin "thaw" have persuaded most Soviet citizens that they are now living under a "rule of law" wherein substantial "justice" is usually achieved in both criminal and civil cases. This dispensation, to be sure, is a blessing conferred, and subject to possible withdrawal, by the oligarchs of the Party. But for the present, and probably for the long future, Soviet jurisprudence, with inevitable exceptions, is equated in the minds of most citizens with consistency, equity, and fairness—the more so as current penal practices aim at the rehabilitation, rather than the punishment, of criminal offenders.

No scheme of law and justice can do more than this. Many do less. The current Soviet system of settling disputes and protecting society from aberrated personalities bears favorable comparison with the best of its counterparts in other parts of the world. Dreams of Utopia, happily, will always be with us. But so long as human nature and the human condition remain what they have always been (and the Russian Marxists have effected no major revolution in these matters, despite all their efforts), every community must make provision for resolving quarrels and dealing with delinquents. The Marxist rulers of Russia, in recent years at least, have done tolerably well in dealing with these facets of human relations.

6 - The Purposes of Power

Ends and Means

Ever since human beings some 7,000 years ago arrived at "civilization" by inventing written language and building cities, all literate and urban peoples have lived under "government" and accepted the institution of "the State." These devices whereby the few command obedience from the many have ever been mixed blessings, giving rise to timeless disputations as to what their forms and functions ought to be. In the modern democratic credo, rulers are expected to promote the "common defense" and "general welfare" and to represent the majority will of the ruled. During the long past, power has rested in most of the polities of mankind with aristocracies, plutocracies, or other oligarchies whose members have sometimes selflessly served the "public interest" and more often sought to maintain and enlarge their privileges through the exploitation and oppression of the voiceless masses of their economic and social inferiors.

What objectives have the Marxist oligarchs of the USSR striven for in the use, or abuse, of the formidable power at their disposal during the turbulent decades since 1917? Answers have varied widely both among outside observers and inside participants. In 1936, on the eve of the "Blood Purge," the amiable and brilliant Fabian Socialists, Sidney and Beatrice Webb, in their two-volume work, *Soviet Communism: A New Civilization?*, persuaded themselves and many of their readers that the Party of Stalin was a beneficent "vocation of leadership" in a "multiform democracy." Trotsky in exile was no less convinced that the Stalinist tyranny represented an utter betrayal and negation of the ideals of the Revolution. In 1957 Milovan Djilas, Marxist critic of Marxism and heretical foe of schismatic Tito, was certain that the Party had become *The New Class,* dedicated to power and pelf at the expense of the people. The Webbs were naïve in mistaking shadow for substance. Trotsky and Djilas may be deemed equally naïve in taking the part for the whole.

Human motives are always mixed and ambivalent, among rulers and ruled alike. If our question admits of any answer, it can best be found not by contrasting or confusing theory and practice but by examining critically the accomplishments and failures of the rulers of the Soviet State in their unending effort to remold man and society.

As Marxists, these rulers were committed to the view that the major evils of Western civilization in the 20th Century were attributable to an obsolete "capitalism" which must inevitably give way—via social revolution, the "dictatorship of the proletariat," and a planned transition to "socialism" and ultimately to economic "communism"—to a "cooperative commonwealth" in which Everyman, emancipated from exploitation and oppression, would contribute by his labor in peace and freedom to the welfare of all. This generous and inspiring vision, derived from the Utopian hopes of Israel, Athens, and Rome and from contemporary Western "liberalism," was from the outset corrupted and polluted in Marxist minds by a savage doctrine of "class war." The transit to the Millennium, moreover, was conceived in the Marxist gospels as a possibility only in advanced, wealthy, mature, and decadent "capitalist" societies. Russia in 1917 was backward, poor, illiterate, rural, and still semi-feudal. To what ends, then, should the Russian Marxists, who seized power in a wholly un-Marxist "historical accident," devote the power which they had grasped?

This dilemma was resolved in three ways, all of them momentous for the future fortunes of Russia and of all mankind. The first was the concept of "World Revolution," implicit in the original Marxist mission of "revolutionary proletarian internationalism" but rendered explicit and imperative by the Communist conviction (almost, but not quite, validated by the Allied and American military assault of 1918–21 and by other events elsewhere during these years of battle) that Marxist rule of Russia could not survive without "proletarian revolution" in Germany, France, Britain, and the USA. This hope came to nothing, despite the agitational and subversive activities of the Third or Communist International (1919–43), since the Marxist prognosis of the destiny of "capitalism" proved to be wrong— a circumstance which, to be sure, no "true believer" can ever admit. Marxist rulership of Russia continued.

The second way by which the Red masters of Muscovy resolved their dilemma was to bring into being, as a method of defense in civil and foreign war, the first totalitarian police-

state of our century. The result was victory, albeit in a desperately impoverished and war-wasted land. The third way
whereby Russia's rulers resolved their dilemma was to apply
the methods of the totalitarian police-state (with initially horrible but ultimately successful results) to the task of building
"Socialism in One Country"—i.e., bringing into being, by coercion and propaganda, a collectivized agriculture and a highly
urbanized and industrialized economy, based on total socialism
and total planning and aspiring to equal Western European
and American standards of productivity and affluence.

The first and second methods of resolving the dilemma are
of no enduring significance—or so, at least, it appears to opti-
mists in the 1960's. The third method has long since transformed the USSR into the second greatest industrial Power of
the world. Its background is therefore worthy of recall. In the
wrecked and famine-stricken Russia of 1921 Lenin perceived
that economic recovery would require an abandonment of the
policies of coercion, requisitioning, and printing-press inflation
which had marked the regime of "War Communism" (1918–21)
and a temporary return to "capitalist" incentives. In March,
1921, at Party Congress X, he proposed a "New Economic
Policy," the essence of which was the abolition of the State
monopoly in grain trading; the substitution of taxes, in money
or in kind, for prior seizures of food supplies from the peasants;
the restoration of a "free market" for crops; and official permission for private entrepreneurs (Nepmen) to engage in retail
trade and small-scale manufacturing for profit, while the State
retained control of the "commanding heights" of foreign trade,
transportation, and heavy industry. The Party endorsed this
"strategic retreat toward capitalism" as a regrettable but inexorable necessity.

By 1927, thanks to the NEP and to the enterprise of kulaks
and Nepmen, agricultural and industrial productivity had been
restored to the levels of 1913. Amid much wrangling among the
comrades (see pp. 58–64 above), Stalin led the Party into a
"resumption of the socialist offensive" in the first Five Year
Plan (1928–32), designed to liquidate Nepmen and kulaks alike,
to collectivize farming, and to create a massive industrial base
for a new social order. Appalling were the material and human
wastes involved in a trial-and-error experiment in pushing a
miserably poor community into lifting itself by its bootstraps
toward some semblance of plenty. Shocking were the stresses and
strains of the process, the injustices and atrocities which ac-

companied it, and the emergence of Stalin as a paranoid and bloody-minded tyrant. Yet, paradoxically, something new under the sun emerged out of darkness at noon: a consciously planned and completely socialized industrial economy.

The Building of Socialism

Industrialization is clearly no phenomenon unique to Soviet experience. The business began in England in the late 1700's, got well under way in Germany and the USA during the 1800's, transformed Japan, France, and Italy in later decades, is currently going forward in China and India, and has in our time become a magic symbol of hope and wealth for all the world's poor. The industrialization of the USSR is, nonetheless, unique, in comparison with earlier instances, in at least three respects: (1) its extraordinary speed, which compressed into ten years (1929–39) processes of change which required several generations in England, Germany, and the USA; (2) the absence of investments of foreign capital; and (3) the total lack of private property, private enterprise, and private profit. With all means of production socialized, land, labor, and capital are allocated among the sundry segments of the economy not through the "automatic" mechanisms of supply and demand and of price and profit in a competitive market for goods and services but through the directives of a nation-wide Economic Plan.

The planned and socialist industrialization of the USSR has been, thus far, the prime objective of the Marxist oligarchs, along with the still distant goal of matching and surpassing the USA in production and living standards. Most Western commentators in the 1930's contemptuously dismissed the program as utterly impossible of accomplishment. As usual in matters Russian, such judgments were wrong. The rulers and people of the Soviet Union have long since devised a system of socialist planning which works very well, indeed—or well enough to achieve an appreciable measure of prosperity by 1940; to defeat the lethal assault of Fascist Europe in World War II; to repair and rebuild and recover pre-war levels of output by 1950 after the incredible devastation inflicted by the invaders; and to maintain quite consistently during the 1950's and early 1960's a rate of economic growth roughly double that of the USA and Western Europe. Space is here lacking for an account of the Soviet system of planning and for a history, description, and evaluation of the Soviet economy. Yet a few general observations are in order.

The aim of the planners from the initial launching of their enterprise, and still so today, has been rapid and large-scale accumulation of capital and rapid and large-scale industrialization through the productive investment of the capital thus accumulated. In method, direction, and purpose, the Soviet system of acquiring and using capital bears little resemblance to the ways of the West, where saving and investment are motivated by private gain, or the hope thereof. In any and all economies, capital can be accumulated only by inducing people to consume less than they produce or to produce more than they consume. Under "capitalism," capital for investment flows from the voluntary savings of individuals and from the profits of corporations. Under Soviet socialism, individual savings and the profits of firms, all publicly owned and operated, also play a role in the garnering of capital, albeit a minor one. The principal source of investment capital (which in the Soviet scheme of things is identical in origin, if not in destination, with public revenues) has long been the "turnover tax," whereby consumers pay for the goods they buy roughly twice the cost of production and distribution—more than twice for "luxury" items and much less for the necessities of life.

Unlike American "sales taxes," the turnover tax is not added to, but is included in, the purchase price. By this device Soviet consumers—in the beginning, the mass of the peasantry and later the ever-waxing ranks of the urban proletariat and the middle- and upper-class intelligentsia—are obliged willy-nilly to contribute a major share to the process of capital formation. But the capital thus accumulated does not flow into the pockets or bank accounts of private retailers, wholesalers, and producers for spending, saving, or reinvestment. All revenues are "socialized" and are at the disposal of the planners to pay for public services and, above all, to invest in the expansion of the national economy.

So much for the question: where does capital come from? As for the question of where does capital go to, the answer is to be found in the elaborate and complex program of goals formulated by the *Gosplan* or State Planning Commission on the basis of detailed studies, reports, and consultations down to the local level regarding past performance and future potentialities for every economic enterprise throughout the country. Under "capitalism," private savings and private profits are allocated, by the price mechanism of the market, into profitable enterprises and away from unprofitable enterprises, with the distinction reflected in constantly changing quotations for corporate stocks and bonds—which, in turn, mirror actual or expected dividends and interest payments flowing from anticipated profits or losses. Under ideal conditions, these arrangements will result, theoretically, in the most efficient allocation of funds among enterprises seeking capital. Under Soviet socialism, where no such arrangements prevail, the decisions of the money market are replaced by the decisions of the planners—as approved, disapproved, or modified by the Presidium and Central Committee of the Party and formally ratified by the Council of Ministers and the Supreme Soviet of the USSR.

The final result of the planning process comes to fiscal expression in the annual "Consolidated State Budget of the USSR," which, quite unlike governmental budgets in "capitalist" communities, constitutes for all practical purposes a balance sheet of input and output for the entire national economy. It includes the budgets of all the Union Republics and of all their subdivisions down to municipalities and villages and comprises a summation of revenues and expenditures for all enterprises and services throughout the land. Statistics are fascinating to most Russians and boring to most Americans. A few figures are, nevertheless, in order.

The budget for 1933 provided for 40 billion rubles of revenue, of which 23 billions were derived from the turnover tax and 17 billions from other sources. Expenditures were totaled at 36 billion rubles, of which 25 billions were devoted to the "National Economy," 2 billions to "Social and Cultural" activities, and 1 billion to "Defense." Fifteen years later, in 1948, following the vast expansion of the Soviet economy in the 1930's, the agony of World War II, and the post-war tasks of reconstruction and economic growth, the budget postulated 429 billions of rubles in revenue (of which 281 billions were derived from the turnover tax and 148 billions from other sources) and expenditures of 388 billion rubles, of which 149 were devoted to the "National Economy," 116 to "Social and Cultural" activities, and 66 to "Defense." For 1954, with the American-Russian arms race in full blast, "Defense" expenditures were set at 100 billion rubles out of total appropriations of 563 billions, with 216 billions devoted to "National Economy" and 141 to "Social and Cultural" enterprises. Revenues were calculated at 572 billion rubles, of which 230 were derived from the turnover tax and 342 from other sources.

By 1960 expenditures totaled 744.8 billion rubles, of which

255.5 represented investment and operating costs of the "National Economy," 247.4 for "Social and Cultural" services, and 96.1 billions for "Defense." Revenues for 1960 were tabulated at 772.1 billion rubles, of which 317.1 were derived from the turnover tax, 203 from the "profits tax," 57.2 from direct taxes, and the balance from miscellaneous imposts. More recent figures are comparable—with all reduced to one-tenth of earlier totals by virtue of the introduction in 1961 of the new ruble, exchangeable for the old in the ratio of 10 to 1 with all prices and wages proportionately reduced. The budget for 1961 envisaged revenues of 78,993,741,000 rubles and expenditures of 77,589,829,000, of which 33,907,835,000 were to be devoted to the "Natural Economy," 27,152,242,000 to "Social and Cultural" enterprises, and 9,255,450,000 to "Defense."

Other figures may be more meaningful. By the end of the Fifth Five Year Plan (1950–55), the annual output of steel was 45 million metric tons, of pig iron 33 millions, of coal 390 millions, and of oil 70 millions. The Sixth Five Year Plan set targets of 50 million tons of pig iron and 60 million tons of steel for 1960. In 1958 this Plan was superseded by the current Seven Year Plan of 1959–65. Industrial output during 1960, scheduled to increase by 8%, actually increased by 10%, with annual steel production of 65,300,000 tons, oil 148 million tons, and other outputs of heavy industry at comparable levels. Contemporary programs aim at annual outputs by 1965 of steel, 90 million tons; pig iron, 70 millon tons; oil, 235 million tons; and electric power, 500 billion kwh. Longer range plans contemplate a Soviet economy by 1970 which will surpass current American levels in both total production and per-capita output.

Only those who are foolish or ignorant will dismiss these goals as fantasies impossible of attainment. Yet realism requires recognition of the fact that the Soviet economy in the early 1960's, while vastly more productive than the economies of Asia, Africa, and Latin America and even of the "backward" regions of Western Europe (e.g., Southern Italy, Spain, and Portugal), was still poor in comparison with the USA, particularly in agriculture and in the output of "durable" consumers' goods. Even during a recession the USA produces at least 5,000,000 passenger cars per year. The USSR produced fewer than 200,000 annually in recent years. In 1960 American industry turned out 3,544,000 washing machines, 3,500,000 refrigerators, and 5,716,000 TV sets. In the same year Soviet industry produced 1,000,000 washing machines, 500,000 refrigerators, and 1,700,000 TV sets.

As regards some representative wages and salaries and some representative prices of goods in stores—and these are all the same throughout the whole territory of the USSR—figures are best put in the new rubles, introduced in January, 1961, each of which has a theoretical value of $1.10. Unskilled workers earn on the average 50 rubles per month and skilled workers 80 rubles. Physicians, a relatively unprivileged group, earn some 100 to 200 rubles per month. Three-quarters of them are women. Aeroflot pilots receive 380 rubles a month and hostesses on planes c. 120 rubles a month. Army Marshals, Cabinet Ministers, factory managers, and industrial executives often earn 500 rubles a month or more, some of it in prizes and bonuses. Popular composers, ballerinas, actors, and novelists may earn as much as 3,000 or 4,000 rubles a month. As for a few prices, all including the turnover tax: most cigarettes, 40 kopeks a pack; beer, 50 kopeks, or half a ruble, a bottle; women's hose (kapron) $1\frac{1}{2}$ to $2\frac{1}{2}$ rubles; simple women's dresses, 30 rubles; theater and opera tickets, 1 to 3 rubles; chocolate bars, $1\frac{1}{2}$ rubles; ready-made men's suits, 100 rubles; small cameras, 40 to 90 rubles; TV sets, 200 rubles and up; bicycles, 60 to 80 rubles; motorcycles, 700 rubles.

We are thus in the presence of a still poor society of low wages and high prices, even though this society is less poor each year, rather than of an affluent society of high wages and low prices. It is, nevertheless, needful in considering Soviet living standards to take into full account a number of factors not reflected in wages and prices. Most employees are on a 40-hour week. All receive two- or four-week vacations with full pay. All citizens enjoy the benefits of a very comprehensive system of social insurance. There is no unemployment, save occasionally for people changing jobs. Few Soviet families pay more than 5% of family income for rent and domestic utilities. The huge residential housing industry is conducted more as a public service than as a business enterprise. Dental service, medical service, and hospital care are all free. All education is free, with university students paid living stipends. Soviet living standards, even for the least privileged, are, therefore, appreciably higher than prices and wages would indicate.

Agriculture remains the least productive segment of the Soviet economy. The marketable crop totals of some 50,000,000 Soviet farmers scarcely exceed those of some 6,000,000 American farmers. On state farms (Sovkhozi), numbering c. 10,000 and averaging 40,000 acres each, with many located in the newly opened lands of Siberia and Central Asia, workers are paid

wages as in a factory. On collective farms (*Kolkhozi*), numbering
78,000 and averaging 5,000 acres each, farmers are paid in cash
and kind, according to the work performed, out of total proceeds
(minus taxes, loan payments, and funds set aside for capital,
seed, and fodder) which flow from the sale of part of the output
at fixed prices to State purchasing agencies and of the remainder
at higher prices on the open market. All farmers have individual plots and may sell any surplus output derived therefrom
on the open market. The Seven Year Plan contemplates by 1965
a million new tractors, 400,000 combines, a threefold increase in
mineral fertilizer output and in rural electrification, and increases of farm output, as compared with 1958, as follows: grain
28–30%, sugar beets 40–55%, potatoes 70%, meat 100%, milk
70–80%, eggs 60%, cotton 30–39%, and wool 70%. These goals
may well be achieved, but their attainment poses problems more
difficult of solution than those confronting Soviet industry.

In Search of Freedom

The conviction is widespread among Americans, particularly
among those who have never been abroad, that civil liberties and
political democracy are of the essence of good government; that
both are non-existent in the USSR; that Russians are yearning
for emancipation from tyranny; and that the non-Russian
peoples of the Soviet Union and those of the "satellites" are
hapless victims of Soviet "colonialism" or "imperialism." In the
absence of precise definitions of terms, such generalizations are
likely to be as misleading as are Communist clichés and stereo-
types regarding "capitalism." People who are illiterate, frequently
ill, often hungry, and alienated from the values of their rulers
are apt, in ranking their aspirations, to give high priority to
literacy, health, improved living standards, and a sense of social
purpose, and relatively low priority to civil rights and free elections. Such is the case today with most of the peoples of Asia,
Africa, and Latin America. Such was the case a generation ago
with many of the peoples of the old Russian Empire.

Any meaningful evaluation of the reality or unreality of
"freedom," however defined, in any contemporary society must
take account of these considerations. The Western observer of
the USSR must also take cognizance of Soviet practices, along
with Marxist theories, and must constantly ask at least two
questions with regard to every facet of his most cherished ideal:
freedom *from* what? freedom *for* what? Bearing in mind as best

we can these pre-conditions of fruitful inquiry, what are the rights of citizens in the Soviet Union and which among them are fictitious and which factual?

The "Bill of Rights" in the Soviet Constitution, unlike the first ten amendments to the Constitution of the USA, is embodied in the text of the document, but not all in one place, and comprises a statement of "duties" as well as rights. Art. 12 asserts that "work in the USSR is a duty and a matter of honor for every able-bodied citizen, in accordance with the principle: 'He who does not work, neither shall he eat.' " The source of the principle is unacknowledged. It is St. Paul the Apostle in Thessalonians, 3:10: "For even when we were with you, this we commanded you, that if any would not work, neither should he eat." Arts. 130–33 enjoin all citizens to obey the laws, maintain labor discipline, respect the rules of socialist intercourse, safeguard socialist property, accept military service, and defend the Motherland under penalty of punishment as "enemies of the people." The rights which are elsewhere set forth may be classified as Personal Rights, Political Rights, Property Rights, and Social Rights.

In the first category are "rights for women" and provision for the complete equality of the sexes (Art. 122), which has long been fact and not fiction in the USSR. In all jobs, women workers are paid the same as men, even though it is still true, by choice or by happenstance, that the proportion of women is largest in the less lucrative professions and vocations—e.g., as of 1955 in official Soviet statistics, 85% in health services, 83% of restaurant workers, 68% of teachers, 49% in public administration, 45% in industry, 33% in transport and communication, and 31% of construction workers. Soviet legislation over the decades has fluctuated between extremes, in accordance with demographic considerations and shifts of Party line regarding marriage and the family, in such matters as "free love," contraception, abortion, illegitimacy, divorce, and other areas of ecstacy or misery in the eternal "battle of the sexes." The following generalizations are applicable to the years since 1955: promiscuity is severely frowned upon; mid-Victorian puritanism and even prudery are prevalent attitudes—with tolerated exceptions, to be sure; the family is once more a hallowed institution; prostitution has (allegedly) disappeared; matrimony is dignified by solemn rituals in a growing network of "marriage palaces" for civil ceremonies; church weddings are still popular but have no standing in Soviet law; divorce is no longer easy and cheap and is discouraged if any prospect of reconciliation remains; contraceptives are readily available in cities and towns; no distinctions are made between "legitimate" and "illegitimate" children; any woman, married or unmarried, may by her own choice have an abortion without cost.

By such devices the USSR has come close to achieving the emancipation of women from ancient thralldom. State stipends are paid to unwed mothers and to mothers of more than four children. Some 15,000 maternity centers care for, and advise, expectant mothers—all of whom, if employed, receive maternity leave with full pay for 56 days before and 56 days after childbirth. Public nurseries, kindergartens, hospitals, and summer camps for children are generously available without cost to parents. Infant mortality, ages 0 to 4, was 133 per thousand births in 1896 and 80 in 1926. In recent years the figure has been less than 40. In all such matters the USSR has given "freedom" a new dimension for women which compares favorably with the best that has been achieved in the same direction anywhere else in the world.

A generally favorable verdict, albeit less favorable, is warranted by the record of Soviet efforts to protect Personal Rights from the age-old curse of racial and national discrimination, exploitation, and oppression. Art. 123 of the Soviet Constitution seeks to assure the equality of all citizens regardless of racial or national origin. The USA is also officially committed to this goal, but has thus far failed to achieve it. Failure at home should induce modesty abroad regarding comparable failure in a common purpose. Soviet failure, apart from Stalin's barbarous deportations of sundry minority peoples during World War II, is of minimum proportions compared to American failure, as all the colored world knows. Soviet successes in vanquishing the old ghosts of racial and national prejudice are striking. The preliterate aborigines scattered about the periphery of the Soviet realm have been given written languages, originally in the Latin alphabet and currently in the Cyrillic alphabet. Along with other minority groups in Asia as well as in Europe, they have acquired schools, universities, factories, mechanized farms, hospitals, and other means toward dignity and equality, along with rapidly rising living standards. To regard these peoples as in any sense victims of Soviet "colonialism" or Communist "imperialism" is to misconstrue totally the story of their advance since 1917.

At the same time a black tradition of anti-Semitism came to new expression in Stalin's last years of paranoia when, quite apart from the fantastic fabrication of the "Jewish Doctors' Plot" of January, 1953 (see p. 87 above), the Marxist oligarchs at Stalin's direction undertook to liquidate the rich Yiddish culture of the Jewish communities of the USSR. This purpose was couched in terms not of anti-Semitism but of "anti-cosmopolitanism" and "anti-Zionism." The means included false accusations and the physical liquidation of many intellectuals, some of whom were posthumously "rehabilitated" (i.e., restored to respectability) after Stalin's demise. Even today, despite many confessions of past mistakes, the Party leadership has not wholly emancipated itself from a dark past. People of Jewish origin are not, *per se,* discriminated against. But Yiddish art and literature are still discouraged, if not altogether suppressed, in the name of opposition to "Zionism" and "cosmopolitanism." The Communist ideal of racial and national "equality" has come closer to realization than its counterpart in the USA. But it will continue to remain incomplete so long as vestiges of old attitudes persist.

As for other Personal Rights, Arts. 124–128 of the Constitution purport to guarantee those civic freedoms for which the liberal revolutionaries of the Atlantic democracies fought in the 17th, 18th, and 19th Centuries: freedom of conscience, freedom of speech, press, and assembly, freedom of association, and inviolability of persons, homes, and correspondence. During the two decades of Stalin's police-state tyranny, these "guarantees" were meaningless save as vague expressions of future hopes or as empty imitations of Western models. During the post-Stalin decade these "guarantees," as we have seen, have been given some content, at least in the sense that Soviet citizens no longer need fear arbitrary accusation, arrest, imprisonment, exile, or execution at the hands of an irresponsible political police and may rely with some confidence on the "rule of law" in a reformed judicial and legal system. But the Soviet State, albeit no longer a police-state, is still a totalitarian one-party oligarchy in which competitive political activity is forbidden and "freedom" of expression is permissible only within the limits of the current "Party line." These limits have expanded appreciably since 1953. Given good fortune, they will expand further in the years to come. But they will continue to be fixed by the calculations and assumptions of the Party leaders as to what is expedient and desirable in the way of enlarging the dimensions of public criticism and public participation in policy-making, rather than by any prevailing consensus that truth and error should be free to compete for public support in an open market for divergent ideas and opinions.

As for "freedom of religion" (and of "anti-religious propaganda"), the Communist rulers of the USSR are all atheists committed to the Marxist postulate that religion is the "opium of the people" and should play no role in a rational society. Amid the miseries of World War II, Stalin and his colleagues, nevertheless, "made peace" with believers by dissolving the mass propaganda association of the "League of the Godless" in 1943 and turning its publishing facilities over to the Orthodox Church. In recent years all cathedrals and churches throughout the USSR which have any historical or esthetic significance are scrupulously kept in repair by appropriate cultural authorities, with some converted into "anti-religious" museums. Any congregation—Orthodox, Catholic, Protestant, Jewish, or Moslem—which is willing, out of its own resources, to support a clergyman may obtain a building for worship and carry on religious services. But organized religious instruction of children is still forbidden. Opportunities for graduate training of clerics are few. The *Komsomols* and the Party continue, as of yore, their anti-religious propaganda. The result is that functioning churches are few and far between in all major cities and are largely attended only by the rapidly diminishing members of the older generation.

As for "freedom of association," most Soviet citizens, like their counterparts in other industrial societies, belong to a bewildering variety of organized groups dedicated to a vast range of shared interests—professional, vocational, esthetic, recreational, athletic, etc. But none is tolerated which is "subversive" of the *status quo*. All are controlled or directed by members of the local units of the Party. Such is clearly the case with the nation-wide network of producers' and consumers' cooperatives which play an important part in the distribution of many types of consumer goods. Such is also the case with Soviet trade unions, which include in their membership (which is voluntary) the overwhelming majority of workers and employees. Soviet unions do not engage in "collective bargaining" with management over wage-scales, which are set by the Economic Plan as approved by the Wages Commission of the Council of Ministers, on which government, management, and labor are all represented. Strikes are neither forbidden nor permitted by Soviet law but are almost unknown (or at least seldom reported) on the premise that wage-rates are fixed by the planners in the interest of the national economy as a whole and on the further premise, which is questionable, that in a totally socialized economy the interests of labor and management are identical. Collective bargaining is limited to conditions of work. Under legislation of February, 1957, grievances of employees may be arbitrated, with the right of appeal to the courts. The prime tasks of trade unions in the USSR are to increase productivity, promote the welfare of the workers, and administer the social insurance system.

As for the Political Rights "guaranteed" to Soviet citizens by the Constitution (see Arts. 134–42), all have been scrupulously observed thus far—save, as already noted, that the Soviet citizen as voter has no choice on election day among rival candidates and must vote for (or against) the official candidates in the "Bloc of Party and Non-Party People." These exercises in unanimity serve a social and psychological function, but are without effect on governmental personnel or policies. By procedures and formulas not yet hinted at, it is probable that ways will be found in time to come to achieve a closer approximation to representative government, to broaden public participation in policy-making, and to give citizens as voters a larger voice in public affairs. In the early 1960's, however, the Party leadership was not yet prepared to move in this direction, nor even to follow the example of their counterparts in Poland in offering to the electorate a limited choice among candidates.

Property Rights (see Arts. 7–10) are of two kinds: collective and individual—with both well respected, at least since 1953. Collective farms and cooperatives hold as "common, socialist property" their buildings, tools (including since 1958 the machine-tractor stations), livestock, and produce, with each farm household entitled to a family plot with its house, animals, and implements "as its personal property." The *Kolkhozi* hold their lands "free of charge" and "in perpetuity," but may neither rent nor sell it. Peasants and handicraftsmen may engage in private business, but may not hire labor. All citizens enjoy personal property rights in their incomes, savings, household goods, clothing, and even houses, although most privately owned dwellings, aside from summer *dachas,* will probably be replaced within the decade by publicly owned apartments. All citizens may inherit personal property.

Finally, the Soviet Constitution (Arts. 118–21) sets forth a list of Social Rights which have few counterparts elsewhere. They include the right to "guaranteed employment and payment for work in accordance with its quantity and quality"; to "rest and leisure"; to an eight-hour day, with shorter working days in some industries; to annual vacations with full pay; to maintenance in old age, illness, or disability; to free medical service; and to free education. These rights are not fictions but are living realities for all Soviet citizens. They constitute the great human gains of the Revolution, acquired at the cost of many hard years of sacrifice and suffering. They are the meaning incarnate of "socialism" and of those aspirations or benefits identified in non-socialist societies with the "Welfare State." They bind people, Party, and Government into a functional unity in which Everyman in Sovietland, whatever his discontents may be, has a cherished and enduring stake.

Citizens of the USSR have not as yet gained political freedom. They continue to live under an oligarchy over whose membership and policies they have no direct control in their roles as voters. But the purposes and programs of the oligarchy have gained for them freedom from want, ignorance, and unemployment and freedom for full participation in the exacting but exciting tasks of building a new order. In their own eyes at least, such freedoms are more precious than the civil liberties and competitive politics of the Western democracies—both of which boons, paradoxically, may be brought nearer to realization by the economic and social transformation of Russia between the 1930's and the 1960's. A highly educated, industrialized, and urbanized society cannot be ruled by the methods of the totalitarian police-state—unless most of its people are demented, as were many Germans and Japanese in the 1930's. Such a society, if its people and leaders remain sane, can move in only one direction: toward increasing liberalization and democratization. This in fact, despite occasional backsliding, has been the direction of change in the USSR since 1953. Speculation regarding the ultimate implications of such change is best deferred to the final section of this penultimate chapter of our survey.

The Quest for Excellence

The Millennial vision of the Good Society—seen "as through a glass, darkly" by the Marxist rulers of Muscovy—is a Utopia dimly discerned through the distorting lenses of dialectical materialism. Of this, more anon. The immediate vision of the Good Society in the 1950's and 1960's posits a central and simple goal:

that of equaling and surpassing the USA in productivity and living standards. Since imitation remains the sincerest form of flattery, Americans might be expected, in a world of rational beings, to respond to this mimesis with pleasure and pride and to welcome their Russian emulators as worthy competitors in an amiable contest to determine which of the rivals can contribute more to the fulfillment of human expectations. Since the world of the 20th Century is more irrational than rational and remains trapped in ancient patterns of response to challenge, the American reaction to the Soviet competition has been one of frustration, fear, and recurrent hysteria over Communist plans and plots to "bury" the West and to "take over the world"—all reflected in steadily mounting arms budgets, on the false premise that the Soviet challenge can somehow be met by weapons for "deterrence" or for war.

Our present concern, however, is not with the American response but with the nature of the Soviet challenge itself as defined and pursued by the rulers of the USSR and supported, with more or less enthusiasm, by the people they rule. The enterprise has taken form of striving to "outdo" the USA in all areas of human interest and activities as a symbol of national prestige and as a means of persuading the "uncommitted" nations of the world and, if possible, all mankind that Soviet "socialism" is superior to American "capitalism" in promoting and achieving the good things of life. The mixed record of results admits of no full review in the space here available. Yet a few notations are here in order regarding Soviet accomplishments in "overtaking" America, despite many failures. Successes endure. Failures pass, if transcended by new successes.

In a society inspired, in the words of the U.S. Education Mission to the USSR (cf. Bulletin 1959, No. 16, U.S. Department of Health, Education and Welfare) by "a kind of grand passion for education," the Soviet school system, by common consent, has become one of the best in the world. In 1959–60 more than 40,000,000 people were studying in Soviet schools on all levels, including 2,280,000 children in kindergartens, 31,600,000 boys and girls in elementary and secondary schools, 2,000,000 in technical and specialized secondary schools, 2,100,000 in colleges and universities, and 3,500,000 in part-time or correspondence study. The earlier 7-year and 10-year schools, with the latter combining elementary and secondary education, were replaced in 1960–61 by a scheme of 8-year grammar schools, followed by a 3-year high school, with requirements, particularly in mathematics, sciences, and languages, far more exacting than in typical American 4-year high schools. The experimental innovations introduced since 1958 include "polytechnical" training—i.e., part-time work in industry and agriculture in local school projects or in nearby factories or farms.

High school graduates with work experience and top-level scholastic records are eligible for admission to colleges (institutes) or universities, where most students, on the basis of need, receive living stipends, with bonuses for excellent performance. A five- or six-year course of study leads to a diploma comparable to the American M.A. degree, with three years of post-graduate work earning the degree of "candidate" for the doctorate—which is sparingly awarded in later life on evidence of significant contributions to scholarship. The educational hierarchy includes special schools for talented and retarded children and a new network of boarding schools in which some 2,500,000 pupils will be studying by 1965. On all levels students are required to study more subjects more intensively than their Western counterparts. Slow learners are selected out for transfer to trade schools or to jobs suited to their talents. Gifted pupils, regardless of racial, class, or family background, are carefully recruited for advanced training in the areas of their special aptitudes.

The fruits of this devotion to learning are too rich and varied to permit of more than sparse sampling in these pages. Harvests have been abundant in some fields of creative endeavor fertilized by the work of outstanding precursors in the Russian culture of the 18th and 19th Centuries. They have been poor in other fields similarly enriched by the traditions and styles of the past. In still other fields, hitherto uncultivated, major triumphs have been scored. In the latter category are athletic sports, among which soccer, ice-hockey, skiing, track, gymnastics, swimming, and volleyball have long been most popular, with basketball and tennis attracting increasing interest. In the early 1960's over 20,000,000 Soviet citizens were members of 200,000 sport clubs, most of them with ample facilities furnished by public authorities at no cost to members aside from nominal dues. Guidance is furnished by the Physical Culture and Sports Committee of the Federal Council of Ministers. Youngsters have easy opportunities and strong incentives for early efforts at acquiring skills. The best among them become professional athletes, albeit (somewhat fictitiously) retaining "amateur" status. The USSR became a member of the International Olympics Committee in 1951. Soviet athletes participated in the Olympics at Helsinki in 1952 and at Melbourne in 1956. In Australia they led the world in unofficial points and gold medals. At the 1960 Olympics in Rome they scored 683 points as against the "runner-up" (USA) with 463.5. In 1959 Soviet athletes held 74 of 170 registered world records, with the ratio little changed since.

This record is paralleled in the arts, but with results more uneven and debatable and with no objective measures of accomplishment at hand. The old phrase *de gustibus non disputandum est* conceals the obvious fact that in esthetic matters all disputes are precisely about tastes, even though such disputes are necessarily inconclusive. Soviet artists, composers, and writers are among the privileged in that many of them are paid regular salaries and all receive generous royalties on their accepted works. Despite the post-Stalin "thaw," painting continues to espouse "socialist realism" or purely representational depiction and eschews "impressionism" and "abstract art." The results seem mediocre to most foreign observers. Soviet architecture continues to be dominated by a still-imperfect technology and by Stalin's preference for "wedding-cake" forms. Yet Stalingrad, totally destroyed in World War II, has been rebuilt on Greek models, while a new "functionalism" has been coming to the fore in Soviet building in recent years. In music Soviet art has attained its highest levels of creativity both in new composers— e.g., Shostakovich and Khachaturian—and in brilliant performers—e.g., Gilels, Oistrakh, Richter, et al. Soviet ballet remains superlative, as American audiences recognized with enthusiasm between 1958 and 1961 in viewing the performances of the Moiseyev dancers, the Beryozka ensemble, and the Bolshoi Ballet. Soviet operatic and theatrical performances, even in the provinces, have long since attained a standard of dramatic perfection and esthetic excitement which has few parallels in the West.

As for Soviet literature, this is not the place to attempt an evaluation of the merits of Russian writing in the Stalin era when all writers (if they hoped for publication) were required to conform to the canons of "socialist realism"—i.e., glorification of the accomplishments and aspirations of the Soviet economy. Neither can we attempt a critique of literature in the post-Stalin epoch—e.g., Mikhail Sholokhov's later works, Ilya Ehrenburg's *The Thaw,* Vladimir Dudinstvev's *Not by Bread Alone,* the works of the late Boris Pasternak (poetry, Shakespeare translations, and the highly controversial and widely misrepresented *Doctor Zhivago*), to say nothing of less well-known poets, dramatists, and novelists. More significant for the mass of Soviet

citizens is the advent of universal literacy and an insatiable
hunger for reading. What is available to the general public, apart
from scholars, is still censored and restricted. No ordinary citizen
can secure in bookstores or libraries any of the works of Sigmund
Freud, Alfred Adler, or Carl G. Jung; or of Trotsky or Bukharin;
or of anti-Soviet writers abroad; or, indeed, any publications
which deviate too widely from the current "Party line."

On the other hand, Soviet readers have available at small
cost, in all the major languages of the USSR and in editions of
scores of millions of copies, most or all of the works of Pushkin,
Tolstoy, Turgenev, Dostoevsky, Chekhov, and other giants of the
past, along with multi-millioned translations of Western writers,
including, among Americans, Longfellow, Mark Twain, Jack
London, O. Henry, Walt Whitman, Hemingway, Steinbeck,
et al. Public libraries in Russia numbered 16,000 in 1914 and
400,000 in 1960. Published books have totaled well over a billion
copies a year in recent years. Some 3,000 periodicals are published in 55 languages. Some 8,000 newspapers in 81 languages
are printed daily in the USSR. The literary market is seemingly
inexhaustible. The literature produced to supply the market,
albeit selective, is of sufficiently wide range to enable the average
avid reader (meaning almost everyone) to acquaint himself with
the classics of Russian and Western letters—and to think about
the implications of the teachings of the masters.

The most spectacular successes of the Soviet system of education (which is inseparably integrated with Party, Government,
and the Planned Economy) have been achieved in science and
technology. Here effective use has been made of the contributions of physicist Mikhail Lomonosov (1711–65), after whom
Moscow State University is named; chemist Dmiitri Mendeleyev
(1834–1907); mathematician Nikolai Lobachevsky (1792–1856);
physiologist Ivan Pavlov (1849–1936), who remains the high
priest of Soviet psychology and psychiatry; and sundry other
Russian pioneers in the natural sciences. Their contributions
to knowledge, plus systematic application and advancement of
their knowledge, supplemented by full familiarity with scientific
and technological discoveries and inventions abroad, have made
possible the industrialization of the USSR. All scientific research
is massively supported by public funds and directed by the Academy of Science (originally established by Peter the Great in 1724),
with local units in the Union Republics and specialized branches
and institutes throughout the land.

The total impact, for Russia and for the world, of these

earnest and brilliantly successful endeavors to unravel the mysteries of nature is outside the limits of our present inquiry. For proper perspective on world politics it will suffice to recall the most dramatic Soviet "firsts" along the ever-advancing frontiers of science. Following their breaking of the U.S. monopoly of atomic weapons in 1949 and their testing of the first Soviet H-bomb, November 23, 1955 (the first U.S. H-bomb was tested March 1, 1954), Soviet scientists in 1957 devised the first ICBM. The TU-104 became the first practical commercial jet liner. Thanks to an early lead over the USA in rocketry, the USSR launched the first Sputnik, October 4, 1957; sent the first rocket to the moon, September 13, 1959; and sent the first man into orbit around the earth in the space-ship *Vostok,* April 12, 1961.

On the third of these occasions, amid nation-wide festivities, the press depicted Yuri A. Gagarin, the world's first "cosmonaut," as a typical representative of the "new Soviet man." Aged 27 at the time of his epoch-making journey, he was the grandson of peasants and the son of a carpenter. At school he studied hard, loved sports, and won membership in the *Komsomols.* Beyond school he became a laborer before being admitted to an aviation academy and subsequently becoming a Major in the Air Force. He married a woman doctor. The couple had two children by 1961. Major Gagarin neither smokes nor drinks. He was admitted to the Party in 1960, a circumstance he described as "the biggest and brightest event in my life before this flight into space." As the world's first space traveler, his role will forever remain unique. But in social background, family life, and previous career he may indeed be deemed akin to many millions of members of the new Soviet generation.

Beyond the Horizon

What of things to come? If contemporary mankind refrains from using its new science to commit suicide, Soviet society will continue to evolve into new shapes, since change is the mark of every living and dynamic culture. Beyond the goal of surpassing America in pursuit of the abundant life, what ultimate purpose is sought to be served by the power-holders of the USSR? What design for community life is likely to be arrived at by 1970 or 1984 or 2000? Does the Soviet system of power and planning offer Man an opportunity at long last to become "master of his fate and captain of his soul"?

Such questions admit of no clear answers. But we may plausibly postulate, for reasons already suggested, that the Soviet future will involve no return to Stalinism but will display, in strange ways, a progressive democratization and liberalization of government, politics, and other human relationships—all long cramped within the confines of an intolerant totalitarianism. Such an evolution presupposes what is questionable—namely, continued abstention from the ancient sin of war on the part of all power-holders and policy-makers in all the world's great capitals. Yet we need not speculate about the probable impact of war on the destinies of the USSR, since any resort to war among Great Powers now means, almost certainly, the self-destruction of our common civilization. Far more useful will be a consideration of the vision of the future in the minds of the Marxists who rule Russia and who hope to fashion the future to accord with their dreams.

This image is blurred, as we shall see. It envisages an ultimate economy of super-abundance, a wholly classless and egalitarian society, and a "withering away of the State." Such are the vague lineaments of the "communism" of days to come when the distributive principle is to be: "From each according to his ability, to each according to his needs." The principle is again, without acknowledgment, of Biblical origin (see The Acts of the Apostles, 4:32–35). Meanwhile, under "socialism," the rule of distribution is: "From each according to his ability, to each according to his work." The Soviet socialist society is manifestly neither an egalitarian nor a classless society.

Since the matter is moot and much misunderstood, it is well to notice that neither Marx nor Engels nor Lenin nor Stalin nor Khrushchev nor any true Marxist anywhere ever urged equality of incomes or the end of classes under "socialism." At this stage, inequality of income is deemed inevitable, necessary, and desirable. Classes will persist, but they will not be antagonistic, since none can exploit another. The State will persist, for the State is defined in the gospels as an instrument of class rule, and the Socialist State is, by definition, the "dictatorship of the proletariat." Only with the ultimate advent of "communism" will classes vanish and the State accordingly disappear. Whether incomes will then be all the same is quite unclear, since people's "needs," however regarded, are not all the same—beyond the elementary necessities of life.

Precisely here we may find a clue to the Soviet future. There is no present reason to believe that Soviet society will ever become "classless" and "stateless" in the Marxist sense. But in pursuit of the vision the Marxist oligarchs are more than likely to embark upon further economic and social innovations with interesting consequences. If, as, and when the USSR achieves a super-abundance of goods and services, all housing may be free of rental costs, as all education and medical service are already free. Most or all direct taxes will be abolished. Basic foodstuffs, beginning with bread, will be free, with other goods and services gradually added to the list.

In a socialized and planned economy it is quite possible to supply shelter, a minimum diet, and a minimum wardrobe to all, without direct cost to the individual, by making these services and goods a community charge on the economy as a whole rather than private purchases for a price in the market. If elementary needs are thus met as a public service, the continuing and inevitable competition and emulation among producers and consumers for prestige, status, leisure, luxury, self-understanding, and self-improvement might well be raised to a higher plane than any hitherto known in earlier societies. Whether this would be good or bad, inspiring or demoralizing, creative or corrosive, no one can foresee, including the Marxist dreamers of a joyous tomorrow. Nor need we now try to answer questions which are presently unanswerable.

The fantasy here suggested is not "pie in the sky by and by when you die," but a real possibility in the USSR in the 1960's. Premier Khrushchev at a session of the Supreme Soviet, May 5, 1960, proposed the abolition of all direct taxes by way of graduated steps to raise tax exemptions. The new tax law of May 7 provided for such increases of exemptions until 1965, by which year workers and employees will no longer pay individual income taxes. Other Party directives and governmental measures during 1960 were designed to reduce inequality of income and to achieve a 40-hour week as a maximum for all workers by 1962. Economist S. G. Strumlin speculated in print in March, 1960, that by 1980 food and clothing would be available without charge to all Soviet citizens, free housing would be at hand for urban and rural workers alike, and all would work only four hours a day with leisure time devoted to sports, recreation, and education in a "truly comprehensive development of each person's aptitudes . . . in a society organized so that mankind as a whole will receive unlimited freedom for the harmonious development of creative potentialities."

Pending the advent of Utopia, the processes of mass educa-

tion, industrialization, and urbanization have led to a paradoxical fulfillment of Alexis de Tocqueville's prophecy of 1839
in his *Democracy in America* that Russia and America, "starting
from different points, tend toward the same end." By virtue of
unplanned trends of social change, commonly called "cultural
convergence" by anthropologists, the societies of America and
Russia, despite obvious ideological and institutional differences,
have become more and more alike. Both are societies of Big
Cities, sharing common problems of urban planning, slum clear-
ance, traffic jams, and suburban commuters. Both are societies of
Big Business and Big Labor, with comparable problems of management, public relations, and disputes over working conditions.
Both are under pressure to persuade consumers, through mass
advertising and installment buying, to increase consumption,
even though the pressure is recent in the USSR and has only
lately come to expression. Both are societies of Big Agriculture,
even though the Soviet farm problem is very different from the
American farm problem. Both are afflicted with, and concerned
about, juvenile delinquency; crime and divorce; graft and influence (*Blat* in the Soviet vocabulary) in business and government; alcoholism, hyper-tension, and neuroses among executives, and often among humble folk working under great pressures or confused by the bewilderments of a new and dangerous
era. Communists attribute these problems at home to "bourgeois
survivals" and to "capitalist decadence" abroad. Anti-Communists ascribe them to Soviet tyranny. Both are in error. These
are the common problems of all industrial societies, whether
"socialist" or "capitalist."

By sharing experiences through travel and "cultural exchanges," Russians and Americans can help one another to
cope with these issues and with many others of common concern.
The political leaders and publicists of both communities have
preferred in the 1950's and early 1960's to cry havoc and
preach enmity, fear, suspicion, and hatred—with probable results best deferred for consideration to our final chapter. In
the interim, the ultimate shape of Soviet society, as fashioned
by its rulers and planners, is still obscure. The best laid plans
of mice and men, Robert Burns reminds us, "gang aft agley."
The final goal, often betrayed by stupidity, greed, cruelty, and
irrationality over forty years, is a polity, economy, and society
in which responsible and dedicated rulers can achieve something never hitherto achieved in human affairs: a Good Society
in which, for the first time in the human adventure, men and

women are safeguarded, as far as is possible through organized community efforts, against the vicissitudes of misfortune; are free from want and fear; and are enabled to attain self-expression and self-fulfillment not alone in pursuit of private purposes but together in pursuit of public purposes.

This vision has inspired many crimes on the part of those who have pursued it with fanaticism. It has also inspired many notable contributions to human health, wealth, and welfare. Some among us regard the vision as abhorrent, since it postulates the subservience of the individual to the political and social totality. Others among us view the vision as the possible dawn of a new age in which human beings may find freedom from ancient ills through sharing common aspirations for a good life. The experiences of a single generation since Russia's October Revolution constitute too short a span of time, against the 7,000 years of civilization, to warrant any definitive conclusions. The Marxist masters of Muscovy have perpetrated much evil and accomplished much good, by any available standards of good and evil. As for the end result of their labors (if any finality is possible in such matters), Western observers would be well advised to suspend judgment, to avoid simplicist dichotomies of vice and virtue, and to hope that evils may wane and that goods may wax, and that the creative accomplishments of the rulers and peoples of the USSR will redound, without subjection to Communist tyranny, to the benefit of humanity.

7 - Russia and the World

Portraits of Evil

When neighbors are defined as enemies and enemies are defined as devils, no tolerable human relations are possible. This is as true of Great Powers, nation-states, and disciples of cults and creeds as it is true of lesser communities, families, and individuals. Among the many tragedies of the 20th Century, a central tragedy, contributing in sundry ways to many others, has been the persisting pattern of mutual distrust, fear, and

hatred between the rulers of Russia and the rulers of the
Western Powers. But for this pattern, World War II need
never have come to pass. Should mankind ever commit the final
folly of World War III, the ultimate holocaust will again be
directly attributable to the prevailing American anti-Communist
neurosis and to the prevailing Soviet anti-Capitalist syndrome.

We need not here discuss the problem of whether it is
normal or pathological for human communities to attribute all
virtue to themselves and all vice to their rivals or foes. Suffice it
to note that these ancient impulses of ethnocentrism continue
to thrust themselves upward through the unconscious from a
primitive past into a global civilization where they have no
place. They drive men to dread and to rage and to violence on
a mass scale. Such behavior, more brutish than that of the brutes,
can only spell in our time the total disintegration of the fabric
of culture and the possible self-immolation of *Homo sapiens*.

Any approach to the study of Soviet foreign policy which
postulates a monopoly of virtue on the part of the "Free World"
against a monopoly of vice on the part of the USSR and its
allies—or, conversely, any approach which presupposes the
antithesis of the postulate here suggested—will lead to no light.
Monodiabolism, whether Communist or anti-Communist, can
only promote a holy war for the forcible conversion of heretics
or the violent extermination of infidels. In the thermonuclear
age Western Civilization cannot afford any such ecstasy of brutality.

Equally futile, if we hope for survival, is the widespread
American premise that negotiation with Communists is impossible because Communists are bent upon "world conquest" or
"world domination." The rulers of Russia cherish exactly the
same counter-image of the USA. Communists, like all disciples
of Messianic cults, aspire to the universalization of their beliefs
and practices in the name of saving mankind from sin. No one
who has ever experienced a profound dedication to a value-
system promising human salvation has ever believed or acted
otherwise. Such was the conviction and hope of early Christians,
pristine Moslems, the first Protestants, the French Jacobins, and
various disciples of universalistic creeds ever since, including
democracy, Marxism, Fascism, and all the other competing
ideologies of the 20th Century. None has ever succeeded in
conquering or converting all mankind. All have indulged in
subversion, revolution, and war to promote their goals and
thereby condemned millions to premature death by the violence

of man's inhumanity to man. All have failed to attain their end and at long last have made peace, however reluctantly, with their enemies—as an eventuality finally deemed preferable to an endless and hopeless war of mutual extermination. Once again, contemporary mankind cannot afford any such reversion to crusades and religious wars, since the most probable outcome would not be a belated truce, after the mutual murder of millions of human beings, but the abrupt thermonuclear co-annihilation of most or all of the human race.

An old Russian proverb asserts that soup is never eaten as hot as it is cooked. Those who aspire to "rule the world" and to "bury their enemies" have never achieved success in their enterprise since the long lost days of ancient Rome. There is no reason to suppose that this age-old pattern of failure is likely to be altered in the remaining decades of the 20th Century. Sophisticated Communists are fully aware of this certainty, even if many anti-Communists are not. The latter tend to forget that an affirmation can never be countered effectively by a negation in the minds and hearts of men. The power-holders and policy-makers of the Communist bloc, despite their doctrine and rhetoric, have displayed a disposition to negotiate a *modus vivendi* with their enemies. This stance has been widely interpreted in the West as a more subtle means of victory. So indeed it is.

Western response to challenge has thus far assumed the form of massive military preparations to resist Communist armed aggression—than which nothing was or is less likely. Some dim inklings of the need for a different response were visible on clouded horizons at the turn of the decade—with results, if any, unclear. Meanwhile, the puzzling problems of Soviet foreign policy and of the relations of the USSR with the non-Communist and anti-Communist majority of mankind require—for intelligibility, analysis, and prediction—a frame of reference wholly different from vulgar dichotomies of virtue and vice and popular Western distinction between those who seek to "enslave the world" and those who are defending "freedom."

Such a fresh frame of reference is not easy to come by, nor is it likely to gain wide acceptance in view of persisting habits of old response to challenge. Yet new thought may be devoted, with possibly fruitful results, to an alternative context within which illumination may be sought regarding Russian relations with the non-Russian world. Like all rulers of all "Great Powers" in the Western State System which has long since become global), the Marxist oligarchs of Muscovy have been confronted from the outset of their rule with the problem of security against the hostile designs, actual or potential, of other rulers of rival "Great Powers" seeking security by maximizing the insecurity of Russia. The pattern is as old as the System and long antedates the Russian Revolution. In quest of safety in an insecure world the policy-makers of all "Great Powers" have at their disposal, depending on circumstances, four options: (1) Security by Supremacy; (2) Security by Balance; (3) Security by Coalition; and (4) Security by playing the role of "Happy Third" or *Tertius Gaudens*.

The first option postulates a goal which many policy-makers of "Great Powers" have pursued and none has attained in recent centuries—i.e., the subjugation of all rival Powers and the achievement of global hegemony or "World Government" through the submission of all to one. The second option is "isolationism," which is a safe pattern of policy when other Powers are so evenly balanced against one another as to preclude any imminent danger to the Power adopting such a posture. The third possible policy is one of cooperation with less dangerous rival Powers against more dangerous rival Powers in a Grand Alliance or Great Coalition in the hope (often vain) of deterring aggression or, at worst, winning victory in war. The fourth possibility—*Tertius Gaudens*—is a variant, in desperate circumstances, of the second—i.e., the hope of non-involvement and neutrality when military conflict is imminent among rival Great Powers, with limited aid to the weaker side for the purpose of promoting the mutual exhaustion of the contestants. In the words of a U.S. Senator on the occasion of the Nazi invasion of Russia: "If we see that Germany is winning we ought to help Russia and if Russia is winning we ought to help Germany and in that way let them kill as many as possible" (Harry S. Truman, *NYT*, June 24, 1941).

The Politics of Insecurity

The fluctuating foreign policy of the USSR during the past four decades can be rendered intelligible, as can those of other Powers, by reference to the options suggested above—always bearing in mind that policy-makers, like other humans, are fallible and capable of mistakes of calculation, with results, in a State System based on the assumption of violence, which are often tragic. The history of Soviet diplomacy is readily available in many other books and is no part of our present task. The record may, nevertheless, be usefully reviewed in outline within the context already indicated.

The confusions and miscalculations in foreign affairs which followed the October Revolution have been touched upon above (see pp. 48–53). Between the summer of 1918 and early 1921 Soviet policy-makers actively sought to promote World Revolution while the Allied and Associated Powers strove to destroy the Soviet regime through blockade, invasion, and subsidized civil war. With the failure of both enterprises, the antagonists found themselves stalemated and made a peace of sorts in March, 1921, with British *de facto* recognition of the Soviet Government, the conclusion of an Anglo-Soviet trade agreement, and the signature of the Russo-Polish Treaty of Riga. A year later at Genoa Soviet and Western delegates strove without success to negotiate a settlement of financial claims and counter-claims. Georgi Chicherin and Walter Rathenau made use of the occasion to sign the Treaty of Rapallo (April 16, 1922), whereby Moscow and Berlin canceled all claims against one another, entered into full diplomatic and commercial relations, and embarked upon a decade of German-Russian political and even military collaboration between outcasts against the dominant French bloc on the Continent.

In the 1920's and early 1930's both the USSR and the USA, in their several ways, were committed to Security by Balance, thanks to the stability of relationships among other Powers in Europe and Asia. But there was no collaboration between them in the absence of American recognition—not accorded until November 16, 1933. Soviet policy, unlike its American counterpart, was by no means strictly "isolationist." The *Narkomindel* (People's Commissariat for Foreign Affairs), directed by Chicherin and presently by the wily Maxim Litvinov, sought safety by concluding bilateral non-aggression and neutrality pacts designed to localize any conflicts which might occur and by championing disarmament and the outlawry of war.

The USSR was the first Great Power to ratify the Kellogg-Briand Pact of Paris of 1928 for renunciation of war as an instrument of national policy—and the first Great Power to espouse, at Geneva in 1927 and thereafter, complete and universal disarmament (with tongue in cheek in the certain knowledge that the "bourgeois States" would never assent). These hopes of the 1920's came to nothing, thanks to gross mismanagement of human affairs in Russia and the West alike. This period of Soviet foreign policy reached its culmination in the signature of non-aggression and neutrality pacts with Poland (July 25, 1932) and with France (November 29, 1932) and with Litvinov's signature in early July, 1933, at the otherwise abortive London Economic Conference, of bilateral accords with most of Russia's neighboring states, plus some others, defining and renouncing "aggression."

All these bright words were soon to be reduced to waste paper. They took no cognizance of the realities of power politics in a State System of rival sovereignties nor of the need of somehow bringing into being some semblance of World Federal Government as a substitute for the traditional imperatives of *Realpolitik*. The wasted opportunities of the 1920's were doubly or trebly wasted anew during the dark decade of the 1930's.

The earlier Soviet formula for safety served Soviet interests well so long as other Powers were balanced in a more or less stable equilibrium. The pre-condition vanished with the advent of the Great Depression. The New York stock market crash in the fall of 1929 was soon followed by economic stagnation, mass unemployment for workers, mass bankruptcy for businessmen and farmers, and mass misery and desperation for scores of millions of people in all the "capitalist" economies of the world. This *débâcle* was mistaken in Moscow for a vindication of the Marxist prognosis. New images of proletarian revolution loomed up. But such dreams remained dreams. The major political result of the Great Depression was the coming to power in Japan (1930 f.) and in Germany (1933 f.) of local imitators of the Italian Fascists of the 1920's. The new Caesars "solved" all social problems, in corrupt cooperation with industrialists, aristocrats, and the demented masses of the lower middle classes, by preaching a crusade to "save civilization from Communism," to the tune of massive rearmament, military adventures, and open preparations to take over the world from the faltering hands of the Western democracies.

Hitler in *Mein Kampf* had made it crystal clear that his projected path to world power must lead not only to the subjugation of the West but to the destruction and partition of the USSR. His prospective allies, Mussolini's Blackshirts and the militarists of Nippon, were similarly oriented. In the 1930's, as in the 1960's, in the minds of millions of muddle-headed people in the democracies, anti-Communism was a badge of impeccable respectability—in the name of which sundry lunacies, outrages, and crimes (up to a point) could be condoned and even applauded. The madmen of Berlin, Tokyo, and Rome therefore cloaked their conspiracy from the outset in the garb of the "Anti-Comintern" Pact of November 25, 1936, and shouted daily that their only ultimate objective was "the destruction of Bolshevism." In the face of an ever-mounting menace, Moscow's response was an abrupt abandonment of its previous pattern of policy, a rapid build-up of armed forces, and a search for Security by Coalition.

In the course of the quest, Soviet diplomacy and Communist Parties achieved successes which, had they not later been undone, might well have averted World War II. The Communist International held its 7th (and, as matters turned out, its last) Congress in mid-summer of 1935. The "line" now was no longer "class war" and "proletarian revolution," but a "united front" with Socialists and liberals against Fascism. Anti-Fascist "Popular Front" coalitions won elections in Spain in February and in France in April and May of 1936. Meanwhile the USSR joined the League of Nations (September 18, 1934)—from which Japan (March 27, 1933), Germany (October 14, 1933), and Italy (December 11, 1937) withdrew—and concluded military alliances, in the guise of pacts to uphold Arts. 10 and 16 of the League Covenant, with France (May 2, 1935) and Czechoslovakia (May 16, 1935). France was allied with Britain, Belgium, Poland, and the "Little Entente" of Czechoslovakia, Rumania, and Jugoslavia. The USA was paralyzed by "isolationism," reflected in the "neutrality" laws of 1935–39 which, in the name of keeping America out of "other people's wars," helped to make the world safe for aggression. But the new Grand Alliance had overwhelming power at its disposal to "deter" and "contain" Fascist ambitions of world hegemony.

How and why all of this was thrown away, with resultant tragedy for all mankind, is a problem of human irrationality and political miscalculation which men may debate, inconclusively, from now until doomsday. In any case it is clear from the record that the men of Moscow, despite their many mistakes before and after the advent of disaster, bore no responsibility for impending catastrophe during the middle 1930's. Year after year Litvinov's eloquent voice at Geneva pleaded for "collective security" and the solidarity of the USSR and the Western democracies in resisting Fascist aggression. Year after year policy-makers in London and Paris rejected all proposals for collective action, acquiesced in Fascist aggression, and finally brought their nations to the brink of ruin. Their motives were mixed, as all human motives are mixed. Some, dreading war, sought peace by "appeasement" of the Caesars. Others hoped that the Western Powers could play the role of *Tertius Gaudens* in the war to come, while Hitler's Germany and Tojo's Japan assaulted the USSR. All were mistaken in their evaluation of the Fascist threat. All feared and distrusted the USSR more than they distrusted and feared the Fascist dictators—which attitude in the end was fully reciprocated by Stalin's policy-makers in Moscow, with ghastly results for all concerned.

Only a few highlights need be noted in the mad diplomacy of the wasted years. Japan's warlords seized Manchuria in September of 1931 and subsequently made military probes into Mongolia and Soviet Siberia. Moscow and Peiping pleaded for international action, through the League of Nations, against aggression. London and Paris refused. Washington was impotent. In 1937 Tokyo's militarists launched an all-out assault on Chiang Kai-shek's China. Pleas for help evoked no response in Western capitals. Moscow extended limited aid to China and beat back Japanese incursions in a series of border battles. Meanwhile, Hitler (March 16, 1935) repudiated Part V of the Treaty of Versailles, providing for German disarmament, and reintroduced military conscription in the Nazi Reich. Moscow urged action. London and Paris did nothing beyond diplomatic protests. In October, 1935, Mussolini ordered his armies to conquer Ethiopia. Moscow urged action. London and Paris, behind a hypocritical façade of League "sanctions," did nothing, wrecked the League, and finally accepted the Fascist conquest. Hitler (March 7, 1936) abrogated the Locarno treaties and began the remilitarization of the Rhineland, thereby making impossible any defense by France of its Eastern allies. Moscow urged action. Paris and London did nothing.

The rest of the tragedy was destined to unroll with the inexorability of a Greek drama. Franco, massively aided by Hitler and Mussolini, undertook the overthrow by armed violence of the Spanish Republic in mid-summer of 1936. Moscow extended help to the Loyalists and pleaded once more for concerted action against aggression. London and Paris, in the name of "non-intervention," connived in the Fascist conquest of Spain, as did Washington in the name of "neutrality." When Hitler ordered his *Wehrmacht* to invade, occupy, and annex Austria (March 12, 1938), the pattern was repeated. By the following summer Neville Chamberlain was thrice flying to Germany—on the principle: "If you don't concede the first time, fly, fly

again"—for the purpose of helping Hitler, in the name of
"peace," to destroy Czechoslovakia. Moscow proposed common
action and offered to defend Czechoslovakia, by war if need be,
if the Western Powers would cooperate. Chamberlain and Halifax, Daladier and Bonnet, went instead to Munich and signed
the "Peace" settlement of October 1, 1938, whereby Hitler was
authorized to annex the Sudetenland, containing all the Czech
border fortifications, and to reduce what was left of Czechoslovakia to helplessness. Chamberlain and Halifax signed a
neutrality and non-aggression pact with Hitler, October 1. Daladier and Bonnet did likewise in Paris, December 6, 1938.

With the League Covenant and the Grand Alliance treaties
all thus cast to the winds while the Fascist Caesars triumphantly
rode "the wave of the future," the men of Moscow were obliged
to reconsider their course—as Stalin indicated to Congress
XVIII in his address of March 10, 1939, denouncing the Western
"appeasers" and "Munichmen." Four days later Hitler occupied
Prague and extinguished the remnant of Czechoslovakia. Subsequent British efforts to negotiate a new alliance with the USSR
came to nothing. Western policy-makers so deeply feared and
distrusted Communists, who fully reciprocated their sentiments,
that the common menace of Fascist aggression, threatening all
with destruction, was insufficient to reconstruct the Great Coalition which had so rashly been thrown away. London refused to
pay Moscow's price for an alliance: a joint guarantee of Finland, Estonia, Latvia, Lithuania, Poland, and Rumania—none
of which desired any such guarantee and all of which dreaded
the prospect of being defended by the Red Army. Moscow refused to conclude an alliance on any other terms.

Since Hitler and Ribbentrop were quite prepared to pay a
price for Soviet neutrality which Anglo-French leaders were
unwilling to pay for an alliance, Stalin and Molotov, in an
abrupt reversal of course, abandoned Security by Coalition in
favor of the role of *Tertius Gaudens,* thus out-Chamberlaining
Chamberlain—with equally dismal results. The Nazi-Soviet
non-aggression and neutrality pact of August 23, 1939, con-
tained a secret protocol contemplating a new partition of Poland
and the division of Eastern Europe into German and Soviet
spheres of influence. But contrary to contemporary judgments,
oft repeated since, the Nazi *Blitzkrieg* against Poland, launched
on September 1, was not the consequence of the Nazi-Soviet pact
since, as is now known, the decision had secretly been reached
and even the date had been set by Hitler and his aides in April

of 1939. The pact was the consequence of the decision, and of almost certain Soviet knowledge of the decision, not *vice versa*.

The miseries and horrors which engulfed most of the human race, including above all the USSR, in the wake of the follies which have been reviewed are well known and have been recounted in detail in other places: how the Kremlin sent troops into eastern Poland in mid-September; imposed protectorates on Estonia, Latvia, and Lithuania and, in violation of its own solemn treaty obligations, waged the "winter war" on Finland (with Britain and France absurdly threatening to fight the Soviet Union instead of the Nazi Reich) and, in March, 1940, imposed peace terms and frontier changes designed, like other Soviet moves of 1939–41, to bolster defenses against Hitler; how "phony war" gave way in the frightful spring of 1940 to further *Blitzkrieg*, with the invincible *Wehrmacht* conquering Denmark, Norway, the Low Countries, and France—as Mussolini entered the conflict for the "kill"; how the USA awakened in alarm from its isolationist dream, extended aid to Britain, and soon embarked on "lend-lease" assistance to all of Hitler's foes; how the USSR in alarm annexed Estonia, Latvia, and Lithuania along with Bessarabia and Northern Bukovina while seeking continued peace with the triumphant Reich; how Hitler in 1940, like Bonaparte in 1811, having lost his "Battle of Britain," decided to conquer Russia; how the assault was delayed in the spring of 1941 as the *Wehrmacht* occupied Hungary and Rumania and struck down Jugoslavia and Greece; and how all the combined armies of Fascist Europe hurled themselves against the Soviet Union on June 22, 1941, in the most savage, deadly, and destructive invasion in the history of modern warfare.

Security by Coalition now became, almost too late, the price of survival. The USSR, like the USA after Pearl Harbor, was forced by enemy attack to become the full ally of Britain in a new Grand Alliance. Prospects remained dark in 1941–42. Moscow had contracted out of war in the Far East, as Japan contracted out of Hitler's crusade against Russia, in the Soviet-Japanese neutrality and non-aggression pact of April 13, 1941. In all other respects almost all the world was at war in a far-flung combat for mastery of the planet between the Fascist Triplice and the "United Nations"—most of whose lesser members in 1942 were "governments-in-exile." The *Wehrmacht*, having destroyed or dispersed all the Soviet armies in its path, reached the outskirts of Moscow by December, 1941. But here, for the first time, Hitler's hosts were halted and driven back by new Russian armies defending the Motherland. By mid-summer of 1942, however, Japanese forces had overrun much of China, all of Southeastern Asia and Indonesia, and all of the islands of the Western Pacific, while the armies of the European Axis were threatening Egypt and had reached the Caucasus and the Volga in another victory march—soon to be accompanied by the most hideous atrocities in all the record of human brutality as the Nazi psychopaths undertook the systematic extermination of all Jews and most Slavs who had fallen into their power.

In the sequel we must confine our attention—amid a global phantasmagoria of Fascist insanity, heroic underground resistance in the occupied lands, and massive battles between the largest armies of all time—to the pattern of Grand Strategy which was to determine the shape of the post-war world. Despite pledges and promises and urgent appeals from Moscow, Britain and the USA were unable or unwilling to open any effective "second front" against the Reich in the West until the Normandy landings of June, 1944. The North African and Italian campaign of 1942–43, albeit clearing the Maghreb of the foe and bringing Sicily and southern Italy under Allied occupation, offered no meaningful relief to the hard-pressed defenders of the USSR. Even American lend-lease supplies to the Soviet Union, ultimately totaling $11,000,000,000, still remained a trickle in 1942 and most of 1943. Russia's fighters—who, in Churchill's phrase, "did the main work of tearing the guts out of the German army"—were long obliged to rely for victory on their own valor and on the output of the Soviet war industries. Both were to prove equal to the needs of a time of desperation.

The turning point of the war in Europe was the savage and protracted Battle of Stalingrad, beginning in August of 1942 and ending with the final surrender (February 1, 1943) of the wretched survivors of Von Paulus's encircled Sixth Army. Henceforth the hitherto unconquerable *Wehrmacht* was to suffer defeat after defeat all across the Russian steppes, with Soviet forces finally overrunning Rumania, Bulgaria, and Hungary in late 1944, and, early in 1945, taking Warsaw, Vienna, Prague, and, at the end, Berlin—where Hitler and Eva Braun, following the example of Goebbels and his family, committed suicide on April 30, 1945, a week before the unconditional surrender of the shattered defenders of a now defunct Reich.

Churchill had hoped that Anglo-American forces might liberate the Balkans and much of Central Europe before the arrival of the Russians. Washington vetoed the project as militarily impossible. Making a virtue of necessity, Churchill and Eden journeyed to Moscow in October, 1944, and struck a bargain with Stalin and Molotov for a division of Southeastern Europe into "spheres," with Greece to be in the British zone, Bulgaria and Rumania in the Soviet zone, and influence to be shared in Hungary and Jugoslavia—all of which indeed came to pass, except for Hungary, in ways then unforeseen. Washington was shocked at such "immorality." The tangled tale of the Yalta (February, 1945) and Potsdam (July, 1945) "summit conferences," where vague formulas were bandied about, written ambiguously into solemn agreements, and given wholly different interpretations in Moscow, London, and Washington, cannot here be told. Let us only note that the Grand Strategy of the Great Coalition in World War II brought Russian troops and Russian power to the Adriatic, the Danube, and the Elbe—with consequences still unchanged in the early 1960's.

The Last Question

The first question posed by the fall of the Third Reich and by the subsequent surrender of Japan (August 14, 1945) was the question of whether the USSR, the USA, and the UK could continue to cooperate in making a peace as they had cooperated in winning a war. By prior agreement at Yalta, the USSR played a brief role in the defeat of Japan through a one-week *Blitzkrieg* into Manchuria, while the USA, not to be outdone by its enemies in the science of atrocity, initiated a new and ghastly era in the arts of war by the atomic bombing of Hiroshima (August 6) and Nagasaki (August 9). The first question was soon answered. Immediately after Japanese capitulation, London and Washington, perceiving that Stalin was resolved to impose Communist regimes on all the lands of Eastern Europe, Danubia, and Balkania north of Greece and to establish a *cordon sanitaire* in reverse against the West, began to challenge Soviet policy and to demand "democracy" and "self-determination" for the new Soviet "satellites," as allegedly pledged at Yalta and Potsdam.

The "Cold War" was thus begun. Its history is not our present concern, since here again the details of victories and defeats, advances and retreats, maneuvers and counter-maneuvers, calculations and miscalculations, are readily available in many other books. Its origin, however, is worthy of further comment. Soviet power was imposed on much of Eastern Europe, 1944–48, by virtue of Anglo-American incapacity to get there first. This disability, in turn, was due to the fruits of the "Peace" of Munich in 1938, for at Munich the Western statesmen not only betrayed Czechoslovakia but surrendered Eastern Europe to Hitler without quite knowing what they were doing. The results, as a few of us predicted at the time, would be either a Nazi-Soviet partition of Eastern Europe, Nazi control of Eastern Europe, or, in the event of the final collapse of the Third Reich, Communist control of Eastern Europe. All of these results materialized *seriatim* in the aftermath of Munich.

In world politics, as in other human affairs, decisions have consequences which are often irreversible. The Cold War began with Western efforts to reverse the consequences of Munich and with Soviet efforts to perpetuate, and capitalize upon, the consequences of Munich. Thus far, by the early 1960's, Western attempts to "liberate" Eastern Europe and to "roll back" Soviet power to pre-war frontiers have failed altogether of their purposes, while Soviet attempts to maintain the *status quo* of 1945 f. have been largely successful—with the notable exception of Jugoslavia, where Stalin's misconceived efforts at coercion drove Tito's indigenous Communist regime into "neutralism" in 1948 and acceptance of diplomatic and economic support from the West.

The global pattern of Cold War soon became, once more, the age-old pattern of Security by Coalition in a temporarily bipolar world—in which, thanks to the advent of the thermonuclear age, old patterns and ancient assumptions of violence in international relations are wholly obsolete if the human race is to have any hope of survival. But all humans, Communists and anti-Communists alike, are creatures of habit who, in the face of new dangers, resort to old formulas because they lack sufficient imagination to devise new departures.

In the world following World War II, as in the world preceding World War II, mutual distrust, fear, and suspicion between the Marxist rulers of Russia and the policy-makers of the Western democracies were the dominant themes of their relationships. The Marxists of Moscow feared, with much reason, that the "bourgeois imperialists" of the West were resolved to rob them of the fruits of victory and, if possible, to suppress Communism all over the world and to destroy the Soviet regime in the USSR itself. The leaders of the West feared, with much reason, that the "Communist imperialists" of the East were resolved to "take over the world" and to crush democracy, civil

liberties, and private business enterprise all over the globe. Both
fears, however justified by a selective compilation of supporting
evidence, were unrealistic and, indeed, irrational in terms of
the immense dangers to all concerned in action thus motivated
by fear. But 20th-Century Man, as Spengler, Toynbee, and the
psychoanalysts have long since pointed out, is less rational than
non-rational or irrational and therefore seeks to solve new problems with old solutions.

The result was a new arms race of unprecedented magnitude, intensity, and peril and the emergence of two rival military
coalitions, each determined to "deter" the other from "aggression" by accumulating thermonuclear weapons, and each quite
capable of destroying the other utterly in any test of force. The
West, led by the USA, began the game of "defense" and "deterrence" by seeking to prolong the short-lived American atomic
monopoly, by ringing the USSR with bombing bases in the
name of "containment," by threatening "massive retaliation"
(meaning the thermonuclear massacre of millions of people), and
by concocting a series of anti-Soviet alliances. The sequence
began with the Truman Doctrine of March, 1947, inspired by
Soviet threats to Greece and Turkey, and the Marshall Plan of
1947 f., designed to restore the economies of Western Europe.
The sequence proceeded with NATO (April 4, 1949), following
the Communist coup of February in Czechoslovakia and the un-
successful Soviet blockade, 1948–49, of West Berlin; U.S. and
U.N. defense of South Korea in June, 1950 f., against invasion
from Communist North Korea; and an American treaty of
peace and alliance with Japan (September 8, 1951), postulating
Japanese rearmament against Russia; alliance agreements with
the Philippine Republic (August 30, 1951) and with Australia
and New Zealand (September 1, 1951); a treaty of peace and
alliance with West Germany (May 26, 1952), postulating German rearmament against Russia; SEATO (September 6, 1954),
embracing the USA, Britain, France, Australia, New Zealand,
Pakistan, Thailand, and the Philippines; the Baghdad Pact of
November 22, 1955 (Britain, Turkey, Iran, Iraq, and Pakistan),
renamed CENTO when Iraq withdrew in 1958; alliance with
Chiang Kai-shek on Formosa (proclaimed an American "pro-
tectorate" in June, 1950), December 2, 1954; and a whole series
of other products of American "pactomania," designed to confront the Communist bloc with avowed enemies around all its
frontiers in the name of defense of "freedom"—though many

of the members of the Grand Alliance of the "Free World" had no knowledge of the meaning of the term.

Communist response to challenge (or counter-challenge) assumed a simpler and less ambitious form. Soviet policy-makers in the late 1940's contented themselves with bilateral security pacts with the Communist-controlled regimes of the European satellites. Stalin's miscalculations lost Jugoslavia to the Communist bloc in 1948 through the expulsion of the Jugoslav Party from the Cominform or Communist Information Bureau, a loose association, as successor to the Comintern (dissolved in 1943), of European Communist Parties. (The Cominform was dissolved in 1956 in an effort, only partially successful, to achieve a *détente* with Tito.) When the Chinese Communists, led by Mao Tse-tung, Chou En-lai, and Chu Teh, conquered China in 1948–49, contrary to Stalin's advice and expectations, most Americans, including Dean Rusk, avowed that Russia had "taken over" China, than which nothing could have been farther from the truth. Making the best of an unanticipated and not altogether welcome contingency, the policy-makers of the USSR concluded an alliance (February 14, 1950) with Red Peking, and subsequently gave up Soviet privileges in Manchuria and granted economic and technical aid to their giant ally. Not until May 14, 1955, did Moscow consolidate its ties with its European satellites into the multilateral alliance treaty of the Warsaw Pact.

The complex and confused relationships between the two Great Coalitions, increasingly complicated by the emergence of more and more new nations in Africa and Asia committed to "neutralism," we must leave to other chroniclers and commentators. The "score" admits of no precise calculation. Since all the world is governed with little wisdom, each side has gained more from the mistakes and stupidities of the other than from any successful pursuit of its own purposes.

Thus Western prestige was enhanced by Stalin's vain attempt to overthrow Tito; by the 1953 riots in East Germany; by Khrushchev's "de-Stalinization" campaign, which contributed to bewilderment and defections among Communists elsewhere and to the Polish "revolution" of 1956, acquiesced in by Moscow, and to the Hungarian rebellion of 1956, brutally repressed by Soviet troops—albeit in the latter instance the USA also suffered "loss of face" by virtue of encouragement to the "freedom fighters" via the Voice of America and Radio Free Europe, followed by total inability to give them any aid without risking a world war. By the same token, Soviet prestige was enhanced by the success of American "cloak-and-dagger" operators in overthrowing the Leftist government of Guatemala in 1954, thus reviving hatred of "Yankee imperialism" throughout Latin America; by the incredible ineptitude of the Eisenhower Administration in dealing with the U-2 incident and the ensuing fiasco of the Paris "Summit" in May of 1960; and by the even more incredible ineptitude of the Kennedy Administration in launching the abortive anti-Castro invasion of Cuba in April of 1961. Both lists could be multiplied almost indefinitely from the record of the 1950's and early 1960's—with appropriate attention to Lebanon, Egypt, Formosa, Laos, the Congo, and all other areas of conflict.

But if we are seriously concerned with the survival of Western civilization and of the human race, all such efforts at estimating who is "winning" or "losing" the Cold War and the arms race are irrelevant and futile. The somber fact of the matter is that a perpetuation of the contest on the terms accepted by both sides since 1945 threatens mankind with irreparable calamity, as all "neutralists" know and as some Americans and Russians and even some Chinese begin to suspect. The prospective *débâcle* does not have its source in any likelihood of a deliberate decision to resort to war on the part of policy-makers in Moscow or Washington or Peking or any other major capital. It lies in the inevitability, in the absence of accord among the Big Three to halt the thermonuclear arms race, of the diffusion of atomic weapons to more and more countries within the next few years—Sweden, China, Israel, Egypt, Cuba, Guinea, and . . . ?—and in the certainty that, by accident or design, some of the bombs will be detonated within another few years. The prospect of doomsday is brought nearer by a circumstance which is already a fact and not a fear for the future—i.e., that in the era of the ICBM, "warning time" of enemy attack, real or imagined, is reduced to fifteen minutes, thereby making impossible any decision-making by national decision-makers and leaving the fate of the human race in the hands of nervous bomber pilots, fallible radar scanners, anxious rocket crews, and other jittery technicians—to whose judgments the human race has no right whatever to trust its survival or extinction.

A mythical Man from Mars or Woman from Venus, observing the human scene in the 1950's and 1960's, would take it for granted, on the dubious assumption of human rationality, that responsible leaders on both sides of the prospective battle line would be appalled by the probability of things to come and would exert every effort to negotiate a *modus vivendi* as a last hope for life on earth. Such an outcome seemed improbable. Soviet spokesmen, while preaching "peaceful coexistence," continued, from the loftiest of patriotic motives, to postulate the inevitable triumph of Communism all over the world—i.e., the destruction of capitalism. American spokesmen, while espousing peace, continued, also from the loftiest of patriotic motives, to postulate the inevitable triumph of democracy all over the world—i.e., the destruction of Communism. The slogans on both sides had become meaningless. Mutual hatred, suspicion, distrust, and fear were the governing realities of a new "time of troubles" which threatened the suicide of the human species.

Yet there is assuredly a chance that *Homo sapiens,* however misgoverned and anxiety-ridden, may yet "muddle through," with both armed camps, increasingly influenced by the "third force" of the Neutralists, abandoning in fact, if not in form, neurotic visions of destroying the "enemy" and universalizing an ideology. In this blessed event, the terms of a future settlement are already visible through the fog of past mistakes. The multilateral treaty of 1959, to which both the USA and the USSR are parties, for the denuclearization, demilitarization, and neutralization of Antarctica must become the model for a global treaty on Outer Space. Germany must either remain permanently partitioned, in which case some new status for West Berlin will be unavoidable, or be reunited on the bases proposed by Prime Minister Anthony Eden at the Geneva Summit Conference of July, 1955, derived from the model of the Austrian treaty of May 15, 1955, and subsequently embodied in the Rapacki Plans of 1957–58 which Moscow warmly endorsed —i.e., disengagement, demilitarization, and neutralization. "Liberation" of Eastern Europe from Soviet control is also possible on a comparable basis and not at all possible on any other basis. Moscow must abandon its insistence on total and universal disarmament, which is quite impossible, and accept some form of controlled and inspected reduction and limitation of armaments. Washington must abandon its insistence on 100% "fool-proof" schemes of inspection, which are also quite impossible, and accept some measure of mutual good faith in efforts to end the arms race.

Given these boons, a new Concert of Power can infuse new life into the UN, vastly enhance its political efficacy, and focus serious attention on its gradual transformation in the direction of a limited World Federal Government—under which, in a necessarily diverse and pluralistic world society, all peoples may live in peace. Given these boons, East and West can cooperate, instead of competing, in promoting peace, order, and economic development in the Middle East, Southern Asia, Africa, and Latin America and can find ways and means of readmitting vast China into the community of nations without "loss of face" or increased insecurity for either the USA, the USSR, or any of China's neighbors. Beyond this, bright vistas of constructive collaboration and creative rivalry loom on far horizons in Man's common tasks of replacing anarchy by order in world affairs; controlling the population explosion; conquering disease, illiteracy, and poverty; and making the Planet Earth a fit dwelling place for the children and grandchildren of today's generation.

Is all of this a practicable possibility or a mere Utopian vision? The answer, perhaps mercifully, is concealed from us in the early 1960's. All that is clear is that such a happy outcome as an alternative to disaster will not simply "happen," but will call for dedicated efforts, bold imagination, and a high order of statesmanship by Communists, Anti-Communists, and Neutralists alike. Man still has a choice to make. If Russians and Americans together will set an example to other peoples by facing the challenge of the days to come with a full sense of moral responsibility for the consequences of their acts, the human future may yet be saved.

Constitution (Fundamental Law) of the Union of Soviet Socialist Republics*

I – The Social Structure

ARTICLE 1. The Union of Soviet Socialist Republics is a socialist state of workers and peasants.

* As amended and added to at the Third Session of the Supreme Soviet of the U.S.S.R., Fifth Convocation. Foreign Languages Publishing House, Moscow, 1960.

ARTICLE 2. The political foundation of the U.S.S.R. is the Soviets of Working People's Deputies, which grew and became strong as a result of the overthrow of the power of the landlords and capitalists and the conquest of the dictatorship of the proletariat.

ARTICLE 3. All power in the U.S.S.R. belongs to the working people of town and country as represented by the Soviets of Working People's Deputies.

ARTICLE 4. The economic foundation of the U.S.S.R. is the socialist system of economy and the socialist ownership of the instruments and means of production, firmly established as a result of the liquidation of the capitalist system of economy, the abolition of private ownership of the instruments and means of production, and the elimination of the exploitation of man by man.

ARTICLE 5. Socialist property in the U.S.S.R. exists either in the form of state property (belonging to the whole people) or in the form of co-operative and collective-farm property (property of collective farms, property of co-operative societies).

ARTICLE 6. The land, its mineral wealth, waters, forests, mills, factories, mines, rail, water and air transport, banks, communications, large state-organized agricultural enterprises (state farms, machine and tractor stations and the like), as well as municipal enterprises and the bulk of the dwelling-houses in the cities and industrial localities, are state property, that is, belong to the whole people.

ARTICLE 7. The common enterprises of collective farms and co-operative organizations, with their livestock and implements, the products of the collective farms and co-operative organizations, as well as their common buildings, constitute the common, socialist property of the collective farms and co-operative organizations.

Every household in a collective farm, in addition to its basic income from the common collective-farm enterprise, has for its personal use a small plot of household land and, as its personal property, a subsidiary husbandry on the plot, a dwelling-house, livestock, poultry and minor agricultural implements—in accordance with the rules of the agricultural artel.

ARTICLE 8. The land occupied by collective farms is secured to them for their use free of charge and for an unlimited time, that is, in perpetuity.

ARTICLE 9. Alongside the socialist system of economy, which is the predominant form of economy in the U.S.S.R., the law permits the small private economy of individual peasants and handicraftsmen based on their own labour and precluding the exploitation of the labour of others.

ARTICLE 10. The personal property right of citizens in their incomes and savings from work, in their dwelling-houses and subsidiary husbandries, in articles of domestic economy and use and articles of personal use and convenience, as well as the right of citizens to inherit personal property, is protected by law.

ARTICLE 11. The economic life of the U.S.S.R. is determined and directed by the state national-economic plan, with the aim of increasing the public wealth, of steadily raising the material and cultural standards of the working people, of consolidating the independence of the U.S.S.R. and strengthening its defensive capacity.

ARTICLE 12. Work in the U.S.S.R. is a duty and a matter of honour for every able-bodied citizen, in accordance with the principle: "He who does not work, neither shall he eat."

The principle applied in the U.S.S.R. is that of socialism: "From each according to his ability, to each according to his work."

II – The State Structure

ARTICLE 13. The Union of Soviet Socialist Republics is a federal state, formed on the basis of a voluntary union of equal Soviet Socialist Republics, namely:

The Russian Soviet Federative Socialist Republic
The Ukrainian Soviet Socialist Republic
The Byelorussian Soviet Socialist Republic
The Uzbek Soviet Socialist Republic
The Kazakh Soviet Socialist Republic
The Georgian Soviet Socialist Republic
The Azerbaijan Soviet Socialist Republic
The Lithuanian Soviet Socialist Republic
The Moldavian Soviet Socialist Republic
The Latvian Soviet Socialist Republic
The Kirghiz Soviet Socialist Republic
The Tajik Soviet Socialist Republic
The Armenian Soviet Socialist Republic
The Turkmen Soviet Socialist Republic
The Estonian Soviet Socialist Republic

ARTICLE 14. The jurisdiction of the Union of Soviet Socialist Republics, as represented by its higher organs of state power and organs of state administration, embraces:

a) Representation of the U.S.S.R. in international relations, conclusion, ratification and denunciation of treaties of the U.S.S.R. with other states, establishment of general procedure governing the relations of Union Republics with foreign states;

b) Questions of war and peace;

c) Admission of new republics into the U.S.S.R.;

d) Control over the observance of the Constitution of the U.S.S.R., and ensuring conformity of the Constitutions of the Union Republics with the Constitution of the U.S.S.R.;

e) Confirmation of alterations of boundaries between Union Republics;

f) Confirmation of the formation of new Autonomous Republics and Autonomous Regions within Union Republics;

g) Organization of the defence of the U.S.S.R., direction of all the Armed Forces of the U.S.S.R., determination of directing principles governing the organization of the military formations of the Union Republics;

h) Foreign trade on the basis of state monopoly;

i) Safeguarding the security of the state;

j) Determination of the national-economic plans of the U.S.S.R.;

k) Approval of the consolidated state budget of the U.S.S.R. and of the report on its fulfilment; determination of the taxes and revenues which go to the Union, the Republican and the local budgets;

l) Administration of the banks, industrial and agricultural institutions and enterprises and trading enterprises of all-Union jurisdiction; general guidance of industry and construction under Union-Republican jurisdiction;

m) Administration of transport and communications of all-Union importance;

n) Direction of the monetary and credit system;

o) Organization of state insurance;

p) Contracting and granting of loans;

q) Determination of the basic principles of land tenure and of the use of mineral wealth, forests and waters;

r) Determination of the basic principles in the spheres of education and public health;

s) Organization of a uniform system of national-economic statistics;

t) Determination of the principles of labour legislation;

u) Determination of the principles of legislation concerning the judicial system and judicial procedure and of the principles of civil and criminal codes;

v) Legislation concerning Union citizenship; legislation concerning rights of foreigners;

w) Determination of the principles of legislation concerning marriage and the family;

x) Issuing of all-Union acts of amnesty.

ARTICLE 15. The sovereignty of the Union Republics is limited only in the spheres defined in Article 14 of the Constitution of the U.S.S.R. Outside of these spheres each Union Republic exercises state authority independently. The U.S.S.R. protects the sovereign rights of the Union Republics.

ARTICLE 16. Each Union Republic has its own Constitution, which takes account of the specific features of the Republic and is drawn up in full conformity with the Constitution of the U.S.S.R.

ARTICLE 17. The right freely to secede from the U.S.S.R. is reserved to every Union Republic.

ARTICLE 18. The territory of a Union Republic may not be altered without its consent.

ARTICLE 18-A. Each Union Republic has the right to enter into direct relations with foreign states and to conclude agreements and exchange diplomatic and consular representatives with them.

ARTICLE 18-B. Each Union Republic has its own republican military formations.

ARTICLE 19. The laws of the U.S.S.R. have the same force within the territory of every Union Republic.

ARTICLE 20. In the event of divergence between a law of a Union Republic and a law of the Union, the Union law prevails.

ARTICLE 21. Uniform Union citizenship is established for citizens of the U.S.S.R.

Every citizen of a Union Republic is a citizen of the U.S.S.R.

ARTICLE 22. The Russian Soviet Federative Socialist Republic includes the Bashkir, Buryat, Daghestan, Kabardinian-Balkar, Kalmyk, Karelian, Komi, Mari, Mordovian, North Ossetian, Tatar, Udmurt, Checheno-Ingush, Chuvash and Yakut Autonomous Soviet Socialist Republics; and the Adygei, Gorny Altai, Jewish, Karachai-Cherkess, Tuva and Khakass Autonomous Regions.

ARTICLE 23. *Repealed.*

ARTICLE 24. The Azerbaijan Soviet Socialist Republic includes the Nakhichevan Autonomous Soviet Socialist Republic and the Nagorny Karabakh Autonomous Region.

ARTICLE 25. The Georgian Soviet Socialist Republic includes the Abkhazian and Ajarian Autonomous Soviet Socialist Republics and the South Ossetian Autonomous Region.

ARTICLE 26. The Uzbek Soviet Socialist Republic includes the Kara-Kalpak Autonomous Soviet Socialist Republic.

ARTICLE 27. The Tajik Soviet Socialist Republic includes the Gorny Badakhshan Autonomous Region.

ARTICLE 28. The solution of problems pertaining to the administrative-territorial structure of the regions and territories of the Union Republics comes within the jurisdiction of the Union Republics.

ARTICLE 29. *Repealed.*

III – *The Higher Organs of State Power in the Union of Soviet Socialist Republics*

ARTICLE 30. The highest organ of state power in the U.S.S.R. is the Supreme Soviet of the U.S.S.R.

ARTICLE 31. The Supreme Soviet of the U.S.S.R. exercises all rights vested in the Union of Soviet Socialist Republics in accordance with Article 14 of the Constitution, in so far as they do not, by virtue of the Constitution, come within the jurisdiction of organs of the U.S.S.R.

that are accountable to the Supreme Soviet of the U.S.S.R., that is, the Presidium of the Supreme Soviet of the U.S.S.R., the Council of Ministers of the U.S.S.R., and the Ministries of the U.S.S.R.

ARTICLE 32. The legislative power of the U.S.S.R. is exercised exclusively by the Supreme Soviet of the U.S.S.R.

ARTICLE 33. The Supreme Soviet of the U.S.S.R. consists of two Chambers: the Soviet of the Union and the Soviet of Nationalities.

ARTICLE 34. The Soviet of the Union is elected by the citizens of the U.S.S.R. voting by election districts on the basis of one deputy for every 300,000 of the population.

ARTICLE 35. The Soviet of Nationalities is elected by the citizens of the U.S.S.R. voting by Union Republics, Autonomous Republics, Autonomous Regions, and National Areas on the basis of 25 deputies from each Union Republic, 11 deputies from each Autonomous Republic, 5 deputies from each Autonomous Region and one deputy from each National Area.

ARTICLE 36. The Supreme Soviet of the U.S.S.R. is elected for a term of four years.

ARTICLE 37. The two Chambers of the Supreme Soviet of the U.S.S.R., the Soviet of the Union and the Soviet of Nationalities, have equal rights.

ARTICLE 38. The Soviet of the Union and the Soviet of Nationalities have equal powers to initiate legislation.

ARTICLE 39. A law is considered adopted if passed by both Chambers of the Supreme Soviet of the U.S.S.R. by a simple majority vote in each.

ARTICLE 40. Laws passed by the Supreme Soviet of the U.S.S.R. are published in the languages of the Union Republics over the signatures of the President and Secretary of the Presidium of the Supreme Soviet of the U.S.S.R.

ARTICLE 41. Sessions of the Soviet of the Union and of the Soviet of Nationalities begin and terminate simultaneously.

ARTICLE 42. The Soviet of the Union elects a Chairman of the Soviet of the Union and four Vice-Chairmen.

ARTICLE 43. The Soviet of Nationalities elects a Chairman of the Soviet of Nationalities and four Vice-Chairmen.

ARTICLE 44. The Chairmen of the Soviet of the Union and the Soviet of Nationalities preside at the sittings of the respective Chambers and have charge of the conduct of their business and proceedings.

ARTICLE 45. Joint sittings of the two Chambers of the Supreme Soviet of the U.S.S.R. are presided over alternately by the Chairman of the Soviet of the Union and the Chairman of the Soviet of Nationalities.

ARTICLE 46. Sessions of the Supreme Soviet of the U.S.S.R. are convened by the Presidium of the Supreme Soviet of the U.S.S.R. twice a year.

Extraordinary sessions are convened by the Presidium of the Supreme Soviet of the U.S.S.R. at its discretion or on the demand of one of the Union Republics.

ARTICLE 47. In the event of disagreement between the Soviet of the Union and the Soviet of Nationalities, the question is referred for settlement to a conciliation commission formed by the Chambers on a parity basis. If the conciliation commission fails to arrive at an agreement or if its decision fails to satisfy one of the Chambers, the question is considered for a second time by the Chambers. Failing agreement between the two Chambers, the Presidium of the Supreme Soviet of the U.S.S.R. dissolves the Supreme Soviet of the U.S.S.R. and orders new elections.

ARTICLE 48. The Supreme Soviet of the U.S.S.R. at a joint sitting of the two Chambers elects the Presidium of the Supreme Soviet of the U.S.S.R., consisting of a President of the Presidium of the Supreme Soviet of the U.S.S.R., fifteen Vice-Presidents—one from each Union Republic, a Secretary of the Presidium and sixteen members of the Presidium of the Supreme Soviet of the U.S.S.R.

The Presidium of the Supreme Soviet of the U.S.S.R. is accountable to the Supreme Soviet of the U.S.S.R. for all its activities.

ARTICLE 49. The Presidium of the Supreme Soviet of the U.S.S.R.:

a) Convenes the sessions of the Supreme Soviet of the U.S.S.R.;

b) Issues decrees;

c) Gives interpretations of the laws of the U.S.S.R. in operation;

d) Dissolves the Supreme Soviet of the U.S.S.R. in conformity with Article 47 of the Constitution of the U.S.S.R. and orders new elections;

e) Conducts nation-wide polls (referendums) on its own initiative or on the demand of one of the Union Republics;

f) Annuls decisions and orders of the Council of Ministers of the U.S.S.R. and of the Councils of Ministers of the Union Republics if they do not conform to law;

g) In the intervals between sessions of the Supreme Soviet of the U.S.S.R., releases and appoints Ministers of the U.S.S.R. on the recommendation of the Chairman of the Council of Ministers of the U.S.S.R., subject to subsequent confirmation by the Supreme Soviet of the U.S.S.R.;

h) Institutes decorations (Orders and Medals) and titles of honour of the U.S.S.R.;

i) Awards Orders and Medals and confers titles of honour of the U.S.S.R.;

j) Exercises the right of pardon;

k) Institutes military titles, diplomatic ranks and other special titles;

l) Appoints and removes the high command of the Armed Forces of the U.S.S.R.;

m) In the intervals between sessions of the Supreme Soviet of the U.S.S.R., proclaims a state of war in the event of military attack on the U.S.S.R., or when necessary to fulfil international treaty obligations concerning mutual defence against aggression;

n) Orders general or partial mobilization;

o) Ratifies and denounces international treaties of the U.S.S.R.;

p) Appoints and recalls plenipotentiary representatives of the U.S.S.R. to foreign states;

q) Receives the letters of credence and recall of diplomatic representatives accredited to it by foreign states;

r) Proclaims martial law in separate localities or throughout the U.S.S.R. in the interests of the defence of the U.S.S.R. or of the maintenance of public order and the security of the state.

ARTICLE 50. The Soviet of the Union and the Soviet of Nationalities elect Credentials Committees to verify the credentials of the members of the respective Chambers.

On the report of the Credentials Committees, the Chambers decide whether to recognize the credentials of deputies or to annul their election.

ARTICLE 51. The Supreme Soviet of the U.S.S.R., when it deems necessary, appoints commissions of investigation and audit on any matter.

It is the duty of all institutions and officials to comply with the demands of such commissions and to submit to them all necessary materials and documents.

ARTICLE 52. A member of the Supreme Soviet of the U.S.S.R. may not be prosecuted or arrested without the consent of the Supreme Soviet of the U.S.S.R., or, when the Supreme Soviet of the U.S.S.R. is not in session, without the consent of the Presidium of the Supreme Soviet of the U.S.S.R.

ARTICLE 53. On the expiration of the term of office of the Supreme Soviet of the U.S.S.R., or on its dissolution prior to the expiration of its term of office, the Presidium of the Supreme Soviet of the U.S.S.R. retains its powers until the newly-elected Supreme Soviet of the U.S.S.R. shall have formed a new Presidium of the Supreme Soviet of the U.S.S.R.

ARTICLE 54. On the expiration of the term of office of the Supreme Soviet of the U.S.S.R., or in the event of its dissolution prior to the expiration of its term of office, the Presidium of the Supreme Soviet of the U.S.S.R. orders new elections to be held within a period not exceeding two months from the date of expiration of the term of office or dissolution of the Supreme Soviet of the U.S.S.R.

ARTICLE 55. The newly-elected Supreme Soviet of the U.S.S.R. is convened by the outgoing Presidium of the Supreme Soviet of the U.S.S.R. not later than three months after the elections.

ARTICLE 56. The Supreme Soviet of the U.S.S.R., at a joint sitting of the two Chambers, appoints the Government of the U.S.S.R., namely, the Council of Ministers of the U.S.S.R.

IV – *The Higher Organs of State Power in the Union Republics*

ARTICLE 57. The highest organ of state power in a Union Republic is the Supreme Soviet of the Union Republic.

ARTICLE 58. The Supreme Soviet of a Union Republic is elected by the citizens of the Republic for a term of four years.

The basis of representation is established by the Constitution of the Union Republic.

ARTICLE 59. The Supreme Soviet of a Union Republic is the sole legislative organ of the Republic.

ARTICLE 60. The Supreme Soviet of a Union Republic:

a) Adopts the Constitution of the Republic and amends it in conformity with Article 16 of the Constitution of the U.S.S.R.;

b) Confirms the Constitutions of the Autonomous Republics forming part of it and defines the boundaries of their territories;

c) Approves the national-economic plan and the budget of the Republic and forms economic administration areas;

d) Exercises the right of amnesty and pardon of citizens sentenced by the judicial organs of the Union Republic;

e) Decides questions of representation of the Union Republic in its international relations;

f) Determines the manner of organizing the Republic's military formations.

ARTICLE 61. The Supreme Soviet of a Union Republic elects the Presidium of the Supreme Soviet of the Union Republic, consisting of a President of the Presidium of the Supreme Soviet of the Union Republic, Vice-Presidents, a Secretary of the Presidium and members of the Presidium of the Supreme Soviet of the Union Republic.

The powers of the Presidium of the Supreme Soviet of a Union Republic are defined by the Constitution of the Union Republic.

ARTICLE 62. The Supreme Soviet of a Union Republic elects a Chairman and Vice-Chairmen to conduct its sittings.

ARTICLE 63. The Supreme Soviet of a Union Republic appoints the Government of the Union Republic, namely, the Council of Ministers of the Union Republic.

V – *The Organs of State Administration of the Union of Soviet Socialist Republics*

ARTICLE 64. The highest executive and administrative organ of the state power of the Union of Soviet Socialist Republics is the Council of Ministers of the U.S.S.R.

ARTICLE 65. The Council of Ministers of the U.S.S.R. is responsible and accountable to the Supreme Soviet of the U.S.S.R., or, in the intervals between sessions of the Supreme Soviet, to the Presidium of the Supreme Soviet of the U.S.S.R.

ARTICLE 66. The Council of Ministers of the U.S.S.R. issues decisions and orders on the basis and in pursuance of the laws in operation, and verifies their execution.

ARTICLE 67. Decisions and orders of the Council of Ministers of the U.S.S.R. are binding throughout the territory of the U.S.S.R.

ARTICLE 68. The Council of Ministers of the U.S.S.R.:

a) Co-ordinates and directs the work of the all-Union and Union-Republican Ministers of the U.S.S.R. and of other institutions under its jurisdiction, exercises guidance of the Economic Councils of the economic administration areas through the Councils of Ministers of the Union Republics;

b) Adopts measures to carry out the national-economic plan and the state budget, and to strengthen the credit and monetary system;

c) Adopts measures for the maintenance of public order, for the protection of the interests of the state, and for the safeguarding of the rights of citizens;

d) Exercises general guidance in the sphere of relations with foreign states;

e) Fixes the annual contingent of citizens to be called up for military service and directs the general organization of the Armed Forces of the country;

f) Sets up, whenever necessary, special Committees and Central Administrations under the Council of Ministers of the U.S.S.R. for economic and cultural affairs and defence.

ARTICLE 69. The Council of Ministers of the U.S.S.R. has the right, in respect of those branches of administration and economy which come within the jurisdiction of the U.S.S.R., to suspend decisions and orders of the Councils of Ministers of the Union Republics and of the Economic Councils of the economic administration areas and to annul orders and instructions of Ministers of the U.S.S.R.

ARTICLE 70. The Council of Ministers of the U.S.S.R. is appointed by the Supreme Soviet of the U.S.S.R. and consists of:

The Chairman of the Council of Ministers of the U.S.S.R.;

The First Vice-Chairman of the Council of Ministers of the U.S.S.R.;

The Vice-Chairmen of the Council of Ministers of the U.S.S.R.;

The Ministers of the U.S.S.R.;

The Chairman of the State Planning Committee of the Council of Ministers of the U.S.S.R.;

The Chairman of the Commission of Soviet Control of the Council of Ministers of the U.S.S.R.;

The Chairman of the State Labour and Wages Committee of the Council of Ministers of the U.S.S.R.;

The Chairman of the State Committee of the Council of Ministers of the U.S.S.R. on Professional and Technical Training;

The Chairman of the State Scientific and Technical Committee of the Council of Ministers of the U.S.S.R.;

The Chairman of the State Committee of the Council of Ministers of the U.S.S.R. on Automation and Machine-Building;

The Chairman of the State Committee of the Council of Ministers of the U.S.S.R. on Aircraft Technique;

The Chairman of the State Committee of the Council of Ministers of the U.S.S.R. on Defence Technique;

The Chairman of the State Committee of the Council of Ministers of the U.S.S.R. on Radio-electronics;

The Chairman of the State Committee of the Council of Ministers of the U.S.S.R. on Shipbuilding;

The Chairman of the State Committee of the Council of Ministers of the U.S.S.R. on Chemistry;

The Chairman of the State Committee of the Council of Ministers of the U.S.S.R. on Construction;

The Chairman of the State Grain and Cereals Committee of the Council of Ministers of the U.S.S.R.;

The Chairman of the State Committee of the Council of Ministers of the U.S.S.R. on Foreign Economic Relations;

The Chairman of the State Security Committee under the Council of Ministers of the U.S.S.R.;

The Chairman of the Administrative Board of the State Bank of the U.S.S.R.;

The Chief of the Central Statistical Board under the Council of Ministers of the U.S.S.R.;

The Chairman of the State Council of Economic Research of the Council of Ministers of the U.S.S.R.;

The Council of Ministers of the U.S.S.R. includes the Chairmen of the Councils of Ministers of the Union Republics by virtue of their office.

ARTICLE 71. The Government of the U.S.S.R. or a Minister of the U.S.S.R. to whom a question of a member of the Supreme Soviet of the U.S.S.R. is addressed must give a verbal or written reply in the respective Chamber within a period not exceeding three days.

ARTICLE 72. The Ministers of the U.S.S.R. direct the branches of state administration which come within the jurisdiction of the U.S.S.R.

ARTICLE 73. The Ministers of the U.S.S.R., within the limits of the jurisdiction of their respective Ministries, issue orders and instructions on the basis and in pursuance of the laws in operation, and also of decisions and orders of the Council of Ministers of the U.S.S.R., and verify their execution.

ARTICLE 74. The Ministries of the U.S.S.R. are either all-Union or Union-Republican Ministries.

ARTICLE 75. Each all-Union Ministry directs the branch of state administration entrusted to it throughout the territory of the U.S.S.R. either directly or through bodies appointed by it.

ARTICLE 76. The Union-Republican Ministries, as a rule, direct the branches of state administration entrusted to them through corresponding Ministries of the Union Republics; they administer directly only a definite and limited number of enterprises according to a list confirmed by the Presidium of the Supreme Soviet of the U.S.S.R.

ARTICLE 77. The following Ministries are all-Union Ministries:

The Ministry of Foreign Trade;

The Ministry of Merchant Marine;

The Ministry of Railways;

The Ministry of the Medium Machine-Building Industry;

The Ministry for the Construction of Electric Power Stations;

The Ministry of Transport Construction.

ARTICLE 78. The following Ministries are Union-Republican Ministries:

The Ministry of Internal Affairs;

The Ministry of Higher and Secondary Specialized Education;

The Ministry of Geological Survey and Conservation of Mineral Resources;

The Ministry of Public Health;

The Ministry of Foreign Affairs;

The Ministry of Culture;

The Ministry of Defence;

The Ministry of Communications;

The Ministry of Agriculture;

The Ministry of Finance.

VI – *The Organs of State Administration of the Union Republics*

ARTICLE 79. The highest executive and administrative organ of the state power of a Union Republic is the Council of Ministers of the Union Republic.

ARTICLE 80. The Council of Ministers of a Union Republic is responsible and accountable to the Supreme Soviet of the Union Republic, or, in the intervals between sessions of the Supreme Soviet of the Union Republic, to the Presidium of the Supreme Soviet of the Union Republic.

ARTICLE 81. The Council of Ministers of a Union Republic issues decisions and orders on the basis and in pursuance of the laws of the U.S.S.R. and of the Union Republic in operation, and of the decisions and orders of the Council of Ministers of the U.S.S.R., and verifies their execution.

ARTICLE 82. The Council of Ministers of a Union Republic has the right to suspend decisions and orders of the Councils of Ministers of its Autonomous Republics, and to annual decisions and orders of the Executive Committees of the Soviets of Working People's Deputies of its Territories, Regions and Autonomous Regions, as well as decisions and orders of the Economic Councils of the economic administration areas.

ARTICLE 83. The Council of Ministers of a Union Republic is appointed by the Supreme Soviet of the Union Republic and consists of:

The Chairman of the Council of Ministers of the Union Republic;

The Vice-Chairmen of the Council of Ministers;

The Ministers;

The Chairmen of State Committees, Commissions, and the heads of other offices of the Council of Ministers set up by the Supreme Soviet of the Union Republic in conformity with the Constitution of the Union Republic.

ARTICLE 84. The Ministers of a Union Republic direct the branches of state administration which come within the jurisdiction of the Union Republic.

ARTICLE 85. The Ministers of a Union Republic, within the limits of the jurisdiction of their respective Ministries, issue orders and instructions on the basis and in pursuance of the laws of the U.S.S.R. and of the Union Republic, of the decisions and orders of the Council of Ministers of the U.S.S.R. and the Council of Ministers of the Union Republic, and of the orders and instructions of the Union-Republican Ministries of the U.S.S.R.

ARTICLE 86. The Ministries of a Union Republic are either Union-Republican or Republican Ministries.

ARTICLE 87. Each Union-Republican Ministry directs the branch of state administration entrusted to it, and is subordinate both to the Council of Ministers of the Union Republic and to the corresponding Union-Republican Ministry of the U.S.S.R.

ARTICLE 88. Each Republican Ministry directs the branch of state administration entrusted to it and is directly subordinate to the Council of Ministers of the Union Republic.

ARTICLE 88-A. The Economic Councils of the economic administration areas direct the branches of economic activity entrusted to them, and are directly subordinate to the Council of Ministers of the Union Republic.

The Economic Councils of the economic administration areas issue within their jurisdiction decisions and orders on the basis and in pursuance of the laws of the U.S.S.R. and the Union Republic and decisions and orders of the Council of Ministers of the U.S.S.R. and the Council of Ministers of the Union Republic.

VII – The Higher Organs of State Power in the Autonomous Soviet Socialist Republics

ARTICLE 89. The highest organ of state power in an Autonomous Republic is the Supreme Soviet of the Autonomous Republic.

ARTICLE 90. The Supreme Soviet of an Autonomous Republic is elected by the citizens of the Republic for a term of four years on a basis of representation established by the Constitution of the Autonomous Republic.

ARTICLE 91. The Supreme Soviet of an Autonomous Republic is the sole legislative organ of the Autonomous Republic.

ARTICLE 92. Each Autonomous Republic has its own Constitution, which takes account of the specific features of the Autonomous Republic and is drawn up in full conformity with the Constitution of the Union Republic.

ARTICLE 93. The Supreme Soviet of an Autonomous Republic elects the Presidium of the Supreme Soviet of the Autonomous Republic and appoints the Council of Ministers of the Autonomous Republic, in accordance with its Constitution.

VIII – The Local Organs of State Power

ARTICLE 94. The organs of state power in Territories, Regions, Autonomous Regions, Areas, Districts, cities and rural localities (stanitsas, villages, hamlets, kishlaks, auls) are the Soviets of Working People's Deputies.

ARTICLE 95. The Soviets of Working People's Deputies of Territories, Regions, Autonomous Regions, Areas, Districts, cities and rural localities (stanitsas, villages, hamlets, kishlaks, auls) are elected by the working people of the respective Territories, Regions, Autonomous Regions, Areas, Districts, cities and rural localities for a term of two years.

ARTICLE 96. The basis of representation for Soviets of Working People's Deputies is determined by the Constitutions of the Union Republics.

ARTICLE 97. The Soviets of Working People's Deputies direct the work of the organs of administration subordinate to them, ensure the maintenance of public order, the observance of the laws and the protection of the rights of citizens, direct local economic and cultural affairs and draw up the local budgets.

ARTICLE 98. The Soviets of Working People's Deputies adopt decisions and issue orders within the limits of the powers vested in them by the laws of the U.S.S.R. and of the Union Republic.

ARTICLE 99. The executive and administrative organ of the Soviet of Working People's Deputies of a Territory, Region, Autonomous Region, Area, District, city or rural locality is the Executive Committee elected by it, consisting of a Chairman, Vice-Chairmen, a Secretary and members.

ARTICLE 100. The executive and administrative organ of the Soviet of Working People's Deputies in a small locality, in accordance with the Constitution of the Union Republic, is the Chairman, the Vice-

Chairman and the Secretary elected by the Soviet of Working People's Deputies.

ARTICLE 101. The executive organs of the Soviets of Working People's Deputies are directly accountable both to the Soviets of Working People's Deputies which elected them and to the executive organ of the superior Soviet of Working People's Deputies.

IX – The Courts and the Procurator's Office

ARTICLE 102. In the U.S.S.R. justice is administered by the Supreme Court of the U.S.S.R., the Supreme Courts of the Union Republics, the Courts of the Territories, Regions, Autonomous Republics, Autonomous Regions and Areas, the Special Courts of the U.S.S.R. established by decision of the Supreme Soviet of the U.S.S.R., and the People's Courts.

ARTICLE 103. In all Courts cases are tried with the participation of people's assessors, except where specially provided for by law.

ARTICLE 104. The Supreme Court of the U.S.S.R. is the highest judicial organ. The Supreme Court of the U.S.S.R. is charged with the supervision of the judicial activities of the judicial organs of the U.S.S.R. and of the Union Republics within the limits established by law.

ARTICLE 105. The Supreme Court of the U.S.S.R. is elected by the Supreme Soviet of the U.S.S.R. for a term of five years.

The Supreme Court of the U.S.S.R. includes the Chairmen of the Supreme Courts of the Union Republics by virtue of their office.

ARTICLE 106. The Supreme Courts of the Union Republics are elected by the Supreme Soviets of the Union Republics for a term of five years.

ARTICLE 107. The Supreme Courts of the Autonomous Republics are elected by the Supreme Soviets of the Autonomous Republics for a term of five years.

ARTICLE 108. The Courts of Territories, Regions, Autonomous Regions and Areas are elected by the Soviets of Working People's Deputies of the respective Territories, Regions, Autonomous Regions or Areas for a term of five years.

ARTICLE 109. People's judges of District (City) People's Courts are elected by the citizens of the districts (cities) on the basis of universal, direct and equal suffrage by secret ballot for a term of five years.

People's assessors of District (City) People's Courts are elected at general meetings of industrial, office, and professional workers, and peasants in the place of their work or residence, and of servicemen in military units, for a term of two years.

ARTICLE 110. Judicial proceedings are conducted in the language of the Union Republic, Autonomous Republic or Autonomous Region, persons not knowing this language being guaranteed the opportunity of fully acquainting themselves with the material of the case through an interpreter and likewise the right to use their own language in court.

ARTICLE 111. In all Courts of the U.S.S.R. cases are heard in public, unless otherwise provided for by law, and the accused is guaranteed the right to defence.

ARTICLE 112. Judges are independent and subject only to the law.

ARTICLE 113. Supreme supervisory power to ensure the strict observance of the law by all Ministries and institutions subordinated to them, as well as by officials and citizens of the U.S.S.R. generally, is vested in the Procurator-General of the U.S.S.R.

ARTICLE 114. The Procurator-General of the U.S.S.R. is appointed by the Supreme Soviet of the U.S.S.R. for a term of seven years.

ARTICLE 115. Procurators of Republics, Territories, Regions, Autonomous Republics and Autonomous Regions are appointed by the Procurator-General of the U.S.S.R. for a term of five years.

ARTICLE 116. Area, district and city procurators are appointed by the Procurators of the Union Republics, subject to the approval of the Procurator-General of the U.S.S.R., for a term of five years.

ARTICLE 117. The organs of the Procurator's Office perform their functions independently of any local organs whatsoever, being subordinate solely to the Procurator-General of the U.S.S.R.

X – Fundamental Rights and Duties of Citizens

ARTICLE 118. Citizens of the U.S.S.R. have the right to work, that is, the right to guaranteed employment and payment for their work in accordance with its quantity and quality.

The right to work is ensured by the socialist organization of the national economy, the steady growth of the productive forces of Soviet society, the elimination of the possibility of economic crises, and the abolition of unemployment.

ARTICLE 119. Citizens of the U.S.S.R. have the right to rest and leisure.

The right to rest and leisure is ensured by the establishment of an eight-hour day for industrial, office, and professional workers, the reduction of the working day to seven or six hours for arduous trades and to four hours in shops where conditions of work are particularly arduous; by the institution of annual vacations with full pay for industrial, office, and professional workers, and by the provision of a wide network of sanatoriums, holiday homes and clubs for the accommodation of the working people.

ARTICLE 120. Citizens of the U.S.S.R. have the right to maintenance in old age and also in case of sickness or disability.

This right is ensured by the extensive development of social insurance of industrial, office, and professional workers at state expense, free medical service for the working people, and the provision of a wide network of health resorts for the use of the working people.

ARTICLE 121. Citizens of the U.S.S.R. have the right to education.

This right is ensured by universal compulsory eight-year education; by extensive development of secondary general polytechnical education, vocational-technical education, and secondary specialized and higher education based on close links between school, and life and production; by utmost development of evening and extra-mural education; by free education in all schools; by a system of state grants; by instruction in schools being conducted in the native language, and by the organization in the factories, state farms and collective farms of free vocational, technical and agronomic training for the working people.

ARTICLE 122. Women in the U.S.S.R. are accorded equal rights with men in all spheres of economic, government, cultural, political and other public activity.

The possibility of exercising these rights is ensured by women being accorded an equal right with men to work, payment for work, rest and leisure, social insurance and education, and by state protection of the interests of mother and child, state aid to mothers of large families and unmarried mothers, maternity leave with full pay, and the provision of a wide network of maternity homes, nurseries and kindergartens.

ARTICLE 123. Equality of rights of citizens of the U.S.S.R., irrespective of their nationality or race, in all spheres of economic, government, cultural, political and other public activity, is an indefeasible law.

Any direct or indirect restriction of the rights of, or, conversely, the establishment of any direct or indirect privileges for, citizens on account of their race or nationality, as well as any advocacy of racial or national exclusiveness or hatred and contempt, are punishable by law.

ARTICLE 124. In order to ensure to citizens freedom of conscience, the church in the U.S.S.R. is separated from the state, and the school from the church. Freedom of religious worship and freedom of anti-religious propaganda is recognized for all citizens.

ARTICLE 125. In conformity with the interests of the working people, and in order to strengthen the socialist system, the citizens of the U.S.S.R. are guaranteed by law:

a) freedom of speech;
b) freedom of the press;
c) freedom of assembly, including the holding of mass meetings;
d) freedom of street processions and demonstrations.

These civil rights are ensured by placing at the disposal of the working people and their organizations printing presses, stocks of paper, public buildings, the streets, communications facilities and other material requisites for the exercise of these rights.

ARTICLE 126. In conformity with the interests of the working people, and in order to develop the organizational initiative and political activity of the masses of the people, citizens of the U.S.S.R. are guaranteed the right to unite in public organizations: trade unions, co-operative societies, youth organizations, sport and defence organizations, cultural, technical and scientific societies; and the most active and politically-conscious citizens in the ranks of the working class, working peasants and working intelligentsia voluntarily unite in the Communist Party of the Soviet Union, which is the vanguard of the working people in their struggle to build communist society and is the leading core of all organizations of the working people, both public and state.

ARTICLE 127. Citizens of the U.S.S.R. are guaranteed inviolability of the person. No person may be placed under arrest except by decision of a court or with the sanction of a procurator.

ARTICLE 128. The inviolability of the homes of citizens and privacy of correspondence are protected by law.

ARTICLE 129. The U.S.S.R. affords the right of asylum to foreign citizens persecuted for defending the interests of the working people, or for scientific activities, or for struggling for national liberation.

ARTICLE 130. It is the duty of every citizen of the U.S.S.R. to abide by the Constitution of the Union of Soviet Socialist Republics, to observe the laws, to maintain labour discipline, honestly to perform public duties, and to respect the rules of socialist intercourse.

ARTICLE 131. It is the duty of every citizen of the U.S.S.R. to safeguard and fortify public, socialist property as the sacred and inviolable foundation of the Soviet system, as the source of the wealth and might of the country, as the source of the prosperity and culture of all the working people.

Persons committing offences against public, socialist property are enemies of the people.

ARTICLE 132. Universal military service is law.

Military service in the Armed Forces of the U.S.S.R. is an honourable duty of the citizens of the U.S.S.R.

ARTICLE 133. To defend the country is the sacred duty of every citizen of the U.S.S.R. Treason to the Motherland—violation of the oath of allegiance, desertion to the enemy, impairing the military power of the state, espionage—is punishable with all the severity of the law as the most heinous of crimes.

XI – The Electoral System

ARTICLE 134. Members of all Soviets of Working People's Deputies —of the Supreme Soviet of the U.S.S.R., the Supreme Soviets of the Union Republics, the Soviets of Working People's Deputies of the Territories and Regions, the Supreme Soviets of the Autonomous Republics, the Soviets of Working People's Deputies of the Autonomous Regions, and the Area, District, city and rural (stanitsa, village, hamlet, kishlak, aul) Soviets of Working People's Deputies—are chosen by the electors on the basis of universal, equal and direct suffrage by secret ballot.

ARTICLE 135. Elections of deputies are universal: all citizens of the U.S.S.R. who have reached the age of eighteen, irrespective of race or nationality, sex, religion, education, domicile, social origin, property status or past activities, have the right to vote in the election of deputies, with the exception of persons who have been legally certified as insane.

Every citizen of the U.S.S.R. who has reached the age of twenty-three is eligible for election to the Supreme Soviet of the U.S.S.R., irrespective of race or nationality, sex, religion, education, domicile, social origin, property status or past activities.

ARTICLE 136. Elections of deputies are equal: each citizen has one vote; all citizens participate in elections on an equal footing.

ARTICLE 137. Women have the right to elect and be elected on equal terms with men.

ARTICLE 138. Citizens serving in the Armed Forces of the U.S.S.R. have the right to elect and be elected on equal terms with all other citizens.

ARTICLE 139. Elections of deputies are direct: all Soviets of Working People's Deputies, from rural and city Soviets of Working People's Deputies to the Supreme Soviet of the U.S.S.R., are elected by the citizens by direct vote.

ARTICLE 140. Voting at elections of deputies is secret.

ARTICLE 141. Candidates are nominated by election districts.

The right to nominate candidates is secured to public organizations and societies of the working people: Communist Party organizations, trade unions, co-operatives, youth organizations and cultural societies.

ARTICLE 142. It is the duty of every deputy to report to his electors on his work and on the work of his Soviet of Working People's Deputies, and he may be recalled at any time upon decision of a majority of the electors in the manner established by law.

XII – Arms, Flag, Capital

ARTICLE 143. The arms of the Union of Soviet Socialist Republics are a sickle and hammer against a globe depicted in the rays of the sun and surrounded by ears of grain, with the inscription "Workers of All Countries, Unite!" in the languages of the Union Republics. At the top of the arms is a five-pointed star.

ARTICLE 144. The state flag of the Union of Soviet Socialist Republics is of red cloth with the sickle and hammer depicted in gold in the upper corner near the staff and above them a five-pointed red star bordered in gold. The ratio of the width to the length is 1:2.

ARTICLE 145. The Capital of the Union of Soviet Socialist Republics is the City of Moscow.

XIII – Procedure for Amending the Constitution

ARTICLE 146. The Constitution of the U.S.S.R. may be amended only by decision of the Supreme Soviet of the U.S.S.R. adopted by a majority of not less than two-thirds of the votes in each of its Chambers.

Selected Bibliography

N.B. Since 1917 thousands of books on the Russian Revolution and its aftermath have been published in the English language. Many more thousands have been published in Russian, German, French, and other tongues. The list which follows represents a small sampling of works in English. These titles, without prejudice to many others here omitted, are likely to prove illuminating to students and general readers, as distinct from specialists on Soviet affairs, either because they are "classics" in the field or offer perspectives, interpretations, and factual data meriting attention and reflection. Titles followed by an asterisk (*) are, as of 1961, paperback books or available in paperback editions as well as hard covers.

Bauer, Raymond A., Inkeles & Kluckhohn: *How the Soviet System Works,* * Knopf, New York, 1960.

Baykov, Alexander: *The Development of the Soviet Economic System,* Macmillan, New York, 1946.

Berdyaev, Nicolas: *The Origin of Russian Communism,* Scribner's, New York, 1937.

Berman, H. J.: *The Russians in Focus,* Little, Brown, Boston, 1953.

Biographic Directory of the USSR, Scarecrow Press (for the Institute for the Study of the U.S.S.R., Munich), New York, 1958.

Black, Cyril E. (editor): *The Transformation of Russian Society,* Harvard University Press, Cambridge, 1960.

Brzezinski, Zbigniew K.: *The Soviet Bloc: Unity and Conflict,* Harvard University Press, Cambridge, 1960.

Bunyan, James: *Intervention, Civil War and Communism in Russia, April–December, 1918,* Johns Hopkins Press, Baltimore, 1936.

———, and H. H. Fisher: *The Bolshevik Revolution: 1917–1918,* Stanford University Press, Stanford, 1934.

Campbell, Robert W.: *Soviet Economic Power,** Houghton Mifflin, Boston, 1960.

Carr, Edward Hallett: *A History of Soviet Russia* (Vols. I–V on the years 1917–26), Macmillan, New York, 1951–59.

Charques, Richard D.: *A Short History of Russia,** Everyman (Dutton), New York, 1958.

Cole, G. D. H.: *A History of Socialist Thought* (4 vols.), St. Martin's Press, New York, 1959.

Crankshaw, Edward: *Khrushchev's Russia,** Penguin Books (Atheneum), Baltimore, 1960.

———: *Russia and the Russians,* Viking, New York, 1948.

Curtiss, John Sheldon: *The Russian Revolutions of 1917,* Anvil (Van Nostrand), Princeton, 1957.

Dallin, David J.: *Soviet Foreign Policy after Stalin,* Lippincott, New York, 1961.

Deutscher, Isaac: *The Prophet Armed: Trotsky, 1879–1921,* Oxford University Press, New York, 1954.

———: *The Prophet Unarmed: Trotsky, 1921,* Oxford University Press, New York, 1959.

———: *Russia in Transition and Other Essays,* Coward-McCann, New York, 1957.

———: *Stalin: A Political Biography,** Vintage (Random House), New York, 1960.

Dinerstein, H. S.: *War and the Soviet Union: Nuclear Weapons and the Revolution in Soviet Military and Political Thinking,* Praeger, New York, 1959.

Djilas, Milovan: *The New Class,** Praeger Paperbacks, New York, 1960.

Dobb, Maurice: *Soviet Economic Development since 1917,* International Publishers, New York, 1949

Ebon, Martin: *Malenkov: Stalin's Successor,* McGraw-Hill, New York, 1953.

Fainsod, Merle: *How Russia Is Ruled,* Harvard University Press, Cambridge, 1953.

Feis, Herbert: *Churchill, Roosevelt, Stalin: The War They Waged and the Peace They Sought,* Princeton University Press, Princeton, 1957.

Feuer, Lewis S. (editor): *Basic Writings on Politics and Philosophy by Karl Marx and Friedrich Engels,** Anchor (Doubleday), Garden City, 1960.

Field, Mark G.: *Doctor and Patient in Soviet Russia,* Harvard University Press, Cambridge, 1957.

Fischer, George: *Russian Liberalism: From Gentry to Intelligentsia,* Harvard University Press, Cambridge, 1957.

Fischer, Louis: *Russia, America, and the World,* Harper, New York, 1960.

———: *The Soviets in World Affairs,** Vintage (Random House), New York, 1960.

Fitzsimmons, Thomas, and Others: *USSR: Its People, Its Society, Its Culture,* Human Relations Area Files Press (Taplinger, distributor), New York, 1960.

Florinsky, M. T.: *Russia: A History and an Interpretation* (2 vols.), Macmillan, New York, 1954.

Goodman, Elliot R.: *The Soviet Design for a World State,* Columbia University Press, New York, 1960.

Granick, David: *The Red Executive: A Study of the Organization Man in Russian Industry,** Anchor (Doubleday), Garden City, 1961.

Gunther, John: *Inside Russia Today,* Harper, New York, 1958.

Harcave, Sidney S.: *Russia: A History*, Lippincott, Philadelphia, 1959.

Harper, Samuel N. and Ronald Thompson: *Government of the Soviet Union* (2nd Edition), Van Nostrand, New York, 1949.

Hazard, John N.: *Settling Disputes in Soviet Society: The Formative Years of Legal Institutions*, Columbia University Press, New York, 1960.

————: *The Soviet System of Government* (2nd Edition), University of Chicago Press, Chicago, 1960.

Hill, Elizabeth and Doris Mudie: *The Letters of Lenin*, Harcourt, New York, 1937.

Ingram, Kenneth: *The History of the Cold War*, Philosophical Library, New York, 1955.

Inkeles, Alex and Raymond A. Bauer: *The Soviet Citizen*, Harvard University Press, Cambridge, 1959.

Kellen, Konrad: *Khrushchev: A Political Portrait*, Praeger, New York, 1961.

Kennan, George F.: *The Decision to Intervene*, Princeton University Press, Princeton, 1958.

————: *Russia and the West under Lenin and Stalin*, Little, Brown, Boston, 1961.

————: *Russia Leaves the War*, Princeton University Press, Princeton, 1956.

Khrushchev in America (full texts of speeches, September 15–27, 1959), Crosscurrents Press, New York, 1960.

Khrushchev, Nikita: *Khrushchev in New York* (September–October, 1960), Crosscurrents Press, New York, 1960.

Kohn, Hans: *Pan-Slavism: Its History and Ideology,** Vintage (Random House), New York, 1960.

Lamont, Corliss: *The Peoples of the Soviet Union*, Harcourt, New York, 1946.

Lenin, V. I.: *The State and Revolution*, International Publishers, New York, 1932.

Levine, Irving R.: *Main Street, USSR,** Signet, New York, 1960.

Liberman, Simon: *Building Lenin's Russia*, University of Chicago Press, Chicago, 1945.

Lukacs, John: *A History of the Cold War*, Doubleday, Garden City, 1961.

Lyashchenko, Peter I.: *History of the National Economy of Russia to the 1917 Revolution*, Macmillan, New York, 1949.

McClosky, Herbert and John E. Turner: *The Soviet Dictatorship*, McGraw-Hill, New York, 1960.

Martin, John Stuart (editor): *A Picture History of Russia*, Crown, New York, 1956.

Masaryk, Thomas Garrigue: *The Spirit of Russia*, Macmillan, New York, 1955.

Maynard, Sir John: *Russia in Flux*, Macmillan, New York, 1948.

Mazour, Anatole G.: *The Rise and Fall of the Romanovs,** Anvil (Van Nostrand), Princeton, 1960.

————: *Russia Past and Present*, Van Nostrand, New York, 1951.

Mehring, Franz: *Karl Marx: The Story of His Life* (translated by Edward Fitzgerald), Covici Friede, New York, 1935.

Meyer, Alfred G.: *Leninism*, Harvard University Press, Cambridge, 1957.

Ministry of Foreign Affairs of the U.S.S.R.: *Correspondence between the Chairman of the Council of Ministers of the U.S.S.R. and the Presidents of the U.S.A. and the Prime Ministers of Great Britain during the Great Patriotic War of 1941–1945* (2 vols.), Foreign Languages Publishing, Moscow, 1957.

Moore, Barrington, Jr.: *Soviet Politics—The Dilemma of Power,* Harvard University Press, Cambridge, 1950.

Mosely, Philip E.: *The Kremlin and World Politics,** Vintage (Random House), New York, 1960.

Pares, Sir Bernard: *Russia,** Mentor, New York, 1949.

Perla, Leo: *Can We End the Cold War?,* Macmillan, New York, 1960.

Pope, Arthur Upham: *Maxim Litvinov,* Fischer, New York, 1943.

Rauch, Georg von: *A History of Soviet Russia,** Praeger, New York, 1960.

Reed, John: *Ten Days That Shook the World,** Vintage (Random House), New York, 1960.

Reshetar, John S., Jr.: *A Concise History of the Communist Party of the Soviet Union,** Praeger, New York, 1960.

Rubinstein, Alvin Z. (editor): *The Foreign Policy of the Soviet Union,* Random House, New York, 1960.

Salisbury, Harrison E.: *To Moscow—and Beyond,* Harper, New York, 1960.

Schapiro, Leonard: *The Communist Party of the Soviet Union,* Random House, New York, 1960.

Schuman, Frederick L.: *Russia since 1917: Four Decades of Soviet Politics,* Knopf, New York, 1957.

Schwartz, Harry: *The Red Phoenix: Russia since World War II,** Praeger, New York, 1961.

————: *Russia's Soviet Economy,* Prentice-Hall, New York, 1950.

Schwartzchild, Leopold: *Karl Marx: The Red Prussian,** Universal Library, New York, 1959.

Scott, Derek J. R.: *Russian Political Institutions,* Rinehart, New York, 1958.

Scott, John: *Behind the Urals,* Houghton Mifflin, Boston, 1942.

Seton-Watson, Hugh: *From Lenin to Khrushchev,** Praeger, New York, 1960.

Shub, David: *Lenin,** Anchor (Doubleday), Garden City, 1957.

Spector, Ivar: *An Introduction to Russian History and Culture,* Van Nostrand, New York, 1949.

Stalin, Joseph: *Problems of Leninism,* International Publishers, New York, 1942.

Stipp, John L. (editor): *Soviet Russia Today,* Harper, New York, 1956.

Towster, Julian: *Political Power in the U.S.S.R., 1917–1947,* Oxford University Press, New York, 1948.

Treadgold, Donald G.: *Twentieth Century Russia,* Rand, McNally, Chicago, 1959.

Trotsky, Leon: *The Russian Revolution** (a one-vol. condensation edited by F. W. Dupee), Anchor (Doubleday), Garden City, 1958.

Vernadsky, George: *A History of Russia* (4th Edition), Yale University Press, New Haven, 1954.

Vyshinsky, Andrei Y.: *The Law of the Soviet State,* Macmillan, New York, 1948.

Webb, Sidney and Beatrice: *Soviet Communism: A New Civilization?* (2 vols.), Scribner's, New York, 1938.

Wetter, Gustav A.: *Dialectical Materialism,* Praeger, New York, 1959.

Williams, W. A.: *American-Russian Relations: 1781–1947,* Rinehart, New York, 1952.

Wolfe, Bertram D.: *Three Who Made a Revolution: Lenin—Trotsky—Stalin,* Dial Press, New York, 1948.

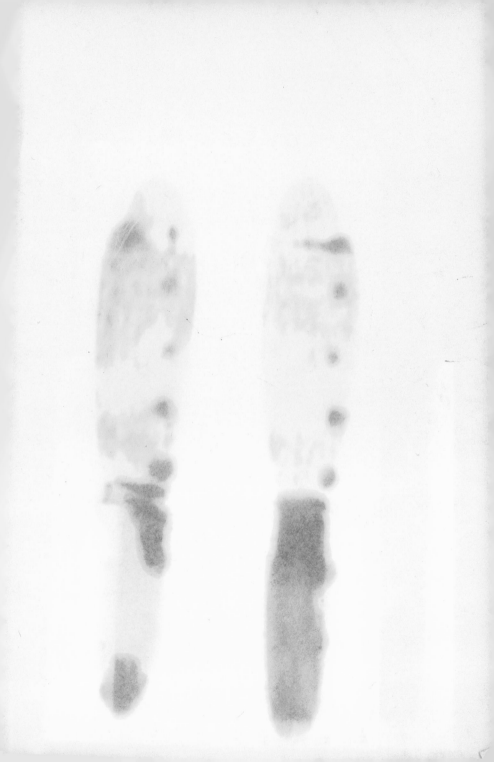

DATE DUE
